Anonymius

Sierra Club Bulletin

Anonymius

Sierra Club Bulletin

ISBN/EAN: 9783743310049

Manufactured in Europe, USA, Canada, Australia, Japa

Cover: Foto ©ninafisch / pixelio.de

Manufactured and distributed by brebook publishing software (www.brebook.com)

Anonymius

Sierra Club Bulletin

THE
Sierra Club Bulletin

Volume V

1904 — 1905

THE SIERRA CLUB
SAN FRANCISCO, CAL.
1905

SIERRA CLUB BULLETIN, VOLUME V.

CONTENTS.

Author.	Title.	Page.
AVERY, RUSS	Mt. Lyell and Mt. Ritter Ascents by Sierra Club Outing of 1904	181
BADÈ, WM. FREDERIC	On the Trail with the Sierra Club	50
	The Water-Ouzel at Home	102
	The Tuolumne Cañon	287
	Book Reviews	262, 322
COLBY, W. E.	The Completed Le Conte Memorial Lodge	66
DUDLEY, WILLIAM R.	Forestry Notes	82, 145, 265, 325
EELLS, ALEXANDER G.	Address at Memorial Exercises	176
GILBERT, G. K.	Variations of Sierra Glaciers	20
	Domes and Dome Structure of the High Sierra.	211
	Systematic Asymmetry of Crest-Lines in the High Sierra of California	279
HANSEN, GEORGE	The Hillside Farmer and the Forest	33
HUTCHINSON, J. S., JR.	First Ascent: Mt. Humphreys	153
JOHNSON, WILLARD D.	The Grade Profile in Alpine Glacial Erosion	271
LE CONTE, J. N.	The Ascent of the North Palisades	2
	The Evolution Group of Peaks	229
McADIE, ALEX. G.	Mt. Whitney as a Site for a Meteorological Observatory	87
McCLURE, N. F.	How Private Burns Climbed Mt. Pinatúbo	26
MONROE, HARRIET	Inscription for the Le Conte Memorial	296
PARKER, FORCE	Over Harrison's Pass from the North with a Pack-Train	297
PARSONS, E. T.	The Notable Mountaineering of the Sierra Club in 1903	44
	The San Francisco Peaks in April	108
PIKE, ROBERT D.	Over Harrison's Pass with Animals	115
RANDALL, MARION	Some Aspects of a Sierra Club Outing	221
RODMAN, WILLOUGHBY	The Ascent of San Antonio	122
SAMPSON, ALDEN	A Deer's Bill of Fare	194

FORESTRY LAW, CALIFORNIA, (1905) 303
NOTES AND CORRESPONDENCE. 76, 138, 254, 314
ORGANIZATION OF THE SIERRA CLUB.................... 70, 133, 238, 310
REPORTS:
    of Secretary 71, 134, 311
    of Outing Committee 74, 240
    of Treasurer 137, 239, 313
    of Custodian of Le Conte Memorial Lodge 241
    on Recession of Yosemite Valley 242
    On Change of Boundaries of Yosemite National Park.................. 250

LIST OF ILLUSTRATIONS.

PLATE		PAGE
I.	The Le Conte Memorial Lodge, Yosemite Valley.............	1
II.	The Palisades, from Woodworth Mountain	2
III.	The Palisades, from the Peak South of Lake Marion	5
IV.	(1) Dumb-bell Lake; (2) Head of the Amphitheater, between the Palisades	11
V.	(1) Summit of the North Palisade, from Mt. Sill; (2) View out from Chimney near Summit of North Palisade................	15
	Map of the Palisades and Vicinity	18
VI.	Lyell Glacier..............................	20
VII.	McClure Glacier............................	23
VIII.	(1) A Fair Stand of Second-Growth Sugar and Yellow Pine of about Twenty-five Years' Growth; (2) A Once Promising Stand of Second-Growth Timber.....................	35
IX.	(1) General Character of Hillside Farming Land; (2) "Thorns also and thistles shall it bring forth"...................	39
X.	Mt. Williamson	44
XI.	The Approach to the Summit of Mt. Williamson	47
XII.	Mt. Whitney, from the Summit of Mt. Williamson	48
XIII.	Mt. Whitney..............................	50
XIV.	Farewell Gap	54
XV.	(1) Kern Lake; (2) Camp Olney....................	58
XVI.	Tower Rock, Kern River Cañon	60
XVII.	(1) Another View of the Le Conte Lodge; (2) Interior View of the Le Conte Lodge........................	66
XVIII.	The Eastern Cliffs of Mt. Whitney...................	87
XIX.	The Water-Ouzel: (1) "Her lubberly husband was still nursing his suspicions," etc.; (2) "With a May-fly in his bill," etc.	105
XX.	The Water-Ouzel: (1) "He likes to stand on a moss cushion," etc.; (2) Where the Water-Ouzel is at Home............	106
XXI.	The San Francisco Peaks from the West	108
XXII.	Over Harrison's Pass: (1) "The very pictures of dejection"; (2) "'Johnny' suddenly fell into a deep snow-hole"	120
XXIII.	General View of the Cucamonga Mountains	122
XXIV.	(1) Head of Cataract Gulch; (2) Among the Redwoods of Sequoia Cañon.............................	136
XXV.	Mt. Humphreys from the East	153
XXVI.	(1) Mt. Humphreys from the Southwest; (2) Lake Frances	158
XXVII.	Looking Down a Gorge on Mt. Humphreys	168
XXVIII.	(1) Descent of Mt. Lyell, 1904; (2) On the Snow-Tongue of Mt. Ritter, 1904	184
XXIX.	Fairview Dome	214
XXX.	(1) Half-Dome at East End of Yosemite Valley; (2) Part of Southeast Wall of Little Yosemite Valley	216

XXXI.	(1) Hill Southeast of Emerick Lake, Upper Merced Basin; (2) A Syncline in Dome Structure	218
XXXII.	(1) Jointed Granite in Kuna Crest, Sierra Nevada; (2) Granite Boulder from which Spalls have been Riven by the Heat of Forest or Meadow Fires	220
XXXIII.	Map of Head-Waters of South Fork of the San Joaquin River	229
XXXIV.	Evolution Basin	232
XXXV.	Evolution Lake	234
XXXVI.	Cirque Bowl and Glacier	271
XXXVII.	Arc of the Cirque Wall Exceeding a Semicircle	273
XXXVIII.	A Step in the Grade Profile	275
XXXIX.	The Bergschrund	276
XL.	Eastward from Mt. Conness	279
XLI.	(1) Eastward from Mt. Gardiner; (2) Southeastward from Alta Meadows	280
XLII.	(1) Near Mt. McClure; (2) Westward from Mt. Hoffman	282
XLIII.	(1) North Side of Goat Crest, Sierra Nevada; (2) South Side of Goat Crest	284
XLIV.	(1) One of the Falls, Tuolumne Cañon; (2) A Series of Cascades, Tuolumne Cañon	290
XLV.	(1) Colonies of Trees, Tuolumne Cañon; (2) Forests, Cliffs, and Cascades, Tuolumne Cañon	292
XLVI.	Kern River and Kaweah Peaks, Looking South from Harrison's Pass	297
XLVII.	Summit of Harrison's Pass	300

PUBLICATIONS OF THE SIERRA CLUB

Number 30

SIERRA CLUB BULLETIN

Vol. V No. 1

JANUARY, 1904

SAN FRANCISCO, CAL.

1904

SIERRA CLUB BULLETIN

Vol. V.   JANUARY, 1904   No. 1

CONTENTS:

	PAGE
THE ASCENT OF THE NORTH PALISADES . . *J. N. Le Conte* .	1
Plates II., III., IV., V.	
VARIATIONS OF SIERRA GLACIERS . . . . . *G. K. Gilbert* .	20
Plates VI., VII.	
HOW PRIVATE BURNS CLIMBED MT. PINA-TÚBO . . . . *N. F. McClure* .	26
THE HILLSIDE FARMER AND THE FOREST . *George Hansen*	33
Plates VIII., IX.	
THE NOTABLE MOUNTAINEERING OF THE SIERRA CLUB IN 1903 . . . . *E. T. Parsons* .	44
Plates X., XI., XII.	
ON THE TRAIL WITH THE SIERRA CLUB . . *W. F. Badè* . .	50
Plates XIII., XIV., XV., XVI.	
THE COMPLETED LE CONTE MEMORIAL LODGE . . . . *W. E. Colby* . .	66
Plates I., XVII.	
ORGANIZATION OF THE SIERRA CLUB	70
COMMUNICATION FROM THE SECRETARY	71
REPORT OF THE OUTING COMMITTEE	74
NOTES AND CORRESPONDENCE	76
FORESTRY NOTES . . . . *William R. Dudley* .	82

All communications intended for publication by the SIERRA CLUB, and all correspondence concerning such publication, should be addressed to the Editor, J. S. Hutchinson, Jr., Sierra Club, Claus Spreckels Building, San Francisco, California.

Correspondence concerning the distribution and sale of the publications of the Club, and concerning its business generally, should be addressed to the Secretary of the Sierra Club, Room 16, Third Floor, Mills Building, San Francisco, California.

THE LE CONTE MEMORIAL LODGE, YOSEMITE VALLEY.
From a photograph by George Fiske.

THE ASCENT OF THE NORTH PALISADES.

By J. N. LeConte.

Of all the vast area of the High Sierra, without doubt the wildest, most magnificent, and most difficult of access is that portion about the extreme sources of the Middle Fork of King's River. This stream above its junction with Goddard Creek (the "head of navigation" for the average camp outfit) drains a basin of about one hundred square miles, nearly all of which is above the timber-line, and which includes about its rim some of the highest points in the State. Through the midst of this rugged area the Middle Fork cuts a profound cañon in granite and black volcanic rock, many points on the west side rising five thousand feet above the stream. This cañon trends almost due north and south. From its edge, extending back four or five miles to the east, is a rough plateau scored by deep transverse gorges which pour the melted snows of the Main Crest into the river. On the north the basin is hemmed in by the Goddard Divide between the King's and San Joaquin rivers, and on the west by a huge spur of the latter terminating in Woodworth Mountain. Except to a man afoot, all these cañons and divides are impassable from the west and north, though it is reported that the Main Crest is crossed by a sheep-trail at a point about six miles north of the Palisades.

To the mountain-climber the main chain of the Palisades is by far the most interesting field of action. For a distance of ten miles this portion of the Main Crest presents toward the west an almost unbroken precipitous front of from two thousand to three thousand feet. At its southern end Split Mountain rises to an elevation of 14,146 feet above sea-level, and, though easy of ascent, the difficulties of reaching its base had until a year ago prevented an attempt to climb it.* Farther north the Middle Palisade touches 14,070 feet, and is still unscaled. At its extreme northern end the mass culminates in a magnificent group of peaks, consisting of the North Palisade (14,282 ft.), Mt. Sill (14,198 ft.), Agassiz Needle (13,945 ft.), and Mt. Winchell (13,817 ft.). These are the North Palisades, and until the ascents described in the following article were made none of their summits had even been attempted.

The Palisades were first mentioned and named by the members of the California Geological Survey in 1864. Professor Brewer in his report says: "At the head of the North (Middle) Fork, along the Main Crest of the Sierra, is a range of peaks, from 13,500 to 14,000 feet high, which we called 'the Palisades.' These were unlike the rest of the crest in outline and color, and were doubtless volcanic; they were very grand and fantastic in shape, like the rocks seen on the Silver Mountain trail near Ebbett's Pass. All doubts as to the nature of these peaks were removed after observing on the east

---

*SIERRA CLUB BULLETIN, Vol. IV., p. 253.

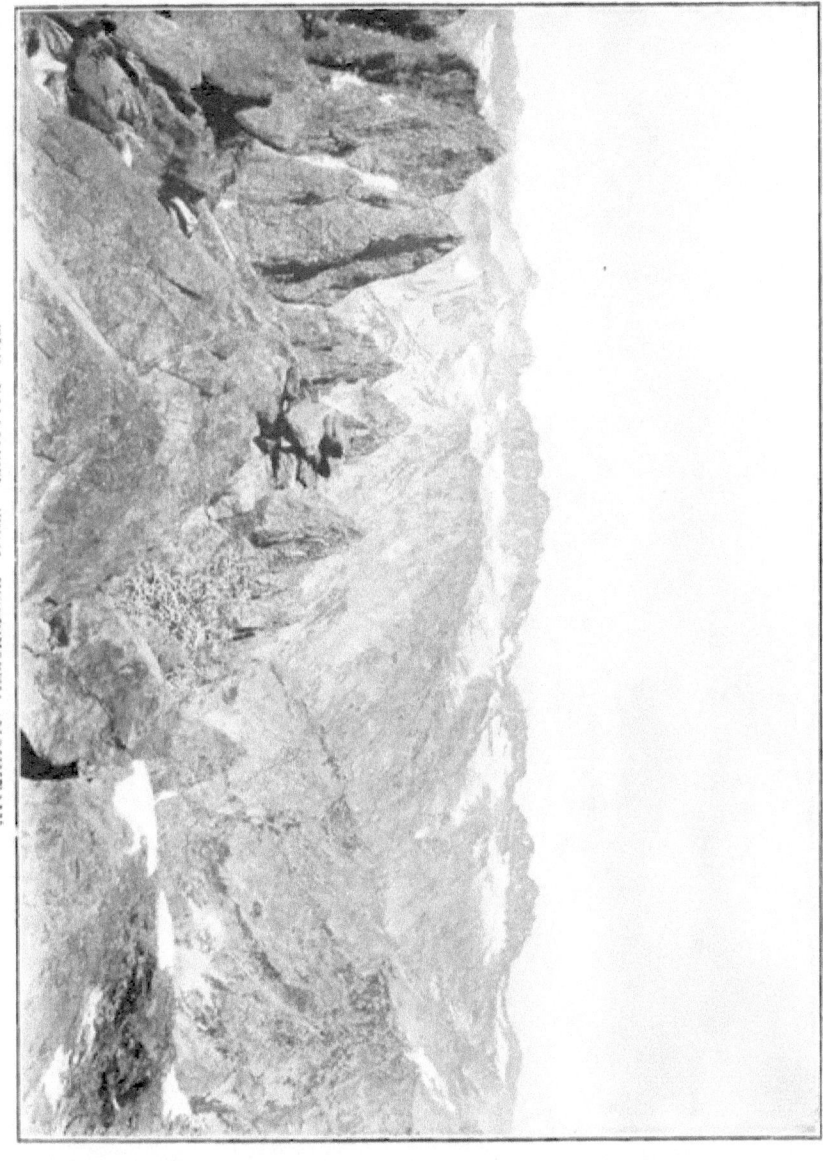

THE PALISADES, FROM WADSWORTH MOUNTAIN.

side of the crest, in the Owen's Valley, that vast streams of lava had flowed down the slopes of the Sierra, just below the Palisades." *

About 1875, the members of the surveying parties under Captain Geo. M. Wheeler, recognized the great height of this part of the range, and determined the altitude and position of two of its high points by traingulation from the "Virginia Base," calling them the N. W. and S. E. Palisades.† These correspond to what are commonly known as the North Palisade and Split Mountain, and their heights as given by him are 14,275 and 14,200 feet.

In 1877 Mr. Frank Dusy, mountaineer, and pioneer of the Middle Fork Sierra, worked his way to the base of the Palisades, and explored the head of the river. In 1879 Mr. Lil A. Winchell, of Pine Ridge, visited the Palisade region, and named the highest point Dusy Peak, the next point north Mt. Winchell, after Professor Alexander Winchell, the geologist, and the most northerly of the group Agassiz Needle.

In 1895 Professor Bolton Coit Brown obtained his first glimpse of the Palisades from the summit of Woodworth Mountain, eight miles to the southwest, and called the highest pinnacle of the northern mass Mt. Jordan.‡ In 1896 I took the liberty of naming the second highest point Mt. Sill.

Until further particulars of the naming of the highest point can be obtained, I shall refer to it as the North

---

* *Geological Survey of California.* J. D. Whitney, State Geologist. Vol. I. Geology, p. 393.

† *Geographical Surveys West of the 100th Meridian.* Capt. George M. Wheeler, in charge. Table of Geographical Positions, etc., p. 19.

‡ SIERRA CLUB BULLETIN, Vol. I., p. 296.

Palisade, leaving to the next BULLETIN the result of this investigation.

The party of the California Geological Survey made no attempt to visit this region. In 1875, Mr. Gustave Eisen and party, of San Francisco, made a knapsack trip up the Middle Fork and Palisade Creek, and climbed one of the points near the Middle Palisade. This and the ascent of Split Mountain already referred to were until last summer the only records of actual ascents amongst the Palisades. To capture the summit of the North Palisade, therefore, had long been a great desire of mine, and a number of trips through the mountains to the west and south of the peak, only furnished a still further incentive to make the attempt.

In the spring of 1903 plans were laid for a trip to the North Palisades. Messrs. James Moffitt and James Hutchinson were to be of the party, men of much experience in High Sierra climbing, and, what is equally important, experienced in the method of traveling necessary in this sort of region. So, after bidding good-by to our Sierra Club friends of the Whitney and Williamson climbs, Mrs. Le Conte and I crossed the Harrison Pass and joined our companions in the King's River Cañon on July 12th. Here also we met Messrs. Robert and John Pike, who decided to join the party.

The start was made at noon of the 17th, and the following evening saw us once more in our beautiful Simpson Meadow, where we remained two days to rest, fish, and prepare our packs for the trip ahead. We reduced our outfit to the simplest possible dimensions, took our three small burros only for packing, and left our little tent and all bulky and heavy articles behind. On the

THE PALISADES, FROM THE PEAK SOUTH OF LAKE MARION.

morning of the 21st we started out early, and followed the trail to Fiske's mine, five miles above, where Cartridge Creek enters the river. Of the rough trip up this cañon I need not speak, as this has already been described in a previous article. We found, however, that all the rock-rolling and brush-cutting of the year before did very little toward improving the route. Triple Fall was made by noon, and we camped for night about a mile or two above without mishap to our pack-animals. Next morning by 10 A. M. we reached the lower end of the Cartridge Creek Lake Basin, and camped again at beautiful Lake Marion, just where the clear stream leaps from the lake over the moraine and into the wild cañon below.

In order to study out a passable route to the North Palisades, and also to make altitude determinations of the many surrounding peaks, the afternoon was devoted to climbing a high slate peak just south of the lake. This peak, which has an elevation of 12,712 feet, is on the divide between the South and Middle Fork of King's River, and is the same which Mr. Lindley and myself ascended last summer when seeking a route to Split Mountain. It commands a splendid view of the head-waters of both streams. By 3 in the afternoon we reached its summit, and immediately turned our attention to the North Palisades, which arose in a forbidding array of jagged spires ten miles to the north. The day was cold, and so perfectly clear that with the aid of the telescope of our transit every rock, chimney, and ledge of the huge wall could be studied with ease. It now appeared that, although the actual summit of the highest peak was on the Main Crest, the whole of the great knife-edge did not constitute a portion of it. Just to the south of the summit a great spur shot off to the east, joined Mt. Sill, and, turning southward, continued the Main Crest in that direction. The great wall of the North Palisade, however, continued directly south from the summit for a mile, and then broke down into some of the tributary cañons of Palisade Creek. Between this wall and Mt. Sill to the east there was included a vast amphitheater draining into Palisade Creek, and it seemed certain that we could make our way into this and climb the great snow-fields within, whose glistening edges could be seen on the very tops of the ridges. To navigate the final knife-edge to the summit appeared by no means so sure. One deep cleft in particular worried us, but of course it was impossible at so great a distance to tell whether or not it was passable. The western face of the mountain appeared to be totally inaccessible, though a few narrow chimneys seamed its savage face. These might, we thought, be taken advantage of as a last resort. The prospect could not be called encouraging, but Mt. Sill might, at any rate, be taken, and from its summit a great area could be mapped. For over an hour we stayed on the summit of our peak studying the chances *pro* and *con*, and had to confess at last that the odds were against us.

After taking a round of angles to all the prominent peaks in sight, and feasting our eyes upon the stupendous panorama, doubly impressive amidst the shadows of the declining sun, we hurried down the mountain, over long stretches of snow, across fields of jagged slate, and around the end of the lake to our camp, where Mrs. Le Conte and Mr. Moffitt had supper ready.

That evening we laid out our supplies for the final

trip. These were cut down to the last extremity. An eider-down quilt apiece, a compact 4 x 5 camera with eighteen plates, a very light plane-table, weighing not more than a couple of pounds, two Sierra Club register-boxes, a small pot and frying-pan for a kitchen outfit, four spoons and four tin cups for a dining-room set, and a rather small three days' allowance of food. After all things were divided up no pack seemed to weigh more than twenty-five pounds. The party consisted of Messrs. Moffitt, Hutchinson, Robert Pike, and myself. Mrs. Le Conte and John were to keep camp till our return.

At break of day the indefatigable Moffitt was astir and getting breakfast before the rest of us could even get our shoes on. By 5:30 everything was packed and we were off. Mrs. Le Conte and John accompanied us to a sheep pass over the north wall of the lake basin, and one of our jacks, "Spotty," carried our packs for that distance without difficulty. Here the knapsacks were adjusted to our own backs for the rest of the trip, and we struck out north, while the others returned with "Spotty" to camp. The descent from the sheep pass was into the basin of a tributary of Cartridge Creek which enters the main stream from the north just below Triple Falls. First it was over hard-frozen snowfields, and then over huge granite fragments to the margin of a lonely lake. This, from its shape, we called Dumb-bell Lake, and made our way around its eastern end, over talus slopes, and then across the complicated topography of the basin toward another pass which could be seen on the divide to the north. In the course of a couple of hours the crest of this was reached by a gradual ascent from the south, but on the north it broke away in steep chutes filled with snow. Far below lay another desolate lake walled in by gigantic cliffs to the east, and the outlet, which entered a deep gorge, was evidently a tributary of Palisade Creek. The immense cañon of this latter could now be seen cutting thousands of feet deep directly across our pathway, and on the farther side rose the Palisades, more savage and forbidding than ever. The snow which choked our pass formed a cornice projecting far over the chute, so it was necessary to first descend by the aid of the rocks on one side, and then take to the snow-field below. Now a swift glissade was a pleasant rest from climbing over talus, and this let us down a couple of hundred feet in a few minutes. At the shore of our Amphitheater Lake we stopped a moment to rest and enjoy the wild outlook, and then entered the cañon through which the outlet stream made its way. The view down this was now unobstructed. Its confluence with Palisade Creek was directly opposite that of the stream which drained the huge amphitheater between the North Palisade and Mt. Sill. Our route could not have been picked better, for all that was now necessary was to descend to Palisade Creek, cross it, and climb out on the other side as far as the timber-line before dark.

This all seems very easy on paper, and looks nice and smooth on the map, but the reality was quite the reverse. The cañon which we now entered was exceptionally rough. Near its head falls blockaded the way, necessitating detours along side ledges. In other places brush choked the narrow space by the stream, or piles of giant débris encumbered the way. Luckily, gravitation was in our favor, and we made fair time, finally reaching the beautiful valley of Palisade Creek by noon.

The cañon of this large stream is typically glacial—a great U-shaped trough, lined along its bottom with meadows and thin timber. The view down its course was very fine. Far across the Middle Fork Cañon rose the black crags of the Woodworth Divide. Great talus-fans and moraines clung to the mountain-sides above, but the lower slopes were clothed with verdure and forests of red fir and tamarack. The meadows were ablaze with flowers; myriads of columbines, castilleias, tiger-lilies, strawberries, and tiny compositæ were everywhere. The place was absolutely untouched. Not since the creation of the forest reserve had human foot trod this glorious wilderness, and even before that time the sheepmen who visited the valley must have been few indeed, for not a blaze, monument, nor corral did we see, and there were but few signs of old sheep-camps.

Here we stopped for noon. A fire was lighted and tea made in our tin bucket. Bread and prunes were produced, and we enjoyed a well-earned rest of two hours. But anxiety as to the outcome of the day's tramp and the sort of camping-place we might run into before nightfall started us out all too soon. The way now lay across the valley and up the side of the great cañon along the course of a tiny stream which we knew drained the distant amphitheater between the Palisades, five thousand feet above. Our path at first lay quite a distance to the left of the stream, which we called Glacier Brook, and the climbing for the most part was through alpine pastures spangled with flowers. But soon we began to leave this region of life, and again to enter that of desolation—of rock and snow. A thousand feet above the valley we passed over the old moraine, and now the grade of the creek decreased, and we entered a wide glacial trough—a "hanging valley,"* tributary to the main Palisade Cañon. By 4 o'clock we had reached the level of the highest trees, consisting of a half-dozen storm-beaten tamaracks, and there threw down our packs for the night. We were completely shut in by high cliffs, and no glimpse of the Palisades could as yet be obtained.

To cook dinner with nothing but a frying-pan, a diminutive pot, and a tomato-can is an art requiring considerable experience and is not an easy one to acquire. First the stones for the fireplace must be put so close together that it is difficult to make the fire burn at all, and, again, to balance the little pots on rough stones requires knowledge of the laws of equilibrium which can never be gleaned from books on mechanics. The operation, though laborious, was finally brought to a successful conclusion, when we ate canned beef (so-called, but in all probability canned horse) off heated fragments of glaciated granite, and canned tomatoes and coffee in turn from cups. The dish-washing consisted in throwing away the plates and rinsing the cups.

As the chill of the approaching night began to settle over our desolate camp we built a huge fire near a big boulder, cut our stogies in two to prolong their period of usefulness, smoked, and were at peace. The outlook was across the great valley of Palisade Creek and directly up the rugged gorge by which we had descended from Amphitheater Lake. Down its middle tumbled the foaming stream, a long line of silver, lost here and there amongst the talus-piles. Cataract Creek, we called it, and

---

* Valleys which enter the trunk cañons far above, so that their streams form falls or cascades, are called "hanging valleys."

DUMB-BELL LAKE.
Photo by J. N. LeConte.

HEAD OF THE AMPHITHEATER, BETWEEN THE PALISADES.
Photo by J. N. LeConte.

marveled at its wonderful setting. About its head was a mighty array of snow-clad peaks, now flashing in the rays of the setting sun. It was far more pleasant to enjoy this view than to think of the difficult day ahead and of those left behind in camp so far away.

We were up again by dawn the morning of the 24th. After considerable trouble with our primitive stove, we finally got breakfast, and, shouldering camera, plane-table, and lunch, took our way up Glacier Brook, determined to work into the great amphitheater, try the North Palisade from the southeast, and if unsuccessful to ascend Mt. Sill. After an hour's climb over talus-piles, meadows, glaciated slopes, and snow, we obtained a glimpse of the ragged western front of our mountain through a gap in the northern wall of the cañon. Soon this was lost sight of; the cañon turned in behind the Palisade ridge, and we were at the entrance to the amphitheater. The slope of Sill plunged down into it rather precipitously from the east, and was bare of snow, with the exception of three long stripes just below the summit. The side toward the Palisade ridge was, to our surprise, not so precipitous, nor was it rough toward the head on the cross-divide between the peaks. The floor, western side, and head was covered with a continuous field of snow, changing into ice at the lower end. We climbed over pile after pile of great talus fragments, and gladly took to the snow at the earliest opportunity. At first it was hard and comparatively smooth, but higher up it became indescribably rough. The unequal melting of the snow cut the whole mass up into a labyrinth of great knife-blades, which were sometimes four feet high and two or three feet apart. We were forced to step from blade to blade, balancing on the sharp edges, and often falling into the spaces between. I have frequently seen this ice-blade structure on Sierran snow-fields, particularly on Mt. Lyell, but never so highly developed as here. We made straight for the point where the cross-divide joins the Palisade ridge, and our spirits rose as we climbed. The way was clear as far as we could see. Soon the magnificent summit appeared peeping over the ridge ahead. The final approach seemed also passable. We were sure of success,—so sure in fact that I, who was at that moment ahead, called out, " Boys, we shall make it." A dozen steps more brought us to the top of the cross-divide, and in an instant was swept away every chance, every hope of success.

Such a stupendous view I never expect to see again in the Sierra. We were on the edge of a precipice which sank for a thousand feet absolutely sheer to the head of a splendid glacier, the largest in the Sierra Nevada, but never before described. Just to the left our ridge joined the Palisade ridge not more than a hundred yards from the summit, and that last portion was a serrated knife-edge. The only possible route was along this edge, and this might have been feasible had it not been gashed in one place by a notch a hundred feet deep. We spent over an hour here examining every crack in the rock and discussing every possible way out of the dilemma. Hutchinson crossed with danger one small notch of the knife-edge, went to the very edge of the great chasm, and with his field-glasses scanned carefully the opposite side, but came to the conclusion that even had one been able to descend to the bottom, not a single fingerhold could be found on the other wall. Furthermore, one could not go around the notch, for it continued on down each side of the mountain as a vertical walled gorge, running out into nothing on the face of the cliff above the glacier.

It was hard to give up when within almost a stone's throw of the top, but it was clearly "no go." We took a long rest, enlivening it somewhat by rolling huge boulders down the precipice on to the glacier. It was really a thrilling sight to watch them go thundering down the cliff, leaping across the berg-schrund, and then end over end through the snow till only distinguishable by the snow-foam when they struck. We then turned our attention to Mt. Sill, and after a rough scramble of an hour along the ridge to the east arrived without serious difficulty on that hitherto untrodden crest.

The view in every direction was unparalleled in grandeur and extent, particularly along the Main Crest to the north and south. Close by rose the apparently inaccessible spire of the North Palisade across the profound cirque containing the Palisade Glacier. This latter was of the greatest interest. Its area seemed fully a square mile, perhaps more,—for distances are hard to estimate in such a locality. All along the base of the cliff below was a berg-schrund, probably a mile in length. Against the mountain-side the slope of the snow was very steep, but lower down it eased off, and the glacier was crossed by fifteen or twenty crevasses far more perfect and much larger than any I have ever seen on Mt. Lyell. The lower end swept to the right around a buttress of Mt. Sill, and was lost to sight, but farther down were two beautiful lakes of milky white water which contrasted in a most striking manner with the clear emerald lakelets scattered all about. To the south stretched away the long line of Palisades, all guarded by sheer cliffs on the east. Along their bases lay three or four small residual glaciers, which, with the large one, form the head-waters of Big Pine Creek. The prospect to the west was cut off by the jagged crest of the North Palisade, but far to the north rose that airy pinnacle, Mt. Humphreys, and I could not but recall a state of affairs similar to our present one when attempting its ascent in 1898.

The height of Mt. Sill as given by triangulation from surrounding summits is 14,198 feet, and checks fairly with the reading of the aneroid, 14,100 feet. It is the fourth highest in the range, being overtopped by Whitney, Williamson, and the North Palisade only. We built a monument and deposited therein our Sierra Club register-box No. 43.

About 3 in the afternoon we started down the western face of the mountain. Some difficulty was encountered in getting around immense granite blocks, but finally the floor of the amphitheater was reached without the necessity of traversing any of the rough snow, made doubly difficult on account of the softening effect of the afternoon sun. After turning down into the cañon of Glacier Brook, Hutchinson climbed out of the notch on the west side and examined with the glasses the front cliff of the North Palisade. We then returned to camp.

After supper that evening we discussed the advisability of making an attempt at the western side of the mountain. It appeared a useless venture as well as a rather dangerous one. But finally it was decided to give one more day to the work—to at least creep around the foot of the giant and get an idea of the country at the head of the river.

Next morning, with rather doubting hearts and very

SUMMIT OF THE NORTH PALISADE, FROM MT. SILL.
Photo by J. N. LeConte.

VIEW OUT FROM CHIMNEY NEAR SUMMIT OF NORTH PALISADE.
Photo by J. N. LeConte.

sore legs and arms, Moffitt, Hutchinson, and I struck back up the cañon again just after sunrise. When opposite the break in the western side, we climbed from ledge to ledge, and finally reached the notch which Hutchinson had investigated the day before. We could now see the whole profile of the great mountain, consisting of crags and precipices piled up for two thousand feet above a vast talus-field along its base. Evidently the first move was to cross this field and reach a point opposite the summit, whence any chimneys that might exist could be examined. This was a great consumer of time, for the blocks fallen from the mountain were of immense size and often the spaces between were filled with soft snow. By 8:30 the field was crossed, and we now saw the entrance of a great chute, or chimney, twenty or thirty feet wide in places, which cleft the western precipice from crest to base. This was evidently the same which terminated in the impassable notch at the top, and which had been the cause of all our trouble the day before. It was useless to follow it all the way up, even if accessible, for we knew that it would be impossible to climb out of the notch in any case. The rest of the front seemed blank, so there was no choice but to start up and look for a point above where the chute could be abandoned on the left-hand side.

At first the climbing was over loose material, tedious but not difficult. Then we struck the rocky bottom of the gorge, and the trouble began. In some places snowbanks were encountered—not so steep but that toe-holds could be kicked out. The containing walls for some distance were inaccessible, till finally we came to a point where a crack ran up the left side, and immediately above this the chimney entered between perpendicular cliffs of great height. This, then, appeared to be the last chance, so Moffitt and Hutchinson both made determined efforts to get up, but without success. On looking down the gorge, however, there appeared to be a ledge along the wall which had been invisible from below. While the others were trying the crevice, I went down to examine this. It appeared to be the only way out of the difficulty; so the others came down and we started across. The ledge was three or four feet wide, but sloped at a high angle away from the wall, so that crawling along it was a somewhat unpleasant operation. Further along it narrowed to but little over a foot, but fortunately became level. Hutchinson and Moffitt came over soon after.

We were now on the rocky front of the mountain, and a glance above showed a narrow chimney parallel to the big one below. Up this we climbed with the greatest care. Sometimes it was only wide enough to admit a man's body, and we had to work up with knees and elbows. In some places it was filled with clear ice, and great icicles hung directly in the way from some lodged boulder above. These had to be avoided by stepping in the narrow space between the rock and ice, or by finding footholds on the walls. After about five hundred feet of this we suddenly came to a widened portion, and there, towering almost in the zenith, a thousand feet above us, was the summit we had so long worked for. Up to that moment we had not hoped for success. Every instant we had expected to be stopped by some impassable barrier, but now on careful examination there did not appear to be any difficulties ahead worse than those that had already been overcome. Oh, the excitement of the minutes that followed! One who has not been in a similar position can never realize our feelings as foot by foot the upward path was won, and nearer and nearer came the tiny rounded cap above. Again we entered a chimney, and again came through in safety. Now we were in a sort of sloping bowl directly below the top. To go straight up was not to be thought of, as the caplike summit almost overhung on that side. We worked up toward the knife-edge just to the south, and instantly the stupendous panorama of precipice, glacier, and desert burst upon us. We were on the main ridge between the impassable notch of yesterday and the top. Even there—even twenty feet below the top we almost failed. The knife-edge was composed of thin blocks standing up on edge, from six to eight feet apart, and equally high. These had to be climbed over one by one, by letting down at arm's-length between two and pulling up over the thin edge of the next. At 11:30 we crawled out upon the crown, victorious at last, after nearly two thousand feet of difficult rock-climbing.

The panorama is nearly the same as that from Mt. Sill, with the exception of the basin of the main Middle Fork, which lay, a lake-dotted plateau scored with cañons, at our very feet. On the other side the course of the Palisade Glacier could be followed farther down than from Sill, and the crest to the north was better shown. The knife-edge to the north of the summit was frightfully gashed, making an ascent from that side wholly out of the question. An approach from the east might be possible, though very doubtful. We had already satisfied ourselves that the southern knife-edge was beyond our powers, so the route up the western front seems to be the only feasible one.

There was no sign of any sort to show that the mountain had ever before been ascended. We built a monument, and left therein our register-box No. 42. My own triangulation places the summit at 14,282 feet, and the aneroid read 14,200, a very fair agreement. This puts the peak third in our Sierra.

We spent an hour on the top, somewhat disturbed, be it confessed, by the prospects of the descent. We had taken careful note, however, of the bad places, and were pleasantly disappointed in finding the return but little harder than the climb. In an hour and a half the ledge was reached and safely passed, and soon after three triumphant tramps were toiling over the boulders of the talus-field headed for "home." When at 4 o'clock we pulled into our little camp at the timber-line, we found Pike fast asleep. There was still time to push on to a more pleasant camping-spot; so, packing up the all too meager outfit, we struck out down the creek, and reached Palisade Valley by 6 P.M.

Here in the midst of this little park was an ideal spot for camping. We made our stop on the peninsula between Palisade Creek and Glacier Brook, surrounded by flower-gardens and sheltered by tall tamaracks. That evening we celebrated by eating up practically everything we possessed that was eatable, and wound up by smoking whole and complete stogies, without the painful necessity of cutting them in two.

If we were eager to start out on this eventful trip, how much more anxious were we at its successful completion to return to those who were left behind! So long before break of day Moffitt was stirring around making coffee, for that was about all we had, except a half-cup of mush

THE PALISADES AND VICINITY.

apiece. But before sunrise we faced the rugged gorge of Cataract Creek and climbed with all the energy that was left. The first few hours were all right, but I confess that for my part I was pretty tired when the pass above Amphitheater Lake was reached. Getting over that villainous talus around Dumb-bell Lake was still worse, and the final pull over the snow to the sheep-pass where we had parted with our camp companions was the worst of all. But the sight of Lake Marion inspired us with fresh energy, and at 11:30 we pulled into camp only to find Mrs. Le Conte and John away. In a few minutes, however, they returned from one of a series of unsuccessful bear hunts.

I have no doubt that others will follow our track to the summit of the Palisades. Doubtless, also, scores from the Club's Outings will climb or be pulled and boosted up its rugged face; but never again will any one feel the inspiration, the excitement, and the glory of success that we three experienced when the first ascent was made.

VARIATIONS OF SIERRA GLACIERS.

By Grove Karl Gilbert,
OF THE UNITED STATES GEOLOGICAL SURVEY.

Glaciers are not constant in size. If a glacier is measured year after year, it is usually found to have undergone variation, increasing or diminishing in length, breadth, and thickness. The greatest changes are in the length, and, as the head of a glacier occupies a practically constant position, the changes in length are expressed in the position of the lower or terminal end. When Vancouver visited and mapped the coast of Alaska in 1792-1794, he recorded the positions of several walls of ice, near which lay fleets of icebergs. He did not use the word *glacier*, but we now know that the ice-walls were the fronts of glaciers that flowed down from the mountains and invaded the sea. Within the last fifteen years a number of these glaciers have been remapped, and it is found that important changes have taken place. In Glacier Bay the ice-front has retreated about thirty-five miles, and many ice-streams which were formerly branches of the great trunk stream have now become independent glaciers,—the Muir, the Grand Pacific, the Johns Hopkins, the Reid, the Hugh Miller, etc. On the other side of the Fairweather Range the variation has been of opposite character, and the Brady Glacier now extends several miles nearer to the ocean than when Vancouver saw it. Similar changes have been observed in

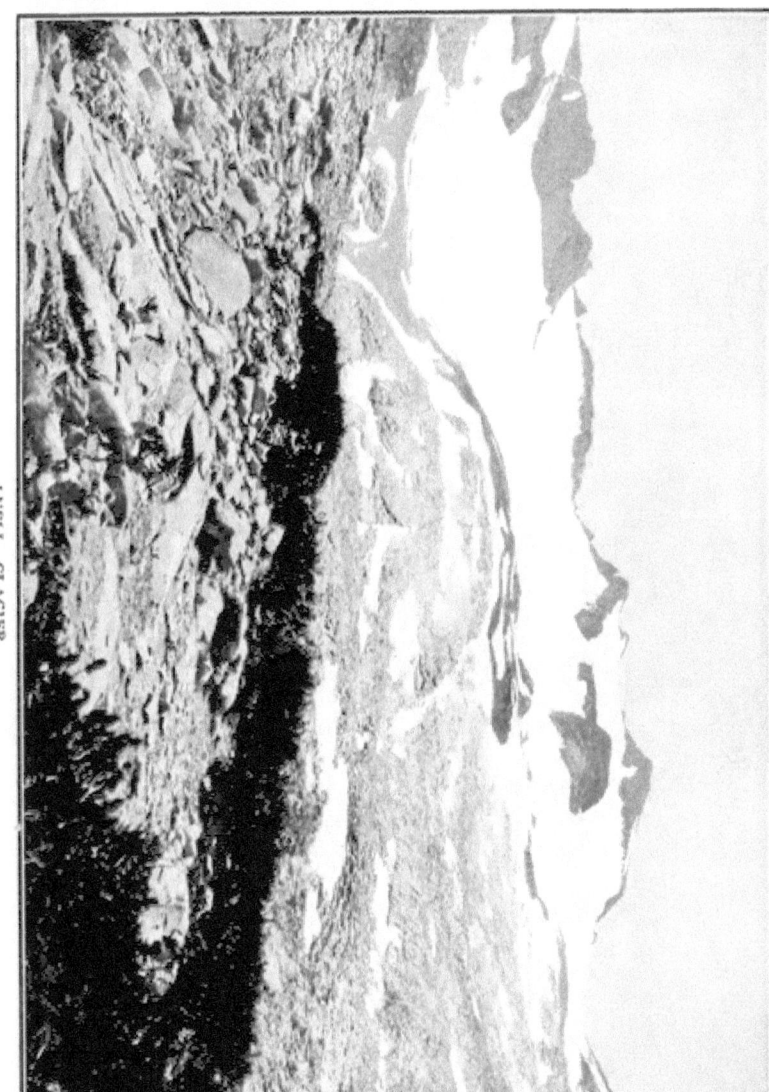

LYELL GLACIER.
From a photograph by Grove Karl Gilbert, August 7, 1903.
The high peak is Mt. Lyell.

various glaciers of Europe and Asia, and the fuller records of Switzerland and other inhabited mountain-lands show that the front of a glacier will often advance continuously for several decades, and then for another long period continuously retreat.

It is easy to get some inkling of the cause of these changes if we consider the essential nature of a glacier. It originates in a mountain valley where the accumulation of winter snow is greater than the summer heat can dissipate. The excess of snow piles up year after year, is compacted into ice, and creeps down the slope, constituting a slow but continuous stream of ice. As it descends it meets new climatic conditions, the winter snow becoming gradually less and the summer melting gradually greater, until at length a region is reached where there is an annual loss of material, instead of an annual gain. In that region it wastes away and comes to an end. So long as there is a balance at the lower end between the supply, through forward motion, and the loss, through melting (or, more strictly, melting and evaporation), the end of the glacier is constant in position; but whenever one of these factors overpowers the other the glacier either grows longer, when it is said to advance, or grows shorter, when it is said to retreat. But while these elementary propositions are simple and easily understood, there are various modifying factors as to which much less is known, and the full theory of glacier variation has not yet been reached, although it has received much attention from geographers. The problem is of such interest that records of glacier variation are carefully made in most regions of ready access, and the reports of changes are annually summarized. In this country the summary is made each year by Professor H. F. Reid, of Baltimore, and published in the *Journal of Geology*. I present the subject here in the hope that the members of the Sierra Club will make use of the opportunities afforded by their excursions to secure for science a record of the changes of Sierra glaciers. It is true that the Sierra glaciers are small, and their changes from year to year are probably much less than in the case of the relatively large glaciers to which such studies have usually been restricted. But this fact does not interfere in the least with the value and interest of comparative observations, if they shall be made. It is desirable that the studies of glacier variation be not limited to a single district, and the greater the variety of general physical conditions under which the observed variations occur the better the prospect of reaching a theory of causation which shall be entirely general.

In 1885 I. C. Russell published, in the Fifth Annual Report of the United States Geological Survey, an account of the existing glaciers of the United States, and his paper not only summarized what was then known of the glaciers of the Sierra Nevada, but gave references to the earlier literature. The most important contributors to that early literature were John Muir, Galen Clarke, and Joseph Le Conte. Russell himself made an important addition, and all later contributions, so far as I know them, have been published by the Sierra Club.

Russell's paper gives several illustrations of the Dana Glacier, from photographs made in August, 1883, and the original negatives are still accessible in the files of the United States Geological Survey, so that it will be possible, by means of new photographs, to determine how far

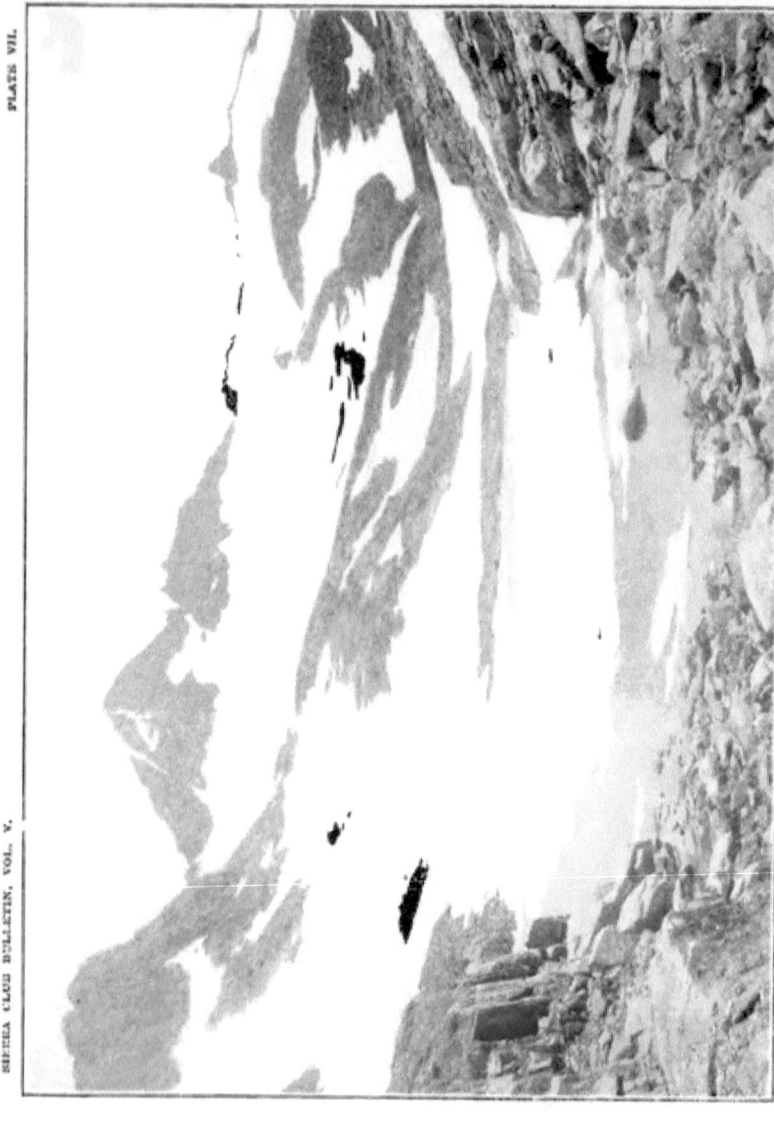

the glacier has grown or shrunken in the last twenty years.

The Lyell Glacier was not only photographed but very fully described by Russell; and he published an excellent map which had been prepared by his assistant, Willard D. Johnson. During the past summer I made a photograph, here reproduced in Plate VI., and with the aid of Russell's photograph have been able to compare the appearance in 1883 with that in 1903. The glacier seems now to have almost precisely the same size as at the earlier date, the only suggested change being a slight shrinkage near the west end. The arrangement of the numerous moraine ridges is precisely the same as in 1883. from which it may be inferred that the glacier has not in any later year been materially larger than then. It might, however, have diminished and afterward increased.

The McClure Glacier, lying close to the Lyell, was included in Johnson's map, but it was sketched from a single station only, and its outlines were not determined with the same accuracy. No photograph was made at that time, and so far as I am aware the view I obtained last summer (Plate VII.) is the first one showing the glacier at short range. Comparing it with the map made twenty years earlier, I noted important differences, and these were the subject of correspondence with Mr. Johnson. It is his definite recollection that the ice was then continuous down to the edge of the lake, where it ended in a cliff about twenty feet high. At the present time the lake is bordered only by snow-banks, and the glacier is evidently limited by the large V-shaped moraine. As Johnson did not map the large moraine, although he did represent other details, we may safely assume that the moraine was not then visible; and the suggestion that the moraine was then concealed by snow is discountenanced by the fact that the neighboring Lyell Glacier was quite as free from snow in the summer of 1883 as in 1903. While the evidence is not altogether conclusive, I regard it as probable that the ice Johnson saw at the margin of the lake was actually continuous with and part of the glacier, and that the glacier has retreated several hundred yards since the making of his map.

One of the best methods of recording the position of a glacier-front is through photography, and this method is by far the most available. Points of view should be chosen which command the relation of the ice to fixed objects of the landscape, and especially to objects immediately in front of it. To enable the future photographer to reoccupy the same station, and thus secure the best possible view for purposes of comparison, the spot should be marked in some way, as by the building of a cairn; and it is well to include in the view something of the immediate foreground. Both these means of identification are available in the case of the views of Lyell and McClure glaciers. It is of primary importance to record with the photograph the date of its taking. This should include not only the year, but the month and day, for it is probable that most glaciers undergo an annual oscillation. It is well to make two negatives from each station, timing and developing one so as to show the details of the ice, and the other to show the details of rocks and other dark objects. The best month for such records in the Sierra is probably September, because at that time the outline of the ice is least apt to be obscured by snow.

It is, of course, desirable that copies of all views be systematically preserved by the Club, so that they may be accessible at all times, and that those who are planning excursions to glaciers may readily acquaint themselves with the earlier work. This suggestion applies not only to views that may be made in the future, but to views now in existence. Valuable records are doubtless already contained in the photographic collection of the Club, and others are in the possession of members and their friends. A little work by some officer or committee of the Club would bring together the available views and discover, at least approximately, the dates of their making.

HOW PRIVATE BURNS CLIMBED MT. PINATÚBO.

By Capt. N. F. McClure.

During the first five months of the year 1903 I was stationed at Camp Stotsenburg, Philippine Islands.

About the middle of May two coming events suddenly aroused me to the fact that any contemplated mountain-climbing must be done immediately. One of these events was the rapid approach of the rainy season, and the other was the probable departure of my regiment in June for the United States.

Camp Stotsenburg lies between two noted mountains. To the east, a distance of fifteen miles, rises Arayat, a lone peak about three thousand feet in height; while to the west, Mt. Pinatúbo, twenty miles away, dominates the Zambales Range. For months I contemplated trying to ascend one or both of these great sentinels, but never seemed able to find the time. About May 20th there was a kind of a lull before the storms that were soon to break, —viz., the rainy season and our orders to return to "God's country." Seizing the last chance, I obtained permission from the commanding officer to make the attempt on Pinatúbo.

My party consisted of Packer E. A. Schad, Privates Burns, Phillips, and La Casse, of Troops "L," "A," and "E," Fifth Cavalry, respectively. I also had with me two Filipinos, Cesario Tolentino and Martin David, and a Negrito guide called Lawayan, two pack-mules, and five horses. We left Camp Stotsenburg May 23d, and about 4 P. M. we reached the Bamban River at a point some twelve miles west of Stotsenburg. It was a beautiful ride through the cañon and over the wooded foothills, though one must at times dismount and walk through the heavy underbrush and down the steeper slopes.

We went into camp on a picturesque ledge, or bench, about fifty feet above the roaring river which dashed past us, and entered a deep gorge just below. All about us arose pinnacles carved by ages of wind and water from an ancient bed of volcanic ashes partly solidified into rock. In fact, one could scarcely call it rock, it looked so soft; but it must have been more firm than it appeared to have stood in great minarets about us as it did. A small trail at the north end of the bench enabled us to water our stock, and by closing the trail leading from above to our camp we had the animals in a little pasture from which there was no avenue of escape.

During the afternoon Martin and Lawayan went to find some other Negritos. These little people live in huts far up on the mountain-side, and are very shy and bashful about appearing before strangers. Late that evening Martin returned and stated that he had secured some other guides, who would meet us next morning on the road.

In the morning early Packer Schad, Private Burns, Martin, Cesario, and myself set forth. We had emergency rations for two days, a little coffee, a pound of bacon, two bolos, four canteens, and some matches. Besides these, Schad, Burns, and I each carried a revolver. We took no blankets, coats, nor rain-coats, as we felt that every pound of extra weight would lessen our chances of success.

Ascending the Bamban River on the west side two miles, we arrived at the rendezvous where we were to find the Negrito guides. Here we lost two valuable hours waiting for them. At last Lawayan arrived with four other Negritos. Of these Debilano was the chief guide, and his companions were called Segundo, Subero, and Fernando. Segundo was a very little old man, Subero was a fine-looking boy of perhaps eighteen, while Fernando was a lithe, middle-aged man, with no clothing whatever except a very brief breech-clout. All the others wore more or less clothing, from Subero, who had on a calico shirt, to Debilano, who was the proud possessor of a policeman's old coat. For several miles we ascended the Bamban River, leaping from boulder to boulder or wading through pools and rapids. At last we came to a point where the main river is formed by two large forks, each issuing from a deep gorge. We followed the left-hand stream, and were soon in the shades of the cañon. The scenery was grand, one might almost say oppressive. The great towering cliffs on either side caused everything to appear dark and gloomy.

We had gone but a short distance when Debilano, who was in the lead, turned back and announced to us that we could go no farther as a large boulder that had formerly been used as a pathway had become dislodged. I did not like to give up so easily so I asked him, through Martin, our interpreter, if there was not some way to go around. He said no, but in about half an hour Burns and Schad, who had gone back, returned to us and stated that they had found another pathway to the top of the falls. To this day I do not know whether the Negritos wished to turn us back or not, but I suspect that they did; for after we got above the falls we found old camp-fires and other signs which had been but recently made, and our little black companions must have known of them.

Still ascending the stream, we arrived, about 1 P.M., at a point about ten miles from our camp, and here we ate a light lunch of emergency rations. We now left the main stream and turned to the left up a dry wash. I had had all the canteens filled, but I did not then realize how long we would be away from water.

On, on, on over boulders, under the shade of overhanging foliage, in the close, hot atmosphere we traveled. The perspiration poured from us and kept every stitch of our clothing wet. The forests of giant ferns and great vines and hardwood trees of many varieties were beautiful. About 4 P.M. our guide pointed through an opening in the trees at Pinatúbo, rising almost sheer above us, and told us how to proceed. He then stated that he and his companions could go no farther. Whether they feared the bands of Igorrote savages found in these mountains, or whether they had some superstitious dread, I do not know, but not another step would they go. Leaving them, Schad, Burns, Martin, Cesario, and I pressed on. Several times as we ascended we left the dry stream-bed, but each time, on account of the heavy underbrush and vine entanglements on either side, we returned to it.

At length the stream-bed ran out, and we found ourselves on the side of the great mountain, clinging to vines and roots as we cut our way upward. It was slow work, and by the time night began to close in we were pretty well exhausted. To make matters worse, we found that the natives had drunk two of the canteens of water, which was half of our entire supply. Just at dusk it began to rain, and, realizing what a night at that altitude would be without fire, I had every effort made to get one started. Fortunately for us, we succeeded. Schad took one canteen of water and made some coffee, and fried some bacon. These with the emergency rations comprised our meal, which we enjoyed greatly, for we had had a hard day's work. We soon began to suffer terribly from thirst, and, though it rained for three hours and wet us to the skin, we were not able to catch any water to drink. At 8 P. M. our situation was sad, to say nothing of being perilous. A single misstep in the darkness might mean a broken leg or a broken arm; it was nine hours till dawn; there was not a level place large enough to lie down upon; our thirst tormented us, and the dampness chilled us to the bone. I continued to urge all to utilize the light of the fire in searching for more wood, and Schad and I worked for over two hours at this groping in the darkness, and with our bolos cut whatever we could find that was inflammable and much that was not.

About 10 o'clock the rain ceased, and we then set to work to dry our clothes, piece by piece. By midnight we were all thoroughly dried out, and by keeping up the fire we managed to pass a night that might have been far worse with wet clothes and no fire. At early dawn Schad was cooking again, using the remaining canteen of water for coffee. After breakfast there was but little food of any kind remaining, as we had left some with our Negrito friends, of whom there were five, instead of only two, as we had expected. Before sunrise we were again ascending, cutting our way through the wet vines and underbrush. In about an hour and a half we arrived on the west side of the peak, at the foot of the last steep slope, which was well-nigh perpendicular. We were now at an elevation of about six thousand feet. I had with me a Sierra Club register-box, but I was so exhausted that I felt that I could not make the last climb. I gave the box to Schad, thinking that he would surely reach the summit. He and Burns and I now started up the last slope. After several attempts at different points, I gave it up. So did Schad and the two Filipinos. In a short time we heard shouts through the mist, and, the fog lifting a little, we saw Burns standing on the summit. He urged us to come on, but we were done for. It is hard to account for the feeling I had, but I can explain it only by attributing it to the effects of long service in the Philippine Islands.

If Burns had had the record-box he would have placed it on the summit. The view from the foot of the slope where I sat was partly obscured by a rolling mist, but there was much that was beautiful. To the west lay the China Sea, to the south were the peaks of the Zambales Range, while to the east the shifting fog allowed us now and then to see a town. Several times we caught a good view of Mt. Arayat, thirty-five miles away, and it looked like a little mound. Far to the east of Arayat lay the eastern Coast Range of Luzon.

Mt. Pinatúbo reaches an altitude of 6,300 feet, and is the highest peak between the mountains of Benguet, in northern Luzon, and Mt. Banajáo, in southern Luzon. It rises in a sharp point, thus affording a fine view.

In half an hour Burns rejoined us, and, being now

twelve miles from water we turned back, much pleased that one of our party had succeeded. Down, down, down we went. Would we never again reach the dry streambed? Ah! there it is! A short distance below this we found our Negrito friends, who had slept in the rocks. They had discovered a bee-tree and were eating the honey. We found it mighty good, but it did not help our thirst much. On, on, down the dry arroyo. Now and then our guides stopped to suck a few drops of water which they found on curled leaves, or to pick leeches from their bare ankles. These disgusting little worms were numerous and ravenous and annoyed the natives greatly. About 1 P.M. the welcome roar of rushing water was heard. The next quarter of a mile was a steeplechase over logs and boulders, and we established the record for that course. How good the life-giving fluid tasted as we lay on the great flat stones and drank our fill!

At 4 P.M. we reached our camp, finding all in good shape. An hour later we sat down to an enjoyable meal, and our Negritos, not now so shy, helped us to eat it. After supper they departed, and next day we returned to Camp Stotsenburg.

To Private Burns, Troop "L," Fifth Cavalry, probably belongs, then, the honor of being the first white man that ever set foot on the summit of Mt. Pinatúbo—and he deserves it, for a tougher or a pluckier little man does not wear Uncle Sam's uniform. Martin and Cesario both assured us that Mt. Pinatúbo had never before been ascended. My attempt had not been a moment too soon, for the day after my return heavy rains set in, and ten days later I was *en route* to the United States, "God's country."

THE HILLSIDE FARMER AND THE FOREST.

By George Hansen.

With all our embellishment of country seats and city parks, as well as with scientific forestry, we make only slow progress in the effort to cover the cruel scars with which civilization has defaced the landscape of our continent. The plow stirs the valley soil, the log-team drags deep furrows over hillsides, and ax and powder assist the weak arms of man in his struggle to cultivate. But of all the agencies that combine to subserve such purpose, none has shown itself of such fierceness as fire. Even when employed as an ally, it is such a treacherous power that no words but condemnation can be heard about its employment.

Far be it from me to look for an excuse for the setting out of fires. It is a grewsome sight to see the fierce flames lick up in hellish glee a magnificent stand of timber. Also are those fires to be condemned which the cattleman sets out in the fallen logs as he travels valleyward in the fall months. Yet, if we again, and ever again, see these columns of smoke rise heavenward so near our settlements, there surely must be some reason, some weighty reason, for such proceedings. It is the mountain rancher who sets them out, the man who struggles to create pastures in the timber-belt, and of his reasons and ways I write in explanation.

The man who first entered the forest had none to ask whether he could girdle the timber and wantonly destroy it, or fell it for some use. Nature had set out those woods, and man had arrived to appropriate them. But as soon as land laws were laid down ownership began, and the sawmill man set up his rights. As long as choice timber was to be had for the cutting he had to press forward. In his trail followed the miner, who was glad to take what had been culled over. But for him, too, certain requirements ruled, and he left what proved below his standard. Under such attacks only select timber was taken, inferior claims and odd quarter-sections never were filed upon. If the latter contained spots of grand stands of trees, the loose conscience of man never hesitated to appropriate what could be grasped with ease by the lumbering methods of the woodsman. The next "owner" of such lands never intended his entry at the land-office to be more than a mere filing. He hires a set of nomadic wood-choppers to bring down in the shortest time possible what was fit to be slain for cordwood, and the squeak of the brake on his last load is the last sound from him that disturbs the stillness of the landscape.

Under such reckless management of three distinct owners some fifteen or twenty years have passed by. A settler of different trend has now arrived—the home-seeker. Nobody opposes him when he sets to work to establish a homestead and strands his wire around the one hundred and sixty acres. But what is it that he finds on the ground where once a dome of graceful build spread over the first-comer? Mighty stumps are scattered through the thicket of spiny shrubs and second-growth timber; gullies are washed across the gentle slopes

A FAIR STAND OF SECOND-GROWTH SUGAR AND YELLOW PINE
OF ABOUT TWENTY-FIVE YEARS' GROWTH.

A ONCE PROMISING STAND OF SECOND-GROWTH TIMBER.
"The fire spread so swiftly that even twigs escaped the singeing flames."

once covered with forest sponge retaining moisture and soil. Those loads of lumber that pass his door were cut twenty, or even thirty, miles above his ranch. A team of ten or twelve mules, swung by a jerk-line, moves eight, or even nine, cords of wood piled solidly on a Washoe rack and back-axle. That kind of wood used to bring six dollars and a half at the mine. But competition has lowered the price to five dollars. And when the home-seeker inquires what his second-growth wood commands he learns that four dollars is all there is " in it." " In it " for whom? Surely not for him. It is worth a dollar and a quarter to cut it,—and where can the profit come in when blacksmith bills are squared and feed supplied to the stock, and only one trip a day can be made to the mine?

It is the exception, therefore, when we find that a rancher has gone to work in a systematic manner to clear his ground by cutting the wood. In the thick litter of pine needles not a blade of grass can grow—the rosin is " poisonous," as the old legend has it. The timber must go, to permit of the sprouting of wild feed, the sowing of grain, and the fallowing of the field. The first illustration shows a fair stand of second-growth sugar and yellow pine of about twenty-five years' growth. The wood is sleighed off and the limbs piled up preparatory to burning in winter-time. The oaks are left standing to furnish shade and shelter for the cattle when feeding on the stubble during the summer. Pleasant hills beyond now show grain-fields where conditions like those described prevailed years since. This is the most favorable result.

But what if a rancher lives so far from the mine

that it would not pay him to "fool" with the wood? What now, since strings of greasy tanks with blackish oil are winding their way like monstrous snakes over the railways to the furnaces of hoist and reduction-works? What is the rancher going to do for a living? He cannot afford to feed hay to any stock except his working horses. Even if he gets from fifteen to twenty dollars a ton for what he succeeds in marketing, there is very little profit to be made. It takes one hundred and thirty pounds of wheat or one hundred and eighty pounds of barley to sow one acre on fields that are only patches, where stumps and rocks have to be avoided when plowing. The only branch of ranching which can be depended upon for a cash income is the raising of cattle, and that pays only as long as large holdings can be acquired under loose land laws. It takes from seven to fifteen acres of such mountainous country to support one head of stock, and a summer range in high altitudes is needed in addition. It, therefore, is plain that additional clearing has to be resorted to to prevent the accumulation of pine needles and thickets of manzanita. How shall we accomplish this at a small cost?

A tremendous cloud rises against yonder hills. Now black, now red, now white. It is only a few minutes since we noticed it. But hear the roar and sish, the crackle and swish! Now in fury drives the tempest over a stretch of low shrubbery, now it rears in grewsome glory over the thick verdure of these promising young pines, now it spreads over the massive bower of a live-oak with a voracity as if oil and grease had been hurled in the path of the devouring monster.

When did this wind arise? What causes this terrific

fire? How did it get a start so near the ranch that we know so well? Did somebody blast stumps, and did some treacherous fuse set fire to the grass? Have children caused it by carelessness? Has a traveler on the road thrown a lighted cigar in the neighboring field? Enough, that it "got away" from somebody. Let us turn out, then, and lend a hand as best we may to stay the progress of the hungry element as it gathers into its maw everything alive, everything burnable, everything devourable, even soil and rock. The whole neighborhood assists, and as evening comes, cool and quiet and calm, backfires are run towards the terrific blaze, and trails are cut with hoe and shovel to stay the wild run.

But circumstances do not always favor the settler; some fires have refused to be stilled so quickly. The wind that is raised with every blaze has carried embers to places where no brand should spread. When the rancher would have been satisfied to have acres burned over, square miles have been laid waste. The heat was so great that nobody could get near the path of the fury, and fencing and buildings have had to be sacrificed. Only when bare fields and wide roads intervened the fire stopped and burned itself out. The next picture shows a once promising stand of second-growth timber that had been ruined but two weeks previous to the taking of the photograph. The fire spread so swiftly that no limbs were burned, even twigs escaped the singeing flames. If timber thus burned happens to be near enough to market to bid for fair returns, the rancher sets to work trimming and cutting up the charred wood ere it has time to become worthless.

With such burning over only the first step towards

clearing the land has been taken. The rest of the work would be easy, if the stumps of the pines were all that had to be reckoned with. No second-growth timber is permitted to exceed eighteen inches in diameter, and stumps of such strength rot out in from three to four years at most. But meanwhile a new crop has grown up amongst them. As if under a magic spell, millions of seedlings of chaparral and manzanita appear. Whence the seeds came nobody has yet explained. Perhaps they had been lying dormant since the majestic timber first sheltered plants of their kind; perhaps wind and birds and animals have scattered them for all these years from adjoining hills, and heretofore the thick cover of pine needles made sprouting impossible. It is a fact that the fire seems to have liberated their latent lives, and now no seed-bed of a nurseryman could be planted closer than these burned-over districts. But a danger arises from this growth when the ground is covered with the thickest stand of young pines imaginable. They cannot increase in size and girth, as they rob each other of light and air. If a cow strays into their shelter, the hunting herder has to dismount ere he can follow her, and that means much in a country where every boy grows up a woodsman and a horseman. This tract of pines was considered a nuisance, and the entire neighborhood was glad when fire "got into it." It is reported to have been the hottest blaze ever known in that part of the mountains, and nobody would ever have thought it possible that a tree or a shrub could withstand such hellish breath. Yet a tree here and there survived the waste, and if only ax and fire would spare them they could reach maturity and spread seed from their opening cones.

GENERAL CHARACTER OF THE LAND WHERE SUCH CONDITIONS PREVAIL.

"THORNS ALSO AND THISTLES SHALL IT BRING FORTH."

Again the crop of worthless shrubbery grows here as elsewhere, and what looks like a close-cropped lawn is one enormous field of matted manzanita. Even the smallest blade of grass is prevented from unfolding under such usurping mass, and the area is now as worthless as it was when covered with the thick, useless pines. No attempt at concealment is thought of when the next fire is set out to burn this struggling shrubbery.

Yet we find that even now, after the second firing, much rubbish and fallen timber remain that require gathering and refiring ere the plow can break the soil or the grazing cattle can pick the scant feed unhindered.

The third picture shows the general character of the land where such conditions prevail. The settlements range along the creek-beds, and the houses crowd to the roadsides. Vineyards occupy some hillsides, and small orchards are set out where the soil promises fair returns. The tailings in the mined-out channels have been leveled and dams are thrown up to retain the good soil that passes with the winter rains. Here sufficient garden-stuff is raised for the home, and enough surplus to warrant peddling in the neighboring towns.

But if it were not for favorable conditions that prevail here and there, such as a roadside tavern, a "station," or the setting up of a blacksmith-shop, thus insuring an extra income, few of these settlements would offer enough inducement for the establishment of a homestead. The hard-laboring son of Italy, with few needs and a numerous family to assist him in the rough work, finds his way to a competence, and even to the accumulation of a heritage, especially when trade in the product of the vine adds to his savings.

But what becomes of many of these "ranches"? The young folks have started out for new fields, and the pioneers, the aging settlers, find the grubbing-hoe and the pulling-rope too hard to handle in their declining days. "Thorns, also, and thistles shall it bring forth," seems to be true even here, where never an Eden blossomed. The owner of cattle has his eyes on places of just such character, and his opportunity is ripe on the day when one of the old couple is borne to the grave and the other leaves to end her days with the young folks in town. The ranch is now added to the large area of the neighbor's already princely holding, and only by old boards and scantlings can the spot be traced where once a home sent the curling smoke to heaven.

Well might the question be put: What profiteth all this? What eventually happens to this uncultivated land? As time goes by, wild "shoestring" oats and bronco-grass flourish. Too tough to offer food for stock, they survived the continuous close cropping and hold the ground once occupied by sweet clovers and tender grasses. Next we see a gaping cut through the deep soil. Here the miner's "giant," the tremendous force of the two-inch nozzle, has cut the channel following the lead on the bedrock below. The gold that was found has been minted in distant communities, and the abyss laughs at man's attempts to restore the old conditions. And this was once a glorious piece of forestland! The giants were cut down to fill the riffles of the miner's sluice-boxes. Being then cleared of stumps and rocks, it was fenced, and yielded an annual crop of grain. It paid for cultivation as long as the owner found occasional employment, ere the work in the timber round about had given out.

But the value of the property decreased, and the place was sold for the mortgage and accumulated interest. It now is under control of a stockman. He turns his cattle into the place, and little cares whether there a home has gone to wreck or not. Notice, then, how the rains have washed out the traces of the last furrows and created in time cuts deep enough for a calf to disappear in. Nature charitably clothes the slope with a dense growth of manzanita lest the wanderer behold the cruel scars here inflicted. Beyond the field of manzanita a promising lot of young pines rise in vigor—to develop into a forest? No; to be cut for cordwood, or to be burned in useless destruction.

Let us imagine that we have a sweeping view over part of one holding of a stockman. It is the result of long years of the acquirement of deserted ranches. Nothing seems to disturb the harmony of the landscape, and to the casual observer it seems to serve its purpose,—that is, the support of the cattle that are scattered through the trees. But nature has decreed differently. It is only a transitory condition that this region passes through, and no matter how slow the change comes about, it is bound to come. The running fires have rendered the soil so hard that a plow can no longer cut its furrows as it could when humus kept the crust mellow. The rills and creeklets that years ago contained water during the summer have been cut into rocky gullies by the unimpeded torrent of winter rains as they hasten to the lowlands. Here and there we meet with traces of a ditch system that years past furnished irrigation for garden and orchard. Where is the water that used to flow within their banks? Why does it no longer come down those creeks that used to harbor ferns and moss? The very home established by the owner of the holding has not command of sufficient water to support his cattle after the first of July, and that on more than one thousand acres.

There is system in all of this, but does it devolve to the good of the country? Will not the very prince of this domain find some day that his sleek band of cattle, as it passes bellowing to the subalpine range, can no longer compete with the stock that goes valleyward to feed on alfalfa farms? It is an absolute fact that the very man who drives a band of from one hundred and fifty to two hundred and fifty head of stock to the mountains has, at times of every year, not a drop of milk for his table. Gradually will he find that the profits of his enterprise decline. Like the roving and robbing gravel-miner, he lives for the time being in affluence, and when his claim no longer "pans out," he too will strike out for new ground; he too will realize that nature forbids the harvesting where no sowing has taken place; and as he sees his very poverty in the vastness of his lands, he will be ready to make way for those destined to replace him. Looking to lands of older civilization, and knowing the present conditions here, we can predict with positiveness who those parties will be. One shall be a new home-seeker, who once again looks for the most promising spots, and will be satisfied to cultivate his small area with thoroughness with toil and tool, neither knowing firebrand nor powder. The other, the holder of the rough ground of the wide open ranges, will be the community of interests represented in the government, local or federal, the very one that never should have been dispossessed of what nature decreed should develop and devolve for the good of all. This shall be replanted. And then—once again—shall God's sun and heaven's rain filter through leafy domes upon a blessed earth.

THE NOTABLE MOUNTAINEERING OF THE SIERRA CLUB IN 1903.

By E. T. Parsons.

After several days of preparation, the main party of Sierrans started for Mt. Whitney, leaving the camp by the Kern on July 9th. Our trail led along the course of Volcano Creek, in which abound the golden trout found nowhere else in the world. That our progress might be a feature of the trip, we took it slowly, allowing three days for the forty miles to Whitney's base. We camped at night in beautiful meadows and daily crossed ridges from which wide-spread views of the distant Sierra delighted us. Each afternoon the anglers brought in great catches, and the second evening we had for dinner over six hundred trout. The third afternoon we reached Crabtree Meadows, where we camped on Whitney Creek in sight of the delectable mountain.

Some started at midnight for the climb, but the main party set out at 4 A.M., after a good breakfast. The long line in single file strung along the trail, and repartee and badinage enlivened the tramp. The morning was invigoratingly cool, and as we progressed to higher elevations the coloring and detail of distant ranges, as well as the nearer lake, ridge, cliff, and crag, came out into distinct view until sunlight burst forth on the far Kaweahs and the Sawtooth group to the westward.

We passed the camp at the base of Whitney where Langley carried on his experiments and tackled the flank of the mountain. The ascent, while toilsome, was not dangerous nor difficult, and we made frequent short halts to enjoy the magnificent alpine scenery. By 8:45 we stood on the top of the highest mountain summit in the United States proper. The others kept coming up, until, numbering one hundred and three, it was the largest party ever assembled at one time on a California mountain-top. We looked out over the great valley to the eastward and the Inyo Range beyond, and plainly distinguished Lone Pine and the meandering green lines of the river and irrigating systems nearly eleven thousand feet below us. To the southward we saw the end of the Sierra where it breaks off into foot-hills and the lower ridges; to the westward in the clear morning light the Kaweahs and the Sawtooth Range, serrated and snow-flecked. But it was to the northward the grandest view lay,—peak after peak and crag after crag, the highest Sierra in all their nobility and grandeur. Near, and perhaps most striking of all, was Mt. Williamson, its almost perpendicular side ridged and fluted in rich dark reds and browns, its summit dentated, and apparently defying all attempts at climbing.

Seven of the advance party, however, under the guidance of the untiring mountaineer, Le Conte, had conquered it after much toil and hardship. As we gazed at its forbidding mien one of us remarked, "Well, day after to-morrow some of us will stand on that rugged peak," only to be greeted with questioning smiles.

But several of us had long determined that the ascent of Williamson was to be the feature of our summer, and we were not to be discouraged. That evening a party of ten, including four women, were enrolled for the expedition, and we arranged to leave the main party the next day on their return to the cañon of the Kern by the trail down Tyndall Creek. Here we left them, turning up-stream and following Tyndall Valley to the last timber, where we camped on a bleak spot near a small meadow, affording food for our two mules. After a late luncheon, our guide, Gould, led the men to a lake over the ridge back of the camp, where we enjoyed an icy dip and returned to camp. We fortified ourselves that evening with a good meal, in view of the struggle scheduled for the next day.

Breakfasting in the dim light of the dawn, we started up Tyndall Valley to the eastward, and a more rugged forbidding region I've never seen. Immense boulders lay piled in heaps or scattered about among lesser rocks. There were five miles of this until we reached the moraine bordering the cirque to the eastward of Tyndall and lying at the base of our objective point. Here was confusion worse confounded. Broken, sharp-edged granite blocks of immense size heaped up in great masses, some balancing and moving or sliding at the least footfall, made our progress slow and trying. Beyond this and below in the basin lay five beautiful sapphire and turquoise lakes, over one of which we crossed on the ice. Next over a snow-field, and we were at the western base of Williamson. We rested for a space and gazed at the work we had before us. The abrupt and frowning mountain-side was carved into chimney after chimney with rugged rock ridges between. There appeared no possible way up; and here the previous party spent five

THE APPROACH TO THE SUMMIT OF MT. WILLIAMSON.
Photo by E. T. Parsons.

hours trying slope after slope in wearing endeavor, until they finally found the only way, up which one of their number, E. B. Gould, was to guide us.

Entering at the foot of one of these great chimneys, our way led upward for twenty-five hundred feet, at times over small snow-patches, again climbing with hands and feet on the rocks bordering the slope, at times—and here most guardedly—zigzagging across and back over the insecure, shifting floor of the chimney, where a step loosened masses of broken talus, and great rocks, started at a touch, went leaping and bounding to a resting-place at the base of the mountain. By careful dodging and extreme watchfulness we escaped all accident, and finally reached the saddle at the top of the chimney. This indeed seemed the limit of our powers, and our guide waited while we scanned the towering cliff for a way up. Finally he showed us a broken crevice up its face, extending forty feet and ending on a small shelf. Two of the men preceded, and then one by one we followed,—toes, knees, hands, and elbows, all came into play. A rope was let down and looped slackly about the women, who climbed up, thus reassured, without a misstep, and without its aid, except the assurance of safety in case of a slip. From this standpoint we crawled through a hole under a large rock and out upon the final ridge. A last scramble up over great masses of broken granite brought us to the summit beside the two monuments, where we rested and enjoyed the outlook, incomparably grander than that from Whitney, because it includes a view of majestic Whitney itself, and also of the Sierra to the northward, which Williamson hides from the beholder on Whitney.

In the club register we found the names of the previous party—Le Conte, Eells, Parker, Butler, Elston, Cosgrave, and Gould. We registered Misses McBride, Redington, Swett, and Bradford, and Messrs. Rodman, Gould, Eloesser, Haskell, Curtis, and Parsons. The four ladies of our party were the first women to make this ascent, except Miss Skinner * and Mrs. Bolton Coit Brown.†

We arrived at the summit at 11:30, so that on account of the long and difficult return to camp our stay was necessarily short. We lunched and drank from a novel fountain made by setting up a large flat slab of granite, sloping it toward the sun, and plastering over its warm surface snow, which melted at once and ran in streams from its lower edge. Then taking a final lingering view of the grand alpine outlook, we reluctantly started for the return to base camp, which was uneventful and safely made by 6 o'clock.

That night we treated ourselves to a good supper, and the sun was gilding the mountain-tops next morning before we stirred from our sleeping-bags.

Retracing our steps to the Kern Cañon trail, we zigzagged down its precipitous wall and lunched in a beautiful grove not far from Junction Meadow. Here we enjoyed a long siesta until the afternoon shadow crept well up the eastern wall of the cañon, when we repacked our mules and followed the trail down beneath tall trees, beside the beautiful river, gazing with surprised delight at the magnificent many-hued walls revealed in all their graceful beauty by the softened, diffused light of early evening. It would surely take the brush of a Keith or

---

* SIERRA CLUB BULLETIN, Vol. I., p. 91.
† SIERRA CLUB BULLETIN, Vol. II., p. 26.

MT. WHITNEY (14,522 FT.), FROM THE SUMMIT OF MT. WILLIAMSON.

the pen of a Muir to paint or describe them adequately. Mile after mile they extended on each side of the cañon, painted delicate yellows, pinks, and greens, towering three thousand to four thousand feet above our trail, and broken only by the foaming lines of delicate, cascading rivulets falling to reach the Kern.

After a delightful supper of freshly caught trout and a jolly evening about our small camp-fire, we slept that night on softest beds of needles beneath tall pines, and greatly did we felicitate ourselves on not missing the ascent of Williamson, the climax of the outing.

An early morning tramp to Funston Meadows, our mules fording the Kern, and our pedestrians crossing on logs; a long midday rest beneath the trees; and another evening walk through flower-studded glades and past the towering faces of painted cliffs brilliantly beautiful; then our Kern bridge, the soda spring, and home at Camp Olney, welcomed vociferously by our fellow mountaineers.

Parties homeward bound were now leaving at intervals, and so a few more days of fishing on lake and river, a few more dips in Lower Lake, a few more jolly camp-fires, for some of us a few days' delightful sojourn in the Giant Forest, and we departed by various routes for home; there with invigorated zest to enjoy the usual walks of life until the voice of Nature again summons her devotees to the delights of an Alpine Outing.

ON THE TRAIL WITH THE SIERRA CLUB.

By William Frederic Badè.

It is perhaps inevitable that this article should betray an Eastern man's point of view; not, however, that of an indoors man, but of one who by choice and circumstance has experienced much that is best in "God's out-of-doors" in the East and the Middle West. A Californian, rightly or wrongly, will think this but a humble preparation for what may be had in his own fair valleys among misty camps "of mountains pitched tumultuously," where "far down the fragrant cañons sing the green and troubled waters." Suffice it to say, in lieu of the proverbially odious, that the writer found himself too pleasurably engrossed by his new experiences to seek to enhance them by comparison. The fact that the Sierra Club stands for the preservation of "the forests and other natural features of the Sierra Nevada Mountains" will always be its best recommendation with lovers of nature East or West. Both its fame and its aim, together with the desire "to explore and enjoy," induced the writer to seek connection with the Club, and on the evening of the 25th of June he found himself on the rails with an enthusiastic contingent of its membership bound for Visalia, the starting-point of the summer's outing. Superlatives come unbidden to one who would attempt a description of the wonderfully varied cos-

tumes, the camp-fire comradeship, and the splendid pageant of scenes and events which thenceforward trailed its sylvan length through five weeks of matchless summer days. In the nature of the case, this article cannot aim to be even a measurably complete record of the outing, but must confine itself to the more salient features of a great complex of events and activities interpreted through the personal impressions of the writer.

From an eagle's outlook, on Friday morning, June 26th, might have been seen a stretch of country-road, forty-five miles in length, winding across the comparatively level floor of the San Joaquin Valley from Visalia to the foot-hills of the Sierra Nevada and up through them, twenty miles more, to Mineral King; Broder and Hopping's four- and six-horse stages, chased by clouds of dust, passing at regular intervals—the convoy of the advance party of the Sierra Club and its outfit; billowy fields of golden grain seeking the horizon, and along the edges, drawn by processions of thirty or forty mules and horses, great combination machines that threw off sacks instead of sheaves; and in the purple distance still more purple spots that marked flourishing acres of citrus culture. In passing through them the cheering stage-occupants were gleefully pelted from the orchards with the golden fruit. The itinerary lunch at Three Rivers was made especially enjoyable through the generosity of the Visalia Board of Trade and Britten Brothers, who had there provided an abundance of delicious fruit and lemonade.

The first night out from Visalia we camped in the foot-hills of the Sierra. My companion, a man with large knowledge of Californian wilderness ways, superintended the preparations for the bivouac. My five-pound eiderdown sleeping-bag was to receive its initiation. We did nothing very arduous or unscriptural when we took up our beds and carried them to a reasonably level spot on the edge of the river gorge. In a country where rains during a large part of the year are unknown the stars are better than a tent, and contact with the bare ground is more a question of comfort than of health. To get into our bags was the work of a few moments, and—a tired mountaineer needs no sedatives. But the extreme novelty of the situation, assisted by villainous unevennesses of the ground and by prowling mules, had the effect of keeping at least one "tenderfoot" awake for some time. From the bottom of the gorge rose the sound of water plunging along the narrow, boulder-strewn channel of the Kaweah. Strange voices of bird or beast came floating down from the surrounding heights. Suddenly there was heard a stealthy tread. Instinctively his hand felt for a weapon,—when he saw the prodigious ears of a mule silhouetted against the sky-line. A brief skirmish, and the intruder left. But about 2 o'clock in the morning an inexcusable interrogatory snort suddenly broke into the dreams of two sleepers. There in the dim light, his nose almost in contact with their effects, stood a big mule on mischief bent. A stone launched unperceived caught him on the nose, and to his mulish wits it must have seemed that the pile of things he had so loudly interrogated had suddenly responded by biting him in the nose. He reared, almost falling on his back, and charged up the hill with a clatter that must have sent every coyote within a mile of us to cover. To add to his own as well as their excitement, he unwittingly made directly for another group of sleepers on the hillside. Awakened by the din, they saw this avalanche of terrified mule-flesh bearing down on them. There was no time to get out of the bags and no chance to run in them. Each one, bag and all, jumped up like a Jack-in-a-box. The sight of these apparitions springing from the ground not only was sufficient to deflect the disturber from his course but to send him a mile up the cañon, where he was lassoed later in the morning,—a sadder and a wiser mule. This was but a trifling incident, and scarcely worth the telling, except in so far as it was typical of those minor happenings that helped to give spice to the larger experiences.

The next afternoon, after a ride full of interest along the East Fork of the Kaweah and through a sadly hacked sequoia basin at Atwell's Mill, we had reached the terminus of the stage-road in the little village of Mineral King. The discovery of gold in the mountains above the town gave considerable importance to it during the seventies. Now, both in appearance and in population, it is but an echo of former days. Even the soaring eagle must strain his eyes to see the few houses that huddle along the East Fork. But there is reason to be thankful that the hand of man has not seriously marred the pristine beauty of this lovely alpine valley. Ages ago glaciers carved it out of solid granite. In winter avalanches cut wide paths down the precipitous slopes. In summer they are festooned with waterfalls. Far into July great snow-patches whiten the flanks of the warding mountains and water marvelous flower-beds below. Where trees have been able to maintain a footing against the pressure of winter snows extensive forests of mountain pine shimmer through the haze. Four miles above us eastward, between Mt. Florence and Mt. Vandever, loomed the snowy pass of Farewell Gap. It is the gateway to the southern Sierra. On the morrow at break of dawn we and our pack-animals, in single file, took the winding trail that leads to the saddle of the pass,—10,400 feet above the level of the Pacific. Since the altitude of Mineral King is about 7,700, this involved a climb of nearly three thousand feet. All our days in the High Sierra were " strung on sunbeam threads," but this morning of our ascent to Farewell Gap was first among peers, so beautiful that the most generous adjective would only belittle it. Sunday morning, too!—and we stood at the portals of one of the grandest natural cathedrals on the Pacific Slope. From the richly carved granite choir-galleries came the joyous music of many waters, and the deep organ-tones of full-throated waterfalls pealed forth ever and anon as we threaded its aisles on subsequent days. It was past midday when the last of our party of one hundred and ten reached the top of the pass, and every one felt that the ascent was an achievement, whatever else might be in store. Our pack-train, though composed mostly of sure-footed mules accustomed to mountain-climbing, had experienced some difficulty in getting over the snow-fields. By 9 o'clock the snow had softened, making the footing very insecure. One of the animals, overcome by exhaustion and the effects of the altitude, fell dead in his tracks. Once or twice unwary riders were thrown headlong from their plunging horses and had to be extricated from the snow-banks into which they dived head first. These as well as some other incidents of the ascent furnished a deal of good-natured

FAREWELL GAP (10,500 FT.).
Photo by E. T. Parsons.

merriment. Occasionally some floundering mule loosened from his pack a dunnage-bag which usually responded immediately to the pull of gravity. Then one or two packers would slide after it down the steep snowy slope, berating the situation with a volubility that would have amazed a steamboat captain. In the case of one or two of the party the effects of the altitude manifested themselves in accelerated heart-action to such a degree that it was deemed wise for them to proceed only after long pauses. But finally all gained the top of the pass in safety. Ten thousand four hundred feet above the level of the Pacific! Treble the figure and you have not yet measured the altitude of the mountaineer's feelings as he stands for the first time on the cornice of the great snow-wall that spans the mouth of Farewell Gap. Along the line of the descent, eastward, lay the valley of the Little Kern. A long white ribbon that hung on the steep mountain-side marked the path of the stream from its birthplace among the alpine snow-fields to its noisy career in the valley below. On the horizon to the northwest a mountain barrier lay thrown athwart the valley of Mineral King. Behind it gleamed snow-peaks, and a depression in the range, clad with misty pines, was Timber Gap, the crossing of the Giant Forest trail. Reluctantly we turned our backs on this panorama and made a rapid descent into the valley. The proximity of some meadow large enough to provide fodder for the pack-animals usually determines the choice of a camping site. Bullion Flat was made to fill the requirements, although some thought it rattled. Ere the alpen-glow began to glorify the heights our Chinese cooks, under the direction of Mr. Miller, chief of the commissariat, had made toothsome provision for ravenous appetites. Charles Lamb, with all his fulsome praise of "roast pig," knew nothing half so delicious as a camp-fire supper in the High Sierra after a day of strenuous mountaineering. If anything can bring completer satisfaction amid such conditions than good food and pure water, cooled by mountain snows and aerated in a thousand falls, it is the deathlike slumber that enfolds the tired mountaineer before he is done wondering at the unearthly brilliance of the stars that watch over his bed on the blooming heath. Doubtless it was after his experience in the California mountains that Robert Louis Stevenson wrote "Life is far better than people dream who fall asleep among the chimney-stacks and telegraph wires."

That night a brisk, cold northeaster, sweeping down on us from Mt. Vandever, tested the thermic qualities of blankets and sleeping-bags. Long ere the sun peered over the granite walls of our dormitory "rosy-fingered Dawn" found us merrily footing the new trail that leads to the top of the Great Western Divide. It was a stiff climb in places, and not without danger for those who were mounted. One popular lady of our party had a narrow escape when her horse slid off the trail. The crest of the ridge afforded a magnificent view. On the east side we caught a first glimpse of the deep pine-clad cañon of the Kern; on the west side, trending southward, another cañon crept away into the mellow haze. Through it were rolling the songful waters of the Little Kern, racing to round the southern end of the Western Divide and join the greater chorus of the Kern. To the north and east the air bristled with bare crags and snowy peaks—to most of us a wilderness of unexplored mysteries. The trail crosses the divide at a point known as Coyote Pass. Here a titanic art-gallery of Nature's own making contains a varied assortment of fantastic sculptures. Sun, wind, frost, and rain have carved the coarse granite into chimerical forms that excite and haunt the imagination. Now began the descent into the cañon along the gorge of Coyote Creek. At lower and lower levels we doubled our zigzag trail on the steep cañon wall. Waterfalls hung among openings in the trees. Instead of the expected camp, every turn brought glimpses of greater depths and more feathery pine-tops. Indeed, the trees seemed the only evidence that we were not headed directly for the center of the earth. Early in the afternoon most of the party had reached the floor of the Kern River Cañon and the site of our permanent camp. Since leaving the art-gallery we had descended nearly a mile by vertical measurement, and still we were more than six thousand feet above sea-level. In honor of Mr. Warren Olney, one of the pioneers of the Sierra Club, our mountain home was named "Camp Olney." An open stand of beautiful conifers, not least among them the stately sugar-pine, filtered the sunshine and softened the night. Coyote Creek, a cold, pure, alder-screened mountain stream, unfatigued by two wild leaps over cañon walls, raced through the middle of our camp and joined the brimming Kern a few hundred yards below. In the daytime it filled our cups with a beverage that put to shame the "blushing goblet," though "filled with the nectar that Jupiter sips," and at night, together with the Kern, it made the hours of slumber vocal with lullabies such as only Sierra waters know how to sing. For those who desired a little variation in their potations there were numerous soda-springs of such varied flavor and mineral content that the soda-water experts of the camp soon held briefs for the exploitation and defense of favorite springs. Nor must we omit to mention, as a bit of gallantry on the part of Nature, the sudden breaking out one night of a new soda-spring in the women's camp. Where not a drop of moisture was visible in the evening, the morning saw a rill of soda-water merrily trickling down the hill. Many other generosities of Nature that combined to approve the wisdom of those who selected the site of Camp Olney must go unmentioned for want of space. But who can forget the amphitheater where nightly the monster camp-fire blazed; where transfigured by the ruddy glow a great semicircle of expectant faces banked the darkness in the shadow of the pines; where Otto Wedemeyer sang of "Gypsy John" and many other winsome song-creations that peopled his wide repertoire; where music seemed glad to come at the call of the Sherwood Quartette; where addresses, instructive and entertaining, on a wide variety of topics, were delivered by Dr. G. K. Gilbert, of the U. S. Geological Survey, Professors Lawson and J. N. Le Conte, of the University of California, Prof. A. G. McAdie, of the Weather Bureau, the officers of the Club, and a number of others, both men and women, who contributed to these camp-fire entertainments. Sunday services were conducted by President J. K. McLean, of Pacific Theological Seminary, and by the Rev. S. C. Patterson.

The common meals naturally became part of the social apparatus of the camp. The task of satisfying healthy appetites, though engrossing, left room for the discussion of the day's adventures and the planning of new ones.

CAMP OLNEY.

KERN LAKE.

Photos by E. T. Parsons.

Neighboring points of interest invited excursions. Dr. J. K. McLean, whose large knowledge of the California mountains enables him to speak from a comparative point of view, thus describes the immediate environment: " The place is deeply cañoned. Tower Rock, a granite group, rises just opposite the camp, two thousand feet perpendicularly out of the river. As Sentinel Rocks in Yosemite are backed by Sentinel Dome, so is Tower Rock by Kern Dome, two thousand feet higher than itself. This on one side: on the other stand ramparts less imposing, but still lofty, in a deep cleft of which Coyote Creek and nearby Laurel Creek vainly do their best to emulate Bridal Veil and Illilouette. . . . The place is a genuine—though, so far as the walls are concerned, reduced—Yosemite." Upstream the grand cañon extended for sixteen miles. A mile or two below the camp were the Kern Lakes; the upper shows evidence of having been formed by a comparatively recent landslide which obstructed the course of the river. They were full of big lake trout and enormous shoals of despised suckers. Scarcely an evening passed when the gleam of a camp-fire and merry voices on the shore did not tell of fisherman's luck browning in the pan. The lava bridge and the falls of Volcano Creek, the fishing at Funston Meadows, the ten-thousand-foot outlook from Kern Dome, the falls of Coyote Creek, —these and many other opportunities for diversion were among the assets of our camp in the pinery. To it we returned after a day's pilgrimage to some sylvan or riparian shrine, feeling that even weariness was a luxury. Who shall describe the splendor of those crystalline nights when, bedded on a fragrant carpet of pine-needles, we watched the full moon climb slowly over the battlements of Tower Rock, with ever-changing play of opalescent light softening its hard, bold countenance into gentle though magnificent repose! Nor did moonless nights leave a slighter impression, for then the lesser lights, in lone possession of the sky, wheeled their blazing constellations among scintillating galaxies of thickly-strewn stars such as dwellers in the lowlands never see. New glories came with the morning, when the Steller jays, self-appointed alarm-clocks, called the sleepers to witness the first rosy shafts of the dawn striking the gray minarets of rock; to watch unseen hands weaving a tapestry of silver and gold down their scarred sides until, amid a rapid and elusive play of spectrum colors, irrepressible waves of light poured over the eastern ramparts, sifted through the trembling pines, and started a new day of joyous life in the Kern Cañon. But one might as well try to paint the sun with charcoal as attempt to describe adequately the beauty and grandeur that filled those charmed Sierran days and nights.

One of the motives of the Club's officers in selecting the Kern Cañon for last summer's outing was the desire to give mountain-climbers a chance to make the ascent of Mt. Whitney. The second party had arrived at the camp soon after the first, swelling its population to over two hundred. Many had come expressly to join in the dash to "the top of the United States." The distance from the camp to the mountain was about eighteen miles as the crow flies when he has not too much distracting business on the way. But a trail over the extremely corrugated surface of the Sierra Nevada easily doubles an air-line measurement, for it must follow the line of least resistance along the path of rivers, circumvent

TOWER ROCK, KERN RIVER CAÑON.
Photo by E. T. Parsons.

mountains, follow the backs of ridges, hit meadows enough to keep life in the pack-animals, and not miss the fords and the gaps. Thus it was not surprising that the real distance to Mt. Whitney was placed somewhere between thirty and forty miles. A pioneer party, composed of about forty persons under the leadership of Professor Le Conte, started on the 5th of July, making the ascent successfully, and by dint of forced marches returning to Camp Olney in six days. The main party, composed of one hundred and eight persons, started on the 9th of July, and planned to make the trip in seven days. Most of the members of both parties were seasoned climbers, including a number of Mazamas from Portland. The approach to Mt. Whitney was made by the Volcano Creek trail and the return by the Kern River Cañon. The size of the party and the limited number of pack-animals available produced some unexpected complications, with the result that some of us, without our sleeping-bags in a freezing temperature, cheerfully slept away part of the first night between a log and a fire. Onward and upward we went the next day, still following Volcano Creek, whose teeming population of famous golden trout was laid under tribute to our rods and appetites. Volumes might be written on what we saw this and the following day, as our path led over lava-beds, past an extinct crater where but recently Nature blew her volcanic forges, over closely matted rosettes of a rare and beautiful evening primrose (*Œnothera xylocarpa*), over golden acres of *Mimuli*, through zone after zone of vegetation, over the sandy waste of the Siberian outpost, into the deeply carved cañon of Rock Creek, hard by the spire of Mt. Guyot, to the third night's camping-ground on Crabtree Meadows. To-morrow, Mt. Whitney!

A quintet of adventurous spirits started soon after 1 o'clock in the morning, hoping to reach the top by sunrise. Unfortunately the distance of the camp from the base involved loss of time in picking the trail where it led over streams and meadows. Silently we filed on through the night, the leaders changing places occasionally to take turns in picking the trail. Even at that early hour the titanic character of our surroundings was manifest; the deep glaciated gorge, mountainous boulders, the dark depths of Guitar Lake, near where Professor Langley made his famous investigation of the color of the sun, and on our left rose the majestic granite hulk of Mt. Whitney. On its shoulder sparkled the diadem of the Pleiades, displaying a dozen or more brilliants where ordinarily but six are dimly visible. Over all brooded a silence so profound that it seemed as if a bit of eternity had been slipped into the place of one of our noisy days. An easy climb brought us to the "chimney,"—a rift in a five-hundred-foot precipice. This part of the climb called for caution and skill. To start a loose rock was to jeopardize the lives of climbers beneath. The "chimney" surmounted, there was a steady, but comparatively easy, climb of fifteen hundred feet to the summit. When we were halfway up the mountain-side the rising sun threw the shadow of Whitney westward over the cul-de-sac of a valley we had just left and bathed in rosy light the wilderness of snow-ribbed summits to the north and west. To convey an impression of the phenomenon is beyond the power of language. Far down at the approach to the "chimney" 'the main party, under the direction of Secretary Colby and Mr. Parsons, was dimly discernible as a wavering line. A few minutes after 7 the quintet was at the top, and members of the main party kept arriving steadily until, about the middle of the forenoon, all had safely conquered the mountain—one hundred and three persons. Considering the size of the party and the height of the mountain (14,522 ft.), July 12th deserves to be remembered in connection with one of the most remarkable achievements in the history of mountaineering. Thanks to the clearness of the atmosphere, the view from the top, especially in the early morning, was several degrees beyond the reach of superlatives. It would burden my account too much to mention even the more prominent among the countless peaks that lifted their glittering crests to the north, south, and west. On the Nevada side the mountain fell off in sheer precipices, leading to depths so awful that it fairly made one's head swim. Two miles beneath our feet lay Owen's Lake, and a few miles north of it the little town of Lone Pine. Farther southeast, beyond the Panamint Range, lay the expanse of Death Valley, its floor two hundred and eighty feet below sea-level—the sink of the Armagosa River. Here the lowest and the highest places in the United States are within sight of each other. Many lingered for hours over this never-to-be-forgotten panorama. Some added to their record the Needles that form part of Whitney, and visited the glacial lakes at the base. Before nightfall all were back in camp. The next evening saw the party encamped at the head of the Kern Cañon, where under the shadow of Picket Guard the Kern-Kaweah and the East Fork of the Kern lash their foaming waters through precipitous gorges into the grand cañon.

The departure of Mr. Parsons's party to Mt. Williamson and a cut-off down the East Fork made by seven fishermen, headed by Bernard Miller, were incidents of the day. The latter was a wild scramble in the interest of the commissariat, which was in need of replenishment. The result was rare sport and a trout dinner garnished with gentian meadows, pines, and waterfalls. The two following days were taken up with a leisurely and delightful march down the Kern Cañon to Camp Olney. One little party captained by Warren Olney, Jr., made an adventurous dash into the deep gorge of the Big Arroyo. The memories of all are hung with pictures of pine groves, flowery meadows, and lofty cañon-walls decorated here and there with wind-blown white streamers where the Kern's tributaries leaped into space. After more beautiful days at Camp Olney, one morning found us again in Mineral King preparing to take the trail over Timber Gap. In weeks already filled with stupendous scenery and thrilling incident the march from Mineral King to the Giant Forest claims a unique place. In the opinion of many it was the exclamation-point in the summer's outing. But the exigencies of space forbid detailed description. Of all our itinerary camps, those at Redwood and Alta Meadows certainly were incomparably the best. At the former we slept between the plank-roots of mighty sequoias on the margin of a lily-starred meadow, at the latter on a lofty mountain shelf overlooking a wonderful configuration of mountains and valleys. Last of all came the Giant Forest, with its fragrant carpet of lupines, its tuneful streams, and the indescribable majesty of sequoia colonnades that seemed to pillar the skies. It was fitting that our summer in Arcady should end there in Broder and Hopping's delightful "Camp Sierra." Imperceptibly the days sped, and still we lingered among these trees, many of which were saplings when the Pyramids were new. But far away, in teeming cities on the coast, duties were calling. One night, under the great trees they were pledged to protect, the Sierrans gathered once more around the last of many camp-fires to say reluctant good-bys. There ended the trail and our hardy pastimes in the Sierra Nevada.

THE COMPLETED LE CONTE MEMORIAL LODGE.

BY WM. E. COLBY,
SECRETARY-TREASURER OF THE LE CONTE MEMORIAL COMMITTEE.

As the accompanying illustrations will indicate, the Le Conte Memorial Lodge in Yosemite Valley has been completed, and the finishing touches were put on the building during the latter part of last September. The Club is now in possession of an exceedingly beautiful and appropriate structure, which will be used as the Club's headquarters in Yosemite Valley during the summer season of each year. A portion of the Club library, as well as maps and photographs, will be placed there, and a custodian will be in charge during May, June, and July, to give information to visitors concerning the Club and the surrounding mountain region.

The foundation, walls, and chimney of this lodge are built of granite obtained in the vicinity. It is rough-hewn, and as much of the weathered surface as possible was placed so as to face the exterior. Broad granite steps lead to the heavy "Dutch" entrance door. The main reading-room is 36 x 25 feet, and in the further end is a huge granite fireplace surrounded by bookcases and window-seats. The interior roof-beams are left exposed, and are finished in the rough. A very unique table has been constructed for the reading-room; a heavy

ANOTHER VIEW OF THE LE CONTE LODGE.
Photo by Hallett-Taylor Co.

INTERIOR VIEW OF THE LE CONTE LODGE.
Photo by Hallett-Taylor Co.

top, 9 x 5 feet, supported by two sections of the unbarked trunk of a large yellow pine.

The location of the lodge in the valley is most pleasing from a scenic standpoint. It is almost immediately under the towering walls of Glacier Point, on a gentle slope that runs back to the base of the cliffs, and has a background setting of a grove of beautiful trees. From the entrance of the building a fine view of the Half (or Le Conte) Dome is obtained.

Immediately after the death of Professor Joseph Le Conte in Yosemite Valley, the construction of a memorial there in his honor suggested itself to his friends. A committee composed of Professor A. C. Lawson, Professor Wm. R. Dudley, Dr. Edward R. Taylor, Mr. Elliott McAllister, and Mr. Wm. E. Colby, was appointed by the Directors of the Club to accomplish this object. They decided that instead of a monument of conventional type it would be much more appropriate and more in keeping with the wishes of Professor Le Conte, were he there to express them, and also typical of his active and useful life, to erect a lodge which would serve as a memorial and at the same time be of direct benefit to others.

This committee at once undertook the raising of the amount estimated to be necessary to effect this plan. They laid the matter systematically before large groups of the professor's friends and asked them to aid by contributing to the five-thousand-dollar fund necessary. Many prominent San Francisco merchants, the student body, alumni, and faculty of the University of California, many of the faculty of Stanford, mining engineers, geologists, Professor Le Conte's relatives, many others among his personal friends, and last, but not least, the members of the Sierra Club, contributed liberally. It is needless to say that by far the major portion of the fund came from Club members. In this manner the committee raised several thousand dollars, but there was still lacking several hundred dollars. The directors came to the rescue and levied what will probably be the only assessment ever placed upon members of the Club. This one-dollar assessment nearly completed the amount necessary, but there was still over two hundred dollars needed when Professor Le Conte's widow generously provided for the deficiency. I quote from her letter, which is self-explanatory:—

BERKELEY, October 16th.

Mr. MCALLISTER,

Dear Sir—I send through my son twenty-eight nuggets given to Dr. Le Conte on the occasion of his golden wedding, by several of his old pupils in South Africa. I know that they with me will feel that no better use could be made of them than contributing in aid of the Yosemite Sierra Club building. And I take this occasion of expressing through you to the members of the Sierra Club, and to any others interested, my sincere thanks for the loving thought which dedicated the building to the memory of my husband.

Yours truly,

CAROLINE ELIZABETH LE CONTE.

The contract price for the building was $4,714.28. Incidental expenses amounted to $77.14. Besides this, the Club paid over two hundred dollars in postage and for printing the numerous circulars sent out at various times. Every cent of this amount has been raised, so that the building has been completed without debt of any sort. The Club is certainly to be congratulated on the outcome, as the building will be a permanent headquarters, under its care and control, and on account of its picturesqueness and unique character has already attracted great interest and has been praised in the highest terms by those who have seen it.

John White, the architect, is deserving of the highest praise, and by donating his plans and time to the work has thereby become one of the largest contributors.

The Yosemite Commissioners have been very kind in rendering assistance, and many others have aided materially, to all of whom the Club is indebted.

The Outing of 1904 will start from Yosemite Valley in order to give as many members as possible an opportunity to visit the lodge on the occasion of its dedication.

SIERRA CLUB BULLETIN.

PUBLISHED IN JANUARY AND JUNE OF EACH YEAR.

Published for Members.   Annual Dues, $3.00.

The purposes of the Club are:—"To explore, enjoy, and render accessible the mountain regions of the Pacific Coast; to publish authentic information concerning them; to enlist the support and co-operation of the people and the Government in preserving the forests and other natural features of the Sierra Nevada Mountains."

OFFICERS FOR THE YEAR 1903-1904.

Board of Directors.

Mr. JOHN MUIR . . . . *President*
Mr. ELLIOTT MCALLISTER . . . . *Vice-President*
Mr. J. N. LECONTE . . . . *Treasurer*
Prof. W. R. DUDLEY . . . . *Corresponding Secretary*
Mr. WILLIAM E. COLBY . . . . *Recording Secretary*
   Prof. GEORGE DAVIDSON,   Mr. J. S. HUTCHINSON, JR.,
   Mr. WARREN GREGORY,   Mr. WARREN OLNEY.

Auditing Committee,
Directors GREGORY, MCALLISTER, and DUDLEY.

Committee on Publications,
Pres. DAVID STARR JORDAN, *Chairman.*

Mr. J. S. HUTCHINSON, Jr.,   Dr. MARSDEN MANSON,
  Editor Sierra Club Bulletin,   Dr. EMMET RIXFORD,
Mr. A. G. EELLS,   Mr. EDWARD T. PARSONS,
Mr. J. S. BUNNELL,   Mr. R. H. F. VARIEL,
Prof. J. H. SENGER,   Mr. TRACY R. KELLEY.

Committee on Admissions,
Directors DUDLEY, OLNEY, and MCALLISTER.

Committee on Parks and Reservations,
Prof. GEORGE DAVIDSON, *Chairman.*

Prof. W. R. DUDLEY,   Pres. DAVID STARR JORDAN,
Mr. J. M. ELLIOTT,   Mr. ABBOT KINNEY.

Committee on Outing and Transportation,
Mr. WM. E. COLBY, *Chairman.*

Mr. J. N. LE CONTE,   Mr. EDWARD T. PARSONS.

COMMUNICATION FROM THE SECRETARY.

To the Members of the Sierra Club:

During the past three years the Club has nearly doubled its membership, which will number eight hundred before long. This remarkable increase has been mainly due to the annual Club Outings, the third having been taken last summer to the Kern Cañon and Mt. Whitney. Our members should not, however, lose sight of the fact that this feature of the Club's life is but a minor part, and is merely a step toward the attainment of the worthy objects for which the Club was incorporated and the high ideals for which it stands. These Outings have unquestionably aided the Club in many ways besides merely increasing its membership. Because of such increase, they have necessarily added to the finances, and thus enabled the Club to do more effective work through its publications and its headquarters in the Mills Building. They have also made the Club much more widely known and consequently extended its sphere of influence. But the sentiment is becoming too prevalent that the Club exists merely for the purpose of conducting these Outings, whereas it was organized nearly ten years before the first Outing was taken. The preservation of the forests and the natural scenery of our mountains will always be our main work and reason for existence. We want these Outings to be enjoyed by our members, and we are glad that they attract members;

but above all we want our members to be in hearty sympathy with the highest and most important work of the Club, and in order to strengthen the Club in such work they should remain members even if it becomes impossible for them to attend the Outings.

The Club aided very materially in the establishment of our forest reserves, and exercises a powerful moral influence whenever any question arises affecting the welfare of the forests and natural scenery of the Sierra.

Every member of the Club should read President Roosevelt's address delivered at Stanford University last spring. A brief quotation is appropriate here:—

> "I want to-day, here in California, to make a special appeal to all of you, and to California as a whole, for work along a certain line—the line of preserving your great natural advantages alike from the standpoint of use and from the standpoint of beauty. . . . Here in California you have some of the great wonders of the world. You have a singularly beautiful landscape, singularly beautiful and singularly majestic scenery, and it should certainly be your aim to try to preserve for those who are to come after you that beauty; to try to keep unmarred that majesty. . . .
>
> "There is nothing more practical in the end than the preservation of beauty, than the preservation of anything that appeals to the higher emotions of mankind.
>
> "California has for years, I am happy to say, taken a more sensible, a more intelligent interest in forest preservation than any other State. It early appointed a Forest Commission; later on some of the functions of that commission were replaced by the Sierra Club, a club which has done much on the Pacific Coast to perpetuate the spirit of the explorer and pioneer."

The Club is honored by this recognition, and should enter upon the work of the future with redoubled zeal. There is not the slightest question but that the Sierra

Club is destined to be one of the greatest clubs of its kind, for where else, in the civilized world at least, has a club such magnificent opportunities as are presented at our very door for the enjoyment and study of the mountains, with the majestic range of the Sierra stretching from one end of the state to the other, clothed with matchless forests, abounding in marvelous scenery, and crowned with the eternal snows?

    Very respectfully,

              WM. E. COLBY,
          Secretary of the Sierra Club.

REPORT OF THE OUTING COMMITTEE.

The Outing of 1903 to the Kern Cañon had the largest attendance of any Outing that the Club has undertaken. Over two hundred and ten persons made the trip to the Main Camp. This involved a journey of sixty-five miles by stage and nearly twenty miles on foot over a very difficult trail which crossed two mountain-ridges at an altitude of between ten and eleven thousand feet. Thirty thousand pounds of personal baggage, provisions, and camp equipment were packed on animal-back over this same trail.

A side-trip to the summit of Mt. Whitney (14,522 ft.) was made by two parties of forty and one hundred and three persons, respectively. One hundred and thirty-nine of this number reached the top of the highest mountain in the United States, certainly a circumstance to be chronicled in the annals of mountain-climbing. Seventeen of the hardier mountaineers later climbed Mt. Williamson which presented greater difficulties to the climber.

It is fortunate that, though such a large party took so many side-trips over rough and mountainous country, no accident of a serious nature occurred to mar the success of the trip.

We are indebted to the Mt. Whitney Club, the Visalia Board of Trade, and the Supervisors of Tulare County for the very material aid rendered in preparing the way for the Club.

After all disbursements, nearly a hundred dollars remained in the treasury, to be used to meet the preliminary expenses incident to the Outing of 1904. The announcement of this Outing will accompany this BULLETIN or will be sent on application.

      WM. E. COLBY, *Chairman.*
      J. N. LE CONTE,
      E. T. PARSONS,
         Outing Committee.

NOTES AND CORRESPONDENCE.

In addition to longer articles suitable for the body of the magazine, the editor would be glad to receive brief memoranda of all noteworthy trips or explorations, together with brief comment and suggestion on any topics of general interest to the Club. Descriptive or narrative articles, or notes concerning the animals, birds, forests, trails, geology, botany, etc., of the mountains, will be acceptable.

The office of the Sierra Club is at Room 16, Third Floor, Mills Building, San Francisco, where all the maps, photographs, and other records of the Club are kept.

The Club would like to purchase additional copies of those numbers of the SIERRA CLUB BULLETIN which are noted on the back of the cover of this number as being out of print, and we hope any member having extra copies will send them to the Secretary.

Owing to the fact that Mr. J. S. Hutchinson was unable to attend to the editing of this issue of the SIERRA CLUB BULLETIN, Mrs. J. N. Le Conte kindly consented to undertake the work. The Club is indebted to her for this issue, and to Mr. J. N. Le Conte and Mr. Wm. E. Colby, who assisted her.

In the current number of *Water and Forest*, an excellent article by Mr. Marsden Mansen, on "Forest Protection and Extension," is most timely. The practical suggestions contained under the head of "Fire Protection," and the novel suggestions as to silviculture and reafforestation will interest all members of the Sierra Club.

Mr. Mansen has also kindly contributed to the Club library his recent work, entitled "The Evolution of Climates," the objects of which are, to quote from the author, "to investigate and interpret the phenomena and principles of the evolution of climates." Any one interested in this work will find it in the Club-room where it may be read.

EIGHTH INTERNATIONAL GEOGRAPHIC CONGRESS.

The following notice has been received from the Chairman of the International Geographic Congress:—

"Pursuant to the action of the Seventh International Geographic Congress, held in Berlin in 1899, the geographers and geographic societies of the United States are considering plans for the ensuing Congress, which is to convene in September, 1904. It is proposed to have the principal scientific sessions in Washington early in the month, and to have social sessions in New York, Philadelphia, Baltimore, and Chicago, with a final session, in conjunction with the World's Congress of Science and Arts, in St. Louis. It is provisionally planned also to provide an excursion from St. Louis to Mexico, and thence to points of geographic interest in western United States and Canada.

"A preliminary announcement is in press, and will shortly be issued to officers and members of geographic societies in all countries, and to geographers who may express interest in the Congress and its work. Details have been intrusted to a committee of arrangements made up of representatives from geographic societies in all parts of the United States. The officers of the committee are: Dr. W. J. McGee (Vice-President National Geographic Society), Chairman; Mr. John Joy Edson (President Washington Loan and Trust Company), Treasurer; and Dr. J. H. McCormick, Secretary. The office of the committee is in Hubbard Memorial Hall, Washington, D. C., U. S. A., where communications may be addressed."

DESCRIPTION OF A LIGHT, COMPACT ARRANGEMENT OF BEDDING AND PERSONAL EFFECTS FOR A CAMPING-TRIP.

I have been asked to describe the outfit which I use for packing my bedding and personal effects when on a camping-trip where it is necessary to economize space and weight. My personal baggage consists of two pieces,—one a roll of bedding, twenty-eight inches long, ten inches in diameter, weighing less than ten pounds; the other a canvas bag, twenty-eight inches long, fifteen inches wide when empty, and when full weighing even less than the bedding.

The bedding consists of a large eiderdown quilt, on one side covered by a sheet of the lightest calico, of a color which will not crock; on the other by a sheet of light but firm tan-color canvas, both sheets merely basted on with strong thread. Along the edges and bottom of the canvas strong tapes are firmly sewed at intervals of a foot or less in opposite pairs, so that they can be tied together when it is desired to turn the quilt into a sleeping-bag. There is a great advantage in this on a warm night; for the heat becomes intolerable in a close bag; but in this can be alleviated by untying the tapes and allowing the cooling air to enter. Instead of tapes, large safety-pins might be used, but they are liable to be lost, while the tapes, if well sewed to the canvas, will last as long as the bag. Upon the return from the trip I always rip off the calico and have it washed, remove the canvas, cover the quilt with cheese-cloth, and use it again on the bed. The bag when rolled for packing is protected by a canvas flap twenty-eight inches by nineteen, the longer dimension being sewed to the middle of the canvas at the top of the quilt. This flap is also fine for covering the head at night. Two or three long double tapes are sewed to the free edge of the flap. When it is desired to pack the bedding, the two long edges of the quilt are brought together along the middle of the quilt, then the folded quilt is rolled from the bottom up as tightly as possible, and the flap rolled around and tied by the tapes, one of each pair being turned in one direction and the other in the opposite, so that they may be tied firmly together.

The canvas bag for clothing and other necessaries is drawn together at the top by a double draw-string, so that it may be firmly closed. On the outside there are two flat pockets, made of a single piece of canvas, sewed several times on three sides and down the middle. They are covered by flaps which button to the pockets, each by two strong flat buttons. These pockets are very convenient for writing materials, handkerchiefs, ribbons, collars, and other little things which it is desirable to keep from the jumble within the bag. It is surprising how much can be packed into one of these bags, though not enough to do away with the necessity of washing the underclothing and blouses many times during an outing of a month. Both the roll of bedding and bag of clothing could easily be packed in a dunnage bag half the size of those used by the Sierra Club in the outing of 1903. In case of a trip without pack-animals, the roll of bedding could be made much lighter by ripping off the canvas and putting it and the necessities in the canvas bag; or the bedding could be kept covered with the canvas and the necessities could be packed in the roll of bedding. I shall be glad to show the outfit to any one who cares to see it.

This is as good for a man as a woman, and the men with whom I have been camping have had a similar outfit.

ALICE EASTWOOD.

In the *National Geographical Magazine* for November we see that those indefatigable mountaineers, Dr. and Mrs. Workman, have spent another season in the Himalayas. After camping overnight at the great height of 19,355 feet, they made next day the highest ascents ever recorded. The party scaled a peak 22,568 feet in elevation, and while Mrs. Workman and one guide remained on the summit, Dr. Workman and two others ascended another mountain to the height of 23,394 feet. These achievements entitle them to the world record for high ascents. Their general explorations of these lofty ranges, being carried on scientifically, are therefore of great value.

The Club library is in receipt of "True Tales of Mountain Adventure," by Mrs. Aubrey Le Blond, donated by Harrington Putnam, New York. The book is very attractively bound and printed, and the illustrations are very convincing. The author states that she has gathered data and quoted extensively from well-known Alpine climbers, chief among whom is Mr. Edward Whymper, to whom the book is dedicated. Nevertheless, being a good mountaineer herself, and long familiar with the scenes and conditions she depicts, her accounts are very readable, and many little details of mountaineering in the Alps are given for the benefit of those who have never climbed. Her excuse for repeating so many of the fatal accidents which occur there is found in the warning they may convey, but the reader will also confess to a creepy fascination produced by the recital of such horrors.

The Whitney Creek Gorge.

In my paper on the Mount Whitney Creek and the Poison Meadow Trail, published in the BULLETIN of the Sierra Club for February, 1902, the claim was made that Mr. Hopping and myself were the first to make the passage of the Whitney Gorge by mule-train. We examined both sides of the gorge very carefully in the summer of 1900, and were satisfied that no one had preceded us; least of all could we concede the existence of a trail from Mount Whitney to the bed of the Kern Cañon through the Whitney Gorge. Nevertheless a trail is marked for the route described on the map accompanying Lieutenant Clark's report to the Department of the Interior as Superintendent of the Sequoia National Park for the year 1899. The insertion of this trail, however, was an error, and it is a pleasure to me to quote from a letter which I received from him not so long since. The paragraphs quoted, however, have an interest outside of the point at issue.

> In making a little sketch for the Department of the Interior in 1899, I took the liberty to transfer the name "Whitney" to a stream formerly known as Crabtree Creek and I gave the name 'Volcano' to the old Whitney Creek. Some Sierra travelers were calling this latter stream Golden Trout Creek, but as a number of nearby creeks have been stocked with this species of trout I thought the stream should derive its name from

the striking volcanic formation along its course. These changes in names seemed to me thoroughly rational, and I hope, in noting them upon my map, I have not trespassed upon any traditions of the Sierra admirers.

I wish also to say a word about the trail traced along the north bank of Whitney Creek from Crabtree Meadows to the Kern, especially as you speak of attempting that passage. In making the map to accompany my report I endeavored to personally travel over the trails indicated. Now in making my trip to Mt. Whitney in 1899 I went out on Volcano Creek to Monache Meadows in order to climb some of the extinct volcanoes and also for a day's fishing along that stream. From Monache I sent my pack-train and men up the usually traveled trail via Cooper Meadows and the Sand Flats to Crabtree Meadows. In company with Dr. Frederick Pearl and one man, I retraced our steps to the Kern and then up that cañon, hoping to be able to get out at Whitney Creek, and so join our main party at the Crabtree Meadows. As a matter of fact the outlook from the point where Whitney Creek joins the Kern discouraged us, and we moved farther up the cañon and gained the eastern plateau across the stone-fields north of the East Fork, as indicated on the map, and thence down to our pack-train at Crabtree. At the Crabtree Meadows I found a trail leading west along Whitney Creek, and I sent a corporal to follow it down and ascertain if it really reached the Kern. He reported that it was a blind trail ending about one mile down the stream in some meadowland, and was apparently only used to gain better grazing for the stock. The government engraver at Washington completed the trail down to the Kern, and as I did not read the proof, the report and map were issued before I knew of the mistake. So far as I knew at that time, there was no practicable trail from Crabtree down Whitney Creek to the Kern.

The Sierra country is very dear to me and I hope that some time I may have the pleasure of joining one of the Sierra Club outings. I am one of the enthusiastic though necessarily silent members of the Club.

Very respectfully,

HENRY B. CLARK,

GRAND RAPIDS, MICH., May 25, 1093. *First Lt. Arty. Corps.*

As our Sierra members know, new and fine trails are being everywhere opened by the forest-ranger. If his coming lessens in some ways the possibilities of adventure, the forest reserve policy is nevertheless on the whole a boon to Sierra enthusiasts, and as for the industrial welfare of California there can be, of course, but one opinion by thoughtful people as to its wisdom.

BERKELEY, CAL., November 1, 1903. WILLIS L. JEPSON.

The Club is indebted to Dr. G. K. Gilbert, of the U. S. Geological Survey, for an album of fine photographs illustrating geological phenomena of the Kern River and Tuolumne Meadow region. He has also kindly donated several photographs of Sierra glaciers, to form a nucleus for a collection of such photographs to be made by the Club. Both these sets may be seen at the Club rooms.

Mr. Geo. Fiske, the renowned photographer of Yosemite, has kindly presented the Club with a fine set of photographs of the Le Conte Lodge.

Mr. Geo. P. Tallant, one of our members who is at present in Europe, has generously sent the Club, from Switzerland, an Alpine ice-ax and a pair of snow-shoes, besides other articles of interest.

We acknowledge the receipt, with the author's compliments, of "Forest Trees and Forest Scenery," by G. Frederick Schwarz. Unfortunately this attractive-looking volume comes too late for further mention in this issue.

FORESTRY NOTES.

Edited by Professor William R. Dudley.

REPEAL THREE DANGEROUS LAWS.
The most notable discussion of the present year is over the repeal of the Desert Land Act, the commutation clause of the Homestead Act, and the Timber and Stone Act. The central idea of these and similar acts relating to the Government land sales has been the one of the Homestead Law, that of helping the home-builder. Our citizens, both native and adopted, have obtained, at easy terms under these laws, small tracts of public land sufficient for their support, and the prosperity of the country has been built on the prosperity of small, independent homes, established by the hundred thousand among the common people in this way. The laws were framed however to encourage the settler rather than to bar out the speculator. They were framed also when good land was plenty and speculation in wild land could not therefore be very profitable. At present, however, in the language of the late message of President Roosevelt,—

"The character and uses of the remaining public lands differ widely from those of the public lands which Congress had especially in view when these laws were passed. The rapidly increasing rate of the disposal of public lands is not followed by a corresponding increase in home building. There is a tendency to mass in large holdings public lands, especially timber and grazing lands, and therefore to retard settlement."

This has been done by skillfully evading the intent of the laws. Under the Desert Land Law, for instance, a man may acquire three hundred and twenty acres of irrigable land. If there are four in his family, they may acquire two entire sections. The law does not require he shall live on this land, but obliges him to take his oath that he is taking steps to irrigate it, when he can get title to it at an early date at $1.25 per acre. It is easy to see that these people may act as the agents of those who wish to acquire large holdings for grazing or speculative purposes, and sell to such monopolies their easily acquired land.

It will be seen that this law working in this way may seriously interfere with the operations of the National Irrigation Law of June 13, 1902, in which it is contemplated that the Government will establish in arid regions reservoirs for the use of the small landholder by controlling all the neighboring irrigable land until the reservoir is completed, when it will sell to permanent occupants only small tracts from forty to one hundred and sixty acres on the homestead plan.

President Roosevelt in his last two messages has urged the repeal of the three laws or clauses of laws named above, and has been consistently supported by the Secretary of the Interior and the heads of the bureaus most concerned in these questions. It was the subject of the chief debate at the Irrigation Congress at Ogden in September, and a resolution has been introduced into Congress providing for inquiry into the operation of our land laws. The matter will eventually be set right. When a question concerning the welfare of the people and the nation becomes the subject of warm and thorough discussion, with men of the Roosevelt type on one side and the land speculators and land barons on the other, it is in a fair way for an early and just settlement.

We have referred in both numbers for 1903, to the activity of land speculators in their favorite field of fraudulent use of the land laws. The Department of the Interior, after collecting a mass of evidence in this direction, has made a number of arrests; probably more will follow. The arrest causing the greatest comment is that of John A. Benson, of San Francisco, once a Government "surveyor," when he made the notorious "Benson surveys," all of which have been or should be resurveyed on account of glaring inaccuracies. His present arrest is, however, based on accusations of fraudulent use of the land laws in his extensive real-estate dealings. Whether he can be proven guilty or not, his case deserves the most careful and thorough investigation on the part of the Interior Department. His former well-known good understanding with prominent newspapers in the West is still manifest in their allusions to the persecutions he is suffering.

THE NEW YORK STATE COLLEGE OF FORESTRY. This valuable training-school was discontinued on June 17th, by a vote of the Trustees of Cornell University, under whose control the College of Forestry was placed. This action was based on the veto of the annual appropriation from the New York Legislature, by Governor Odell during the preceding May. The Governor based his veto on the report of a legislative committee, adverse to the management of the forestry school lands belonging to the State in the Adirondacks, and the legislative committee in turn were influenced by the personal and somewhat sentimental objection of wealthy owners of large tracts of timber-land adjacent to the State forest to Dr. Fernow's method of cutting the timber in the college forest. We doubt if these wealthy Manhattan proprietors of Adirondack deer-forests are capable of criticising a forester's working plans, or that these plans would involve any real injury to the water-supply of the region; but Director Fernow encountered too powerful neighbors, probably ignorant of the very objects of forestry, and the result is a serious check to forestry education in America. Seventy undergraduates in forestry were obliged to abandon their work at Cornell, and a prosperous school, for whose work and training a nation has pressing need, is destroyed. California should have a cordial sympathy for Dr. Fernow who said at a critical moment some effective words in favor of our California Redwood Park which had more weight with thoughtful men than is generally known. We especially commend to readers of the Bulletin Dr. Fernow's statistical article on the "Timber Supply in the United States," in the *Forestry Quarterly* during the past year. The latter journal is not to be discontinued with the State college, but will be regularly published, with its headquarters at Ithaca, N. Y., as formerly.

TRANSFER OF FOREST RESERVES. Early in the present session of Congress Representative Mondell introduced a bill providing for the transfer of the administration of the forest reserves from the General Land Office to the Bureau of Forestry in the Department of Agriculture. The interest of the Sierra Club in this matter is well known. We believe it means such economy and improved efficiency that it would solve most of our difficulties upon the reserves in California, and obviate most of the dangers connected with the forest reserve policy, and there are dangers if the latter are not made useful to the public. There is little to add to former arguments except to urge California members of Congress to amend this resolution, if it seems likely to fail in committee, by proposing that the California Reserves—a large proportion of the entire amount—be turned over to the Bureau of Forestry. There would be no opposition in this State, and the interest of California would be better subserved if the Bureau, with its limited number of trained men, had only 9,000,000 acres, or a possible 15,000,000, to provide working-plans for instead of the entire 70,000,000 acres, the amount in all the forest reserves of the country at the present time. The Bureau of Forestry has made good its promise of putting a considerable number of men in the field of forest work in California during the past summer, working along the lines indicated in the June BULLETIN. Mr. Pinchot himself spent some weeks here in August and September, giving a number of important addresses. On the evening of August 31st some of the members of the Sierra Club and the University Club gave a banquet in his honor, at which President Wheeler, President Jordan, Mr. Pinchot, Mr. Wm. H. Mills, and others spoke.

THE PARKS OF CALIFORNIA. On September 14th a meeting important in the annals of future San Francisco was held on the grounds of the Tamalpais Country Club. The master spirit was William Kent, of Mill Valley. The object was the establishment of a public park on Mt. Tamalpais. It was a representative meeting, many men and women of wealth and public spirit, and no professional orators, were present. Working committees have since been appointed on which the Sierra Club is largely represented. The park must be established through purchase and private gift, as there is no public land on the mountain. Already Mrs. Emma Shafter Howard and her son, Shafter Howard, have signified their desire to give their interest in the large Shafter property on the mountain to this public park if the project is carried out. It is proposed that the park be under national control.

On November 17th, Mr. Gillett of California introduced a bill providing for the purchase by Congress of the two Calaveras groves of *Sequoia gigantea*, with a view to making a national park thereof. An extraordinary interest has been created in this movement by the Outdoor Art League and the members of the California Club, not only among the women's clubs of America, but among public men all over the United States. The women of California are right; the nation should purchase these groves,—not at an extraordinary price, but at a fair valuation, and the nation should control this property. We wish it could control all the forest park property in the Sierras, thus insuring uniform treatment and care.

Efforts are being made to induce the Government to set aside the "Pinnacles" and a tract adjoining, in San Benito, for a permanent reservation, on the ground of the beauty, picturesqueness, and variety of color of these masses of sandstone. It is an attractive, indeed wonderful, piece of natural scenery and should be carefully treated for its future use as a public resort. It is all on Government land and hence would not call for Congressional purchase.

MT. SHASTA AND THE BLACK BUTTES.

PUBLICATIONS OF THE SIERRA CLUB

Number 31

Sierra Club Bulletin

Vol. V   No. 2

JUNE, 1904

SAN FRANCISCO, CAL.

1904

SIERRA CLUB BULLETIN

Vol. V.   JUNE, 1904   No. 2

CONTENTS:

	PAGE
MT. WHITNEY AS A SITE FOR A METEOROLOGICAL OBSERVATORY.....*Alex. G. McAdie*..	87
Plate XVIII.	
THE WATER-OUZEL AT HOME..... *Wm. Frederic Badè*.	102
Plates XIX., XX.	
THE SAN FRANCISCO PEAKS IN APRIL. *Edward T. Parsons*.	108
Plate XXI.	
OVER HARRISON'S PASS WITH ANIMALS.*Robert D. Pike*...	115
Plate XXII.	
THE ASCENT OF SAN ANTONIO.... *Willoughby Rodman*.	122
Plate XXIII.	
ORGANIZATION OF THE SIERRA CLUB............	133
SECRETARY'S REPORT...................	134
Plate XXIV.	
TREASURER'S REPORT	137
NOTES AND CORRESPONDENCE	138
FORESTRY NOTES............*William R. Dudley*.	145

All communications intended for publication by the SIERRA CLUB, and all correspondence concerning such publication, should be addressed to the Editor, J. S. Hutchinson, Jr., Sierra Club, Claus Spreckels Building, San Francisco, California.

Correspondence concerning the distribution and sale of the publications of the Club, and concerning its business generally, should be addressed to the Secretary of the Sierra Club, Room 16, Third Floor, Mills Building, San Francisco, California.

THE EASTERN CLIFFS OF MT. WHITNEY.
(A SHEER FALL OF ABOUT 6,000 FEET.)
Photo by Professor J. N. Le Conte.

MOUNT WHITNEY AS A SITE FOR A METEOROLOGICAL OBSERVATORY.

BY ALEXANDER G. MCADIE, PROFESSOR OF METEOROLOGY.

(From Monthly Weather Review for November, 1903.)

In reply to a letter dated June 15, 1903, from the Chief of the Weather Bureau, asking for a report on the advantages and disadvantages of Mt. Whitney as a site for a meteorological observatory in connection with the proposed astrophysical observatory, the accompanying notes based on observations made during a hasty trip to the summit in July, 1903, in company with the Sierra Club of San Francisco were submitted.

Accessibility.—Mt. Whitney is situated in latitude 36° 34′ 33″ north, and longitude 118° 17′ 32″ west. It may be reached in several ways.

I. From Lone Pine on the Carson and Colorado Railroad, along the county roads to Carroll Creek, up zigzags of a trail, across Cottonwood Creek to Horseshoe Meadow, a climb of nearly 5,000 feet in ten miles, and thence by trail to Volcano Mountain.

II. By trail from the Kern River, at its southern end, working north along the Kern River to the East Fork, thence south to Crabtree Meadow, thence to Langley's Camp on the eastern side of Mt. Whitney, 2,800* feet below the summit.

III. From the northern end of Kern River, working south to East Fork, thence as in II.

The trails on the western side of the mountain are not steep, nor especially difficult and dangerous. A good climber can go from Langley's Camp to the summit in less than four hours.

On the top of the mountain, or peak, is a flat of several acres. On the extreme eastern edge a small monument of rocks has been erected. The eastern side of the peak is precipitous, a sheer fall of about 6,000 feet sharply marking the mountain. About 11,000 feet below the summit lies the valley of Owens River, with Owens Lake to the southeast. On a clear, quiet day Lone Pine, almost directly east of Mt. Whitney, and distant about fifteen miles, can be seen. Independence, lying to the north-northeast, is hidden by a ridge. Between Independence and Lone Pine six streams flow to the east. The most important of these is Lone Pine Creek, which flows down from Mt. Whitney. According to the report of Mr. Charles C. Garrett, Observer at Independence, Cal., dated June 17, 1903, the quantity of water in this creek is as follows:—

"The flow of the stream varies very much in different years. Measurements taken two days ago at my request showed a flow of 660 miners' inches. The water is now at its highest point, and this is regarded as an average year. It is probable that at the time of lowest water not more than 80 inches flow. Measurements were taken in the months of October and December, 1893, for testimony in a water suit, and flows of 195 and 160 inches, respectively, were found. The principal owner of the waters of Little Pine Creek informs me that, in his opinion, the average flow of the stream for an average year is about 300 miners' inches."

---

* Three thousand feet is probably a more accurate figure.

On the eastern side of the mountain there are at least four lakes within three miles. There is a splendid supply of good water at Langley's Camp. Mt. Whitney is in the Mt. Whitney Military Reservation, and I am under the impression that one of the reasons urged in establishing the reservation was the desire to retain it for use as a station for scientific research.

The peculiar character of Mt. Whitney renders it a good site for meteorological work, inasmuch as comparisons can be made of the conditions in the free air over a confined and heated valley and the conditions existing on the westward slope of the Sierra, or plateau conditions. While we were on the summit a lady's veil was thrown over the eastern edge, and, although the temperature was but 53°, it was plain that there were high temperatures and strong ascensional currents on the eastern side of the mountain. The course of the veil was such as to suggest that with regard to the general flow of the air from west to east the mountain acts as a dam, or weir.

It is probable that for the greater portion of the year the peak is accessible. The average precipitation in this section is not very large. Snow remains in the crevasses until August or September. At the time of our ascent, July 8, 1903, we passed across one crevasse, which, however, could have been avoided by making a detour south of the gully. I do not know that the peak has ever been ascended in winter, but I believe there might be periods when this would be possible. No one of the other high mountains on the Pacific Slope, such as Shasta or Rainier, is so easy to climb as Mt. Whitney. Owing to the fact that the two peaks mentioned lie farther north and in the track of atmospheric disturbances, climbing is almost out of the question in winter, and hazardous even in summer Mt. Whitney, therefore, of all the extremely high peaks on the Pacific Coast, is probably most suitable for a meteorological observatory.

All materials would have to be carried up by pack-train. I made some inquiry as to prices for this work, but could obtain no trustworthy estimates.

The Elevation of Mt. Whitney.—As will be seen below, few mountain elevations have been discussed more carefully than that of Mt. Whitney. Some barometric observations were made on our trip, although it was a hasty one and not altogether favorable for such work. Fortunately the weather conditions were very favorable. The greatest care was taken by Professor J. N. Le Conte and myself to read carefully, and independently of each other, the heights of the mercurial column. Our chief purpose was to correct the prevailing estimate of the height of Mt. Whitney—viz., 14,900 feet, an elevation given on most of the maps in use in California.

Gannett, in his "Dictionary of Altitudes in the United States" (third edition, 1899), gives an elevation of 14,898 feet, and this we believe to be erroneous. The authority given is Whitney, but I am unable to ascertain if Professor Whitney made the ascent and measurement, or, as chief of the Geological Survey of California, used the measurement made by Carl Rabe for the survey. This latter was the first measurement of Mt. Whitney. His readings, as marked on the case of the mountain mercurial barometer (Green No. 1554) used by him, are 17.836 inches, 32°; 17.848 inches, 42°.

The elevation deduced from the above readings was

14,898 feet, or exactly the same as the figures given by Gannett. This elevation, however, does not seem to be in accord with the readings, and if the altitude is determined on the assumption that the correction applied to the barometer was the same as applied in our observations (a doubtful assumption, it is true), the elevation would be about 13,701 feet, the sea-level pressure on that date being 30.01 inches at the given hour, the value of the mean temperature being 37.5° F., and the corrected reading at Mt. Whitney being 17.915 inches.

Two mercurial barometers were carried from San Francisco to Mt. Whitney summit and read at half-hourly intervals by Professor J. N. Le Conte, University of California, and myself. One of the barometers was the same instrument used by Rabe (Green No. 1554). Our readings on the summit were as follows:—

SUMMIT OF MT. WHITNEY, JULY 8, 1903. OBSERVERS: J. N. LE CONTE AND A. G. McADIE.

Pacific Time.	Green, No. 1554.		Green, No. 1664.	
	Barometer.	Attached thermometer.	Barometer.	Attached thermometer.
	Inches.	°F.	*Inches.*	°F.
9:30 a. m.	17.630	51	17.652	54
10:00 a. m.	17.638	51	17.652	55
10:30 a. m.	17.646	55	17.660	55
11:00 a. m.	17.650	55	17.660	54
11:30 a. m.	17.650	50	17.667	52
12:00 noon	17.650	49	17.668	51
12:30 p. m.	17.652	48	17.674	54
1:00 p. m.	17.654	49.5	17.674	53
	17.646	51.7	17.663	
	− 0.036*		− 0.041*	
	17.610		17.622	
	+ 0.088†		+ 0.068†	
	17.698		17.690	

* Reduction to standard temperature.

† Sum total of the probable instrumental error, scale correction, capillarity, and gravity corrections for latitude 37° and for altitude 15,000 feet.

The mean of our pressure-readings on the summit was 17.690 inches, while the mean of the Langley readings was 17.588 inches. There are only four of the series by Langley which were taken at hours comparable with ours,—namely, September 4, 8:30 A.M.; September 5, 12:40 P.M.; September 6, 8:17 A.M.; and September 6, 9 A.M. The mean of these corrected and reduced is 17.609 inches. The difference, therefore, is but 0.081 of an inch. The temperatures also agree fairly well.

Professor Langley gives the elevation of Mt. Whitney as 14,522 feet, or 10,762 feet above his base-station at Lone Pine.*

We found deposited on the summit a record of an ascent made on August 23, 1902, by Professors Kellogg, Hallock, Putnam, and others, in which it is stated that the temperature was then 34° F., and the boiling-point, as determined by William Hallock, 186.4° F. It is interesting to note that the pressure corresponding to this boiling-point would be 17.58 inches.

On October 8, 1895, Hutchings and others ascended the mountain and reported that water boiled at 187° F.

Wheeler's Determinations.—Wheeler gives as the height† determined by the adopted mean of barometric observations made by the observers of his survey party of 1875, 14,471 feet. The mean of three readings, at half-hour intervals, on September 24, 1875, after being corrected and reduced, was 17.796 inches; temperature, 35.3°; wet-bulb reading, 29.0°. A similar mean for October 13, 1875, was 17.840 inches; temperature, 36.7°;

---

* The exact elevation of the station at Lone Pine is uncertain.
† " United States Geological Surveys West of the One Hundredth Meridian." Wheeler, 1889, p. 95.

wet-bulb reading, 32.2°. The corrections applied are not accessible, but the records are probably in the office of the Chief of Engineers, U. S. Army.

"It is," says Wheeler, "the highest point measured by careful barometric observations within the territory of the United States, except Alaska."

The record of the observations made by Rabe in 1873, with the barometer, Green No. 1554, is as follows:—

Barometer.	Attached thermometer.
Inches.	°F.
17.836	33
17.848	42
17.842	38
— 0.015*	
17.827	

* Reduction to standard temperature.

These readings, corrected for temperature only, differ from the values obtained by us, by + 0.217 inches. The difference from the readings of the other barometer (Green No. 1664) was + 0.205 inches.

It will be noticed that in the readings made in 1903 there is a decrease in temperature during the observations, as shown by both attached thermometers, and moreover the temperatures themselves are not similar. Barometer No. 1554 is a small mountain barometer with a scale reading from twenty-four to eleven inches. Barometer No. 1664 has a scale reading from thirty-three to fourteen inches. Both instruments were filled with clean mercury June 23, 1903, and the longer instrument carefully read and compared with station barometer No. 387 in the Weather Bureau office at San Francisco. Its mean correction was + 0.068 inches. It may be questioned whether this correction properly applies to readings at high elevation, but for the present we will assume that it does so.

We must consider next the various simultaneous base readings.

Hour (Pacific Time).	Mount Whitney.	Independence. Elevation 3910 feet.	Mount Tamalpais. Elevation. 2375 feet.	San Francisco. Elevation 155 feet.
10 a. m.	17.680	25.965	27.55	29.90
11 a. m.	17.689	25.953	27.56	29.89
12 noon	17.701	25.936	27.56	29.88
1 p. m.	17.704	25.919	27.56	29.86

The above are the so-called station-pressures,—that is, the observed readings corrected for temperature, scale correction, capillarity, and gravity. Independence is the Weather Bureau station nearest to Mt. Whitney, and the observations were made at that point by Mr. Charles C. Garrett.

The sea-level pressures at Independence and at San Francisco were as follows:—

Hour.	Independence.	San Francisco.
10 a. m.	29.88	30.06
11 a. m.	29.86	30.05
12 noon	29.85	30.04
1 p. m.	29.82	30.02
Mean	29.85	30.04

The observations at San Francisco and at Mt. Whitney are probably the most satisfactory of all, and these we shall proceed to use in determining the true elevation.

Professor Bigelow's modification of the Laplacian equation, as given on page 490, equation 60, of his "Report on International Cloud Observations," (Vol. II of the Report of the Chief of the United States Weather Bureau, 1898–99), or equation 52, p. 66, of his "Report on the Barometry of the United States," etc., (Annual Report of the Chief of the United States Weather Bureau, 1900-1901, Vol. II), is as follows:—

$$h - h_0 = (56517 + 123.3\theta + 0.003h)$$
$$\left(1 + 0.378\frac{e}{B}\right)(1 + 0.0026 \cos 2\phi) \log \frac{B_0}{B}.$$

Using the values for 10 A.M. July 8, $B_0 = 30.06$ inches, as at San Francisco, $B = 17.680$ inches, as on Mt. Whitney, and a mean temperature $\theta = 53°$, we obtain

$$\log B_0 = \log B + \frac{h - h_0}{56517 + 123.3\,(53) + 0.003h}(1-\beta)(1-\gamma),$$

whence $h = 63096 \times 0.230507 = 14,515$ feet.*

Previous Determinations of Altitude.—On page 201 of his "Researches on Solar Heat" (Professional Paper of the Signal Service No. 15), Professor Langley gives what is probably the best series of observations as yet made on Mt. Whitney. The observers were Mr. E. O. Michaelis, Mr. J. J. Nanry, and Mr. J. E. Keeler.

The readings given in Table 173 of his work are as follows:—

---

* Prof. Abbe having kindly pointed out that I had not made full use of the Independence readings, I give herewith the following values: 10 A.M., 14,441 feet; 11 A.M., 14,414 feet; noon, 14,378 feet; 1 P.M., 14,355 feet, which, as the editor remarks, are to be considered as only a portion of a continuous 24-hour series. Having also seen Mr. Heiskell's computations, I would add that the values 14,530 and 14,532 obtained by him by using the Bigelow tables agree with the values obtained above in which the value of θ was 53°, or a degree less than that used by him. Recomputing the elevation, but using a temperature of 54° and sea-level pressure of 30.06, my computation gives 14,572. The sea-level pressure used by Mr. Heiskell was 30.04 inches and the station-pressures 17.694, which, according to the method of computation used above, would give an elevation of 14,534 feet.—A. M., November 20, 1903.

READING OF BAROMETER NO. 2018, SIGNAL SERVICE, ON THE SUMMIT OF MT. WHITNEY.

Date.	Time.	Reading.	Attached thermometer	Reading.*
1881.		*Inches.*	° *F.*	*Inches.*
September 2	6:00 p. m.	17.600	30.0	17.599
2	9:00 p. m.	17.597	26.5	17.603
2	12 midn't	17.569	25.5	17.576
3	3:00 a. m.	17.529	22.5	17.540
3	6:00 a. m.	17.518	22.5	17.529
3	8:15 p. m.	17.514	28.2	17.516
4	8:30 a. m.	17.627	52.8	17.591
5	12:40 p. m.	17.600	62.5	17.546
5	5:07 p. m.	17.680	61.5	17.628
5	6:30 p. m.	17.640	42.0	17.622
5	8:20 p. m.	17.599	38.0	17.588
5	10:22 p. m.	17.558	32.0	17.555
5	12 midn't	17.558	31.5	17.555
6	1:00 a. m.	17.610	30.0	17.610
6	3:00 a. m.	17.610	30.0	17.610
6	5:00 a. m.	17.610	28.0	17.613
6	8:17 a. m.	17.692	52.0	17.657
6	9:00 a. m.	17.680	54.4	17.640

Professor J. N. Le Conte, on July 8, 1903, made measurements of the height by angles of elevation and depression between Old Camp Independence, Lone Pine, and the Peak and return, and obtained a result of 14,470 feet.†

Historical Notes.‡—The mountain was first seen from Mt. Brewer by members of the Geological Survey of California, Brewer, King, and others, in 1864, and named Mt. Whitney. On August 18, 1873, John Lucas, C. D. Bigole, and A. H. Johnson, climbed the peak and called it Fisherman's Peak. On September 1, 1873, Clarence

---

* Corrected for temperature and reduced to Signal Service standard, but not for gravity.

† But this depends upon the height of Lone Pine depot; and this in turn upon the elevation of Mound House on the Virginia and Truckee Railroad.

‡ References: Langley—"Researches on Solar Heat." Wheeler—"Surveys West of One Hundredth Meridian, 1889." Stewart—*Mt. Whitney Club Journal*, Visalia, Cal. Le Conte—SIERRA CLUB BULLETIN.

King, then in New York, learned that the peak which he had climbed in 1871, now known as Sheep Mountain, Old Mt. Whitney, and Mt. Corcoran (Bierstadt), lying to the south of Whitney, was not Mt. Whitney, and hastening West climbed the right peak September 19, 1873. On September 6, 1873, the mountain was climbed by Carl Rabe, and the first mercurial barometer (Green, No. 1554) carried to the summit. Professor Langley's expedition is well known. He reached Lone Pine on July 24, 1881, and left on September 10th by way of Lone Pine Cañon. The journey, in brief, is described in pages 36 to 44, Professional Paper No. 15, Signal Service, published in 1884.

I cannot do better than quote Professor Langley's statement, given on page 44:—

"I do not think the Italian Government, in its observatory on Ætna, the French in that of Puy de Dome, or any other nation at any other occupied station, has a finer site for such a purpose than the United States possesses in Whitney and its neighboring peaks; and it is most earnestly to be hoped that something more than a mere ordinary meteorological station will be finally erected here and that the almost unequaled advantages of this site will be developed by the Government."

COMPUTATION OF THE ALTITUDE OF MT. WHITNEY.

(A report by Mr. H. L. HEISKELL to Prof. F. H. BIGELOW, dated Oct. 2, 1903.)

Relative to the observations made on Mt. Whitney, Cal., by Professor McAdie on July 8, 1903, at 10 A.M., 11 A.M., noon, and 1 P.M., and used by him in connection with simultaneous observations taken at Independence, San Francisco, and Mt. Tamalpais, to determine the height of the summit, I find that the observations are too few, and taken at a bad time of the day, to give any very accurate results.

Three essential elements must be considered in barometric hypsometry: temperature, pressure, and vapor-pressure, and the observations should be taken at different times of the day and on different days, so as to obtain a true mean; an error of one degree in mean temperature causes an error of twenty feet in the height of Mt. Whitney; an error of .001 of an inch in pressure causes an error of one foot in the computed height. In these observations the attached thermometer is read for temperature and there are no hygrometric observations; then again the temperature at Independence, etc., was taken from the thermograph, so that a possible error of from one hundred to two hundred feet is not improbable.

From the data available, using your formula in your Barometry Report, I make the height of Mt. Whitney as follows:

	Feet.
By using the simultaneous observations taken by the observer at Independence and by Professor McAdie at Mt. Whitney, the elevation is	14,651
San Francisco and Mt. Whitney	14,532
Mt. Tamalpais and Mt. Whitney	14,618
Mean	14,600

If we reduce the observations at Independence, San Francisco, and Mt. Tamalpais to sea-level, and then compute to Mt. Whitney, we have—

	Feet.
Independence and Mt. Whitney	14,590
San Francisco and Mt. Whitney	14,532
Mt. Tamalpais and Mt. Whitney	14,595
Mean	14,572

or a difference of twenty-eight feet from the preceding.

Professor McAdie, using observations taken at San Francisco only, calculates the height at 14,515.

On September 2, 3, 4, 5, 6, 1881, Professor Langley had a very accurate and careful series of eighteen simultaneous observations taken at Lone Pine and Mt. Whitney and published in his "Researches on Solar Heat." His barometers were carefully compared, and his temperature and hygrometer observations were made by experienced observers, so that the accuracy of the work can hardly be questioned. In 1900 Mr. Gannett deduced from railroad-levels the elevation of Lone Pine at 3,661 feet above sea-level, but in 1881 the height of Lone Pine was given by Mr. George Davidson to Professor Langley as 3,760 feet, or nearly 100 feet higher. The means of eighteen simultaneous observations at the two points are as follows:—

LONE PINE.	MT. WHITNEY.
Pressure......... 26.018	Pressure......... 17.586
Temperature..... 69.57	Temperature..... 37.20

Using the height of Lone Pine, as given by Mr. Gannett in 1900 (3,661 feet), and the barometric observations of Professor Langley, I make the height of Mt. Whitney 14,423.

Professor Langley, in his report, using 3,883 feet for Lone Pine and his own barometric work, says Mt. Whitney, by barometer observations, is 14,625.

Professor Langley, by using Davidson's altitude (3,760 feet) for Lone Pine and barometer observations at Mt. Whitney, makes the height 14,522.

On August 17 to September 7, 1881, Professor Langley had sixteen simultaneous observations taken at Lone Pine and Mountain Camp to determine the height of the camp. To see how we agree on that height I herewith give the data: Using Davidson's height of Lone Pine

(3,760 feet), the height of Mountain Camp is 11,624; using Gannett's height of Lone Pine (3,661 feet), Mountain Camp is 11,525. Professor Langley makes Mountain Camp 11,625.

From the above, I should say that the approximate heights are: Lone Pine (Gannett), 3,661; Mountain Camp (Gannett and Langley), reduced by me, 11,525; Mt. Whitney (Gannett and Langley), reduced by me, 14,423.

I should, therefore, suggest that the adopted height of Mt. Whitney be about 14,423 feet, as determined by using Professor Langley's observations and Professor Gannett's height in 1900 for Lone Pine.*

COMPUTATION OF THE ALTITUDE OF MT. WHITNEY.

Under date of January 11, 1904, Professor Joseph N. Le Conte, of the University of California, says:—

"The Lone Pine railroad station is on the main line of the Carson and Colorado Railroad, and is on the eastern side of Owens River, close to the base of the Inyo Range. The town of Lone Pine is on the western side of the valley and on the western side of the river also. The distance between the two points is about three miles, and the railroad station bears about north 60° east of the town. I visited the railroad station last September and spent some time with Mr. McGrath, the division superintendent. His memory of the altitude of the rail at the station, namely, 3,658 feet, was afterward corroborated in a letter from him to me after consulting the records of the survey at Carson City, Nev. Mr. Henry Gannett gives the same number in his "Dictionary of Altitudes," evidently obtained from the same source. This, however, is not the altitude of the point occupied by Professor Langley in his determination of the height of Mt.

---

* A letter from Professor McAdie makes it very doubtful whether the hamlet "Lone Pine," occupied by Professor Langley in 1881, is the same as the railroad station "Lone Pine," subsequently established.

Whitney. There has never, to my knowledge, been a line of levels run between the two places, and the only determination of the height of the town that I have ever found is the one given by Captain Wheeler—namely, 3,810 feet; this, however, is barometric.

"There is a 'railroad tangent' at Lone Pine station over twenty miles long. It is absolutely straight and nearly level. It would be easy to measure off a base line four or five miles long, and arrive at a good measure of the elevation of the mountain; this might be still further improved by simultaneous angles observed from the mountain and the station. Such a measurement would depend on the elevation of the rail, of course, but this I think can be checked up. A survey has been run from this point to Mojave on the line of the Southern Pacific near Los Angeles. If the results of this latter survey could be obtained, we would know better how much reliance to put on the figures 3,658. It has long been a desire of mine to make this triangulation, for the angle of elevation is over 6° and the distance fifteen miles only. But I could not put very much faith on the levels over 550 miles of such rough country."

Under date of January 16, 1904, the Director of the United States Geological Survey, says:—

"Regarding the relative elevation of the railway station near Lone Pine, Cal., and the barometric station in that town occupied by Professor Langley, the only information that I have been able to get is to the effect that the difference in elevation is slight, probably not exceeding ten feet, the site of the town being the higher.

"More to the purpose, however, is the fact that this office has run a line of levels from the sea through the San Joaquin Valley, and up the south fork of the Kaweah River to Farewell Gap, thence connecting by vertical angles with the summit of Mt. Whitney, obtaining, as a result, 14,434 feet. I do not consider this result as conclusive, inasmuch as the last link in the chain consists of a single vertical angle at a distance of thirty-four miles."

THE WATER-OUZEL AT HOME.*

By William Frederic Badè.

The avifauna of the Kern Cañon, especially at the head-waters of the Kern and in the neighborhood of the Kern lakes, proved both varied and interesting even to a casual observer during the Sierra Club outing of 1903. The Steller jay (*Cyanocitta stelleri*), the Clarke nutcracker (*Nucifraga columbiana*), the Louisiana tanager (*Piranga Ludoviciana*), the Arctic bluebird (*Sialia arctica*), juncos, several species of hawk and grouse, Brewer's blackbirds (*Scolecophagus cyanocephalus*), and the water-ouzel (*Cinclus Mexicanus*), were among the commonest of the feathered folk seen near Camp Olney. The last-mentioned bird I had seen for the first time on the upper Klamath River—a bobbing, bowing, winking compound of many avian charms. But it was not the winsome bird I learned to know on the banks of the Coyote. One morning (July 2d) I was casting the fly on a few foam-flecked pools near its junction with the Kern. Fed by the melting snows of the Great Divide, every morning found the creek at its fullest, for then it was carrying past Camp Olney the increment of the previous day's thaw. A keen ear could easily detect in the thunder of its falls a fuller crescendo, and the water leaped from the escarpments with greater abandon. True to her name the water-ouzel was there in her favorite environment of alder, pines, and flying spray.

* With photographs by the author.

My efforts to beguile the excessively wary trout made me an object of much suspicion to a pair of these birds, who seemed to claim exclusive hunting rights on that part of the creek. Evidently they had never seen a man do so insane a thing as to whip a stream with a make-believe fly at the end of a long string. Was he fishing for ouzels? Did he expect their nestlings to bite on that fly? Their behavior made it apparent that a brood of nestlings must be hidden away behind one of the many cascades. It required but little observation to locate the nest—a moss-built affair sunk in the floor of a niche behind a heavy sheet of falling water. The site had been cleverly selected. No increase of volume in the stream could endanger the nest, for the pool had enough fall to spill all the water above a certain level. The diaphanous liquid curtain effectually screened it from observation and protected it from attack by bird enemies. Few carnivorous birds would venture to seek their prey behind a waterfall. The ready accessibility of this nesting-site for purposes of observation at once suggested to me the possibility of photographing the birds as they came and went in pursuance of their family duties. Their excessive shyness was the only obstacle. In order to overcome this I continued to fish for two days near their particular cascades, pretending not to see them; and yet it was only the occasional unwary trout that found his way into the creel. My interest for the time being was more ornithological than piscatorial. The ruse succeeded, for the ouzels decided that I was harmlessly interested in my own business, insane though it was, and began to go about theirs with confidence. This probation period afforded abundant opportunity for the study of their habits and manners. My recollection of Mr. Muir's classic study added zest to my observations. What a winking, bowing, busy little creature the "dipper" is! In what far-off period of time did this "humming-bird of California waterfalls" acquire the bowing and scraping habit which one is accustomed to think the peculiar accomplishment of the snipe family and a few other water-birds? The possession of a nictitating membrane, which gives the bird an air of winking at the observer, is evidence of long and intimate acquaintance with the water. In his search after food he often lights in midstream on some rock over which the water dashes at intervals. Not infrequently I saw him swept off the rock into a churning pool. But his short wings enabled him to rise from the water with ease, or he swam complacently to the nearest bank and waded out. Several pair of them had set up housekeeping in more inaccessible places under some of the higher falls. As with short and rapid wing-stroke they darted in and out among the flying spume and spray, often directly through the swaying sheet of water, they seemed the very embodiment of the spirit of the waterfall. The two sprites which I had under particular observation were quite generous in showing off their varied accomplishments. They swam, dived, waded, sang; they pirouetted from rock to rock, slipped into the current by intention or accident, flickered in the sunlight, and washed their slate-colored plumage in the crystal water of the falls. Four hungry mouths kept them extremely busy. Every few minutes they appeared with their bills full of insects that live in and beside the water. In fact, a young water-ouzel seems to be quite as bottomless as a baby robin. Both continue in the begging habit as a fine art long

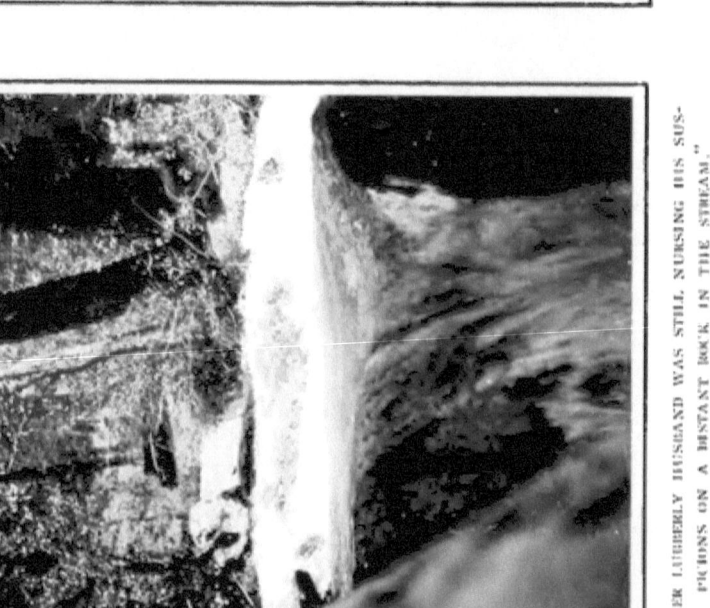

"HER LUBBERLY HUSBAND WAS STILL NURSING HIS SUSPICIONS ON A DISTANT ROCK IN THE STREAM."

"WITH A MAY-FLY IN HIS BILL, READY TO DART BEHIND THE FALL."

PLATE XIX.

after they ought to be finding their own grub. Several young ouzels which I observed on Volcano Creek seemed the most accomplished avian beggars I have ever seen. Not only their voices but every sprouting pinfeather seemed to be saying, "Give a poor beggar something to eat!" Not the least interesting and commendable feature of a water-ouzel's family life is the fact that husband and wife expect to assume equal shares of the family burdens. How they apportion their duties during the period of incubation I was not able to observe. But both minister with equal assiduity to the needs of the fledglings. What is more important, they seem to hold each other to the performance of this duty under untoward circumstances. The following incident occurred at the time when I was preparing to photograph the birds at close range. I had concealed my camera within six feet of a place where they were accustomed to perch before entering the niche behind the cascade. Such close approach again excited suspicion and alarm. For considerably more than an hour they refused to carry food to their nestlings. Then the female began to reconnoiter. Seeing that I was apparently only whipping her home pool as I had whipped many another pool in the neighborhood, she decided to risk a visit to her nest with a load of tidbits. The distribution must have been made with unseemly haste, for she immediately appeared again through her doorway of spray. She was, however, in no haste to leave the neighborhood, but lit on a boulder a few feet away and warbled the equivalent of a "Coast clear" to her lubberly husband, who was still nursing his suspicions on a distant rock in the stream. (See Plate XIX.) He would not come. His bill was full of May-flies. A second and a third time she signaled, and now he very circumspectly approached the cascade that hid the nest, flitting hesitatingly from rock to rock until he was almost beside her. But suddenly his fears again overcame his courage and he darted precipitately back to the place from which he had started. He was n't going to risk his neck, not he! This churlish behavior seemed to rouse the ire of his spouse. Instantly she lit beside him and running her bill several times vigorously into his fluffy plumage she took his catch of May-flies from him and carried them to the hungry nestlings. Her example no less than the little explosion of wifely indignation seemed to recall him to a sense of his duty. My presence was soon ignored, and he came and went as regularly as she. One of the accompanying photographs (Plate XIX) shows him with a May-fly in his bill, ready to dart behind the fall. His whole attitude—the uptilt of the stubby tail, the poise of the head and body—suggest something of the alertness that characterizes the water-ouzel at all times. The grace and swiftness of the mountain stream have passed into the bird's movements. The dash and music of its waters have sung themselves into his being. And there are moments, even in his busy life, when he likes to stand on a moss cushion and watch the stream glide by. (Plate XX.)

The little domestic episode described above, of course, does not embody anything that is peculiar in the water-ouzel's conception or performance of family duty. I have observed a disposition on the part of at least one other pair of birds to hold each other to a certain standard of domestic conduct. This occurred in the case of a pair of red-eyed vireos (*Vireo olivaceus*) who had built their nest in a flowering dogwood on the grounds of the Penn-

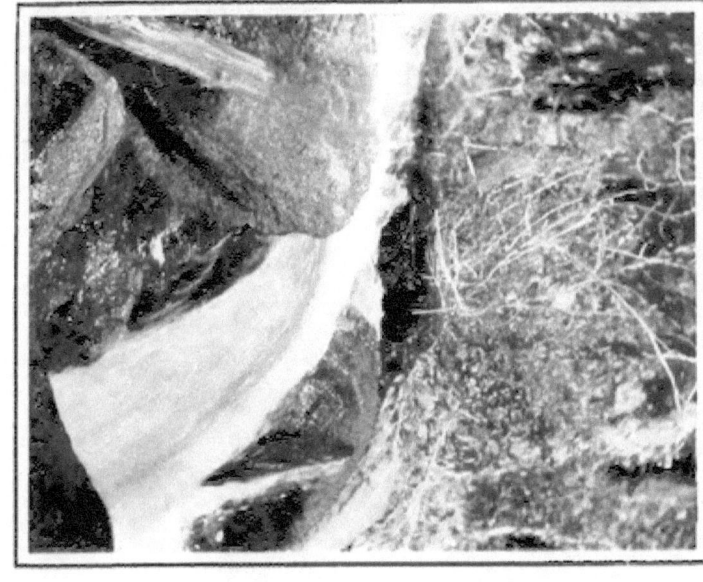

"HE LIKES TO STAND ON A MOSS CUSHION AND WATCH THE STREAM GLIDE BY."

WHERE THE WATER-OUZEL IS AT HOME. (KERN-KAWEAH FALLS.)

sylvania Chautauqua, at Mount Gretna, Pa. From my second-story lecture-room I had them under daily observation during the entire period of incubation and until the fledglings were coaxed from the nest. As soon as the eggs had given place to five cavernous-mouthed nestlings, the work of foraging began. The diet of the young vireos consisted largely of caterpillars. The female always carefully minced hers during the first few days, but the male pushed the whole of his catch undivided down the throat of the luckless nestling that happened to be nearest to him. It was no thanks to his care that some of them narrowly escaped death by choking. Once the female happened to arrive just as he was about to repeat some of his bungling work. At once she flew at him with every sign of indignation, snatched the caterpillar from him and divided it piecemeal among her nestlings. For some time after that she contrived to be at the nest whenever he returned. Apparently she had no faith in his ability to feed her nestlings, for on these occasions she herself distributed the food he brought. Her actions, even as in the case of the ouzels, indicated that she *expected* and *disapproved* certain things in the conduct of her mate.

In the cases observed it was the female whose stronger maternal instincts made the demands on the conduct of the male. But the obligations and the demands are no doubt reciprocal. Such evidences of domesticity give the water-ouzel no mean place among birds that have an admittedly high emotional development. Long may this charming singer continue to dwell in the cascaded mountain fastnesses of the Pacific Coast—his only and inalienable home!

THE SAN FRANCISCO PEAKS IN APRIL.

By Edward T. Parsons.

There is a mountain fever that seizes the nature-lover, inspiring and moving him to seek the mountain-tops, there to delight in the magnificence and glory spread out for the contemplation of those who reach high pinnacles. In fact, the mere sight of a lofty snow-crowned peak is sufficient infection, and never do I gaze on one of those buttressed pillars of the temple of creation without a sudden access of this fever.

Those who have crossed the country on the Santa Fe route, and who, approaching the crest of the continent at Flagstaff, have gazed on the nobly symmetrical mountain group known as the San Francisco Peaks, will understand my feelings as I found myself at that place one Saturday early in April, 1901, with the long-awaited convenient opportunity before me to climb their loftiest summit.

My arrangements were soon completed, and at 4 o'clock in the afternoon I took a horse and buggy for the sixteen-mile drive to a ranch on the western slope of the mountain, where I was told meals could be procured. As the question of lodgings was a dubious one, I took my blanket-roll with me, finding afterwards that I was well advised in so doing.

Skirting the base of the mountain to the north of

THE SAN FRANCISCO PEAKS FROM THE WEST.
Photo by E. T. Parsons.

town, I followed a country road for a couple of hours through sections of Government land timbered with the Coconino pine, and alternate railroad sections that had been sold and all lumbered off. On the remaining timbered sections the snow still lay deeply heaped, and demonstrated the influence of forest preservation in the prolonging of the water supply for the agricultural territory lower down. However, the once-cleared sections had been mostly abandoned after the timber was removed, and since the declaration of the forest reservation had been free from destructive sheep-grazing. Here a vigorous growth of young pines promised well for the future.

Twelve miles out I overtook a large herd of cattle being driven by four Mormon cowboys. After a talk with them, and as I followed along, they, on learning my errand, invited me to join them at camp that night, which I did. It was easy to see that they thought it strange that any one should start out alone to climb a mountain, and they were somewhat suspicious lest I were a timber inspector or secret-service man looking up timber depredations or investigating illicit grazing on the reservation, but when reassured they were very cordial and hospitable.

At dusk we made camp near a little stream on the western flank of the mountain hard by the crude log-cabin at the ranch I was seeking, where the brother and sister of one of them were domiciled, waiting for their ranch to dry up for spring plowing. Before retiring I went up to this cabin and met the young woman and her brother. She insisted on my sharing their supper of bacon and eggs, bread, and coffee. She took pleasure in explaining how she had roofed-in the lean-to with the tin of coal-oil cans and how she had put in the windows. She was about sixteen years old, but her hands were deeply calloused by hard toil, and she seemed to consider it a matter of course to do a man's work.

Returning to my blankets at the cowboys' camp-fire, I rolled up for the night. From the cozy comfort of my sleeping-bag I enjoyed a long and silent contemplation of the mountain in the bright starlight of that clear, vaporless atmosphere. Slumber overcame me as I listened to the murmur of the cowboys sitting about their fire telling tall stories of the ranch and preparing for their early breakfast. As the fire waned with the passing hours, the extreme cold of the early morning penetrated my covering and I woke to suffer and wait in chilly discomfort the slow-coming dawn. Ice froze one and a half inches thick in pools near our camp that night.

But after a steak with the cowboys and a cup of tea and bread and butter at the ranch, warmed by this double hospitality, I loaded up my camera, tripod, and binoculars, pocketed my luncheon of canned deviled ham, graham wafers, seeded raisins and prunes, slung on my canteen, and started for the mountain.

There was no trail, so I took my way across the ranch in the open meadows till I reached the first sparsely grown timber, which was the mountain aspen. The white trunks and symmetrical tops were very striking in the open landscape. Soon I reached the evergreens, and the occasional clumps of aspen contrasted charmingly with the dark-green foliage of the conifers.

That was a glorious morning. The clear, blue sky, the novel and beautiful landscape, and the pure ozone-laden air invigorated me, and with every deep inspiration I drank in happiness and delight.

While thickly timbered for the most part, the way up the flank of the mountain was not impeded by underbrush, and traveling was easy. Approaching deep snow, I picked open spaces where the sun had solidified and hardened it, and so found good footing. I looked for deer and grouse, but saw none, and observed only the tracks of wild turkeys, which were evidently in goodly force about the mountain.

Nearing timber-line the trees were gnarled and stunted, mostly mountain pine and juniper. Traveling slowly, I began to feel some fatigue as I passed the last trees on the rocky spur I was surmounting. The broken rock of the open became more tedious and difficult and the rarity of the air oppressive, so that I proceeded short distances with frequent rests between, and at 10:30 took my first luncheon, on a large rock, from which I overlooked the wide-spread view to the westward. The dark green forests of Coconino County extended far as the eye could see, streaked with desert spaces and dotted here and there with hills and buttes. Mt. Bill Williams was the most prominent landmark, and he should have been a most worthy character to have had so noble a memorial. But I disliked to anticipate the pleasures awaiting me at the summit, so on I went slowly and more slowly, until at last, about 11:30, I stood on the mountain's crest, thirteen thousand feet above sea-level, on a finial point of the continental divide. Words fail me to describe the grandeur and magnificence of the outlook and the depth of my feelings, moved by the thrill of conquest and by the delight of the nature-lover in the sublime vista before me.

Seventy miles away to the northward extended the Grand Cañon of the Colorado. Looking down into it from the mountain-top, its farther wall, fifteen miles beyond its southern edge, showed plainly its immensity and austere grandeur. For nearly two hundred miles it extended in open view; while beyond it, away over in Utah, the Kainab Plateau, an immense mesa, limited the horizon.

Turning my binoculars to the eastward, the bright-colored earth of the Painted Desert lay before me, plainly marked by the course of the cañon of the Little Colorado River to its junction with the Grand Cañon and Marble Cañon. Nearer at hand was the brightly colored volcanic cone, Sunset Peak, with its cuplike crater, into which I looked from my high vantage-point. While close below me, embraced in the horns of the crescent-shaped mountain, extended a small steep-walled valley, in which lay the deep snows—source of many a distant stream and spring.

The nearer view to the southward was cut off by the ridge of the mountain which extended for about a mile, curving round to the eastward. Overlooking the ridge, away to the south, were many small lakes, which I saw for the first time, and which are not visible to the traveler on the railway.

Seventy miles to the southwest was the Verde Valley, on the further slope of which is the great mining town of Jerome, and I saw plainly the dense smoke from the roasting copper ores marking the location of Senator Clark's great smelter. I fancied I could distinguish the large hotel near the smelter, from the porch of which I had often gazed northward across the Verde Valley and the mesa beyond to the snow-capped peak on which I was now standing.

Again I studied the outlook to the westward, noticing for the first time a volcanic cone near the base of the mountain, in the crater top of which was a little crystal-blue lake.

Seating myself in the sun on the east side of a large rock, sheltering me from the strong, cold wind, I enjoyed my remaining luncheon and looked out over the earth. Never before in all my mountaineering had I seen so wide an extent of the earth's surface and noted so varied and numerous examples of the working forces of Nature, volcanic action and erosion, with their evidences,—cones and lava-fields, great plains and deep cañons, timbered regions and desert wastes.

But the creeping shadows warned me of the flight of time, and prudence suggested the start for the descent. I set up my camera and made several exposures to the north and east, and then, seeking new experiences, I concluded not to retrace my steps, but to descend by a different route; so I made my way along the crest of the mountain for half a mile to the southward and started down the southwest spur of the mountain. At first all went well, but on reaching the snow-fields below the bare rock ridge, I found the surface softer and more difficult to traverse than on the route I climbed. For about a mile it lay from five to twenty-five feet deep. However, I made my way slowly but safely until, in an unthinking moment, I attempted a cross-cut through some thick timber where the sun, succeeded by frost, had not had opportunity to harden the surface, and soon I sank over head and ears in the soft snow. My heavy camera and thick clothing impeded me; but finally, by dint of stretching out and wallowing at full length, and so laboriously working myself along, I succeeded in getting into the open again where the footing was more solid.

Swinging along below snow-line, across the opens and through the pines and aspens, I finally reached the cabin again at 5 P.M., tired and hungry. Supper cured the latter feeling, and, bidding my Mormon friends good-by, I was quickly on my way back to town, where I arrived at 9 o'clock, and was soon snug in bed, to rise next morning with an increased respect and appreciation for the noble mountain I had admired for so many years.

OVER HARRISON'S PASS WITH ANIMALS.

By Robert D. Pike.

The evening of July 3, 1901, found us near the head of that large flat, snowy amphitheater where heads the Kern. On the west of this amphitheater rise the lofty peaks of the Great Western Divide; to the north the pinnacles of the King's-Kern divide jut sharply out of long slopes of snow into the dark blue sky, and, contrasted with the glistening white, look dark and forbidding; on the east, rising above snow-slopes and rock terraces, are the great peaks of the Sierra Crest.

That day we had come from the meadows on Tyndall Creek, where for two days our seven animals—four horses and three donkeys—had been feeding on the short but nourishing high mountain grass, preparing, all unwittingly, for the ordeal through which they were to pass. We knew that they would be without feed for one night, but none of us foresaw the additional hardships that were to be their and our share. For the night we bivouacked on one of the occasional granite islands that raise themselves out of the sea of snow. Ours supported a few hardy alpine pines, which furnished good fuel, and quite a level space of decomposed granite sand, which made a comparatively soft bed. We picketed the animals near our camp, and throughout the night the poor beasts were restless with hunger and cold.

We awoke before daybreak the next morning and looked out on a frozen world. The thirteen shots which

Kobbe fired from his shot-gun to celebrate the Fourth rang out on the still, cold air with startling distinctness, and were reverberated in indignation from the surrounding cliffs. Everything was shrouded in the chill gray light of dawn, save where the higher peaks caught the light of the rising sun, and if it were not for the occasional chirp of an alpine bird perfect silence reigned. The cheerless aspect of things, the cold, and the poor hungry animals, huddled together for warmth in dejected attitudes, did not tend to raise our spirits.

We hurriedly prepared breakfast, and, packing up as quickly as possible, started at half-past 6. Our course lay over a gently sloping field of hard-frozen snow, which crunched with a substantial sound under the pressure of our feet. Two and a half hours steady climb up this slope brought us to the summit of the King's–Kern divide. We had chosen the depression between Crag Ericsson and Leland Stanford Peak, but the discouraging sight which met our eyes on reaching the summit made us doubt the wisdom of our choice. There at our feet fell off a precipice, impossible of descent even on foot. We were on the precipitous wall of a deep snow amphitheater, out of which flowed one of the branches of the King's River. The whole aspect took in steep bare cliffs, sawtooth ridges, and ragged peaks partly clothed in snow. Below us the greater part of the deep white basin reposed in the morning shadow, but tongues of light were gradually creeping in and dispelling the shadow along its western edge. The scene, to our eyes, seemed saturnine and forbidding, and we longed with the animals for fresh green meadows and shady trees.

Not much time was lost, however, in bemoaning our

plight. Immediately we started to search along the top of the ridge to the eastward, until, about a hundred yards from our position, we discovered a monument at the top of a very steep snow-chute leading to the bottom of the basin. It was so steep as to almost present the appearance of a cliff, and a snow-cornice at the top made a nearly vertical fall for about six feet. So this was Harrison's Pass! On looking down it we were strongly impressed with the fact that places called "passes" differ widely in character. But there was no alternative but to make our way down, because we could not go back.

Standing at the top, we threw rocks over the brink and watched them rush down with great leaps and bounds until they became dark specks on the still dull white of the bottom. Their hasty manner of descent warned us to be careful with our animals. The only possible way of getting them down was to cut a zigzag trail through the snow. This we began to do with our only tool, a small ax. It was weary work. One of us would chop out blocks of snow with the ax and push them over, while another would follow behind and tramp down the newly made trail. About fifteen feet of trail was all one man could do at a time. He would then be relieved by the one behind and rest until each man had had his turn. For about twenty feet along the first leg of the trail the wall caused by chopping out was about five feet high. Further down, however, the slope was less abrupt. Each leg of the trail entirely crossed the gully and found a turning-place on the rocks, where in one case, at the first turn, some ice was encountered, making it a dangerous spot for the animals. We kept up this chopping until the morning shade had given place to the burning glare of midday, when we lunched on cold mush and prunes and then worked again till the cool shade of late afternoon overtook us. At this time a considerable stretch of snow still remained, but it looked as though the animals could get down over it.

After a few minutes' rest, spent in gazing up the steep white slope half-covered by a jagged-edged shadow, whose edge ran up the middle of the pass, lined by our trail, flanked by jagged brown granite pinnacles, and crowned by the dark blue alpine sky, we started the hard job of dragging and carrying our goods to the bottom, for the animals would have all they could do to manage themselves. The kyaks we dragged along the trail, because it was easier than carrying them, and it helped to pack the now softened snow. Our clothes-bags we tied up tightly and rolled over the top. Immediately, charmed by gravity, they seemed to become animate, and with great leaps sped along until they reached the level and were ordinary clothes-bags again. This work necessitated each man going up and down the pass—a vertical distance of about seven hundred feet—three times, which well-nigh exhausted us all.

With our outfit packed safely on the rocks at the bottom, we turned our attention to the last and most difficult undertaking. All day long our minds had looked forward in nervous apprehension to taking the animals down the trail. The events of the day had not made us optimistic, and with our bones aching and our skins burning we looked for the worst. On reaching the top we saw the poor horses with their heads hung low and their ears in noncommittal attitudes, the very pictures of dejection. Our hearts went out to them, for we knew they would have another night without feed. Two of the donkeys, however, "Johnny" and "Jumbo," little beasts with much worldly wisdom in their heads, stood with a look of evil contentment in their eyes. They slowly munched their jaws, and yellow bits falling from their mouths, together with yellow blotches on their noses and on the snow, and a torn corn-meal bag, showed us the nature and extent of their theft. A short way from them, and not so fortunate in breaking loose, stood "Pete," our third donkey, tugging at his rope with watering mouth and ears bent forward in a piteously expectant attitude. This corn meal we had neglected to bring down; so we took the blame for its loss on ourselves.

After this funny little incident we started to lead the animals down the trail. Three of us led off, each leading a horse; and the three donkeys were driven behind us by Halloran, who led the fourth horse. The horses occasionally plunged belly-deep in the soft snow, but always managed to lunge out and keep on the trail. Their efforts to free themselves from the snow were sometimes so violent that we had to give them a long rope to prevent being trodden upon. On coming to the end of the trail we turned the horses loose, expecting that they could go down the remaining slope easily. But each one of them rolled head over tail for about a hundred yards, and then, gradually picking themselves up, stood around as though nothing unusual had happened. They were too exhausted to even be nervous. On this last stretch the donkeys fared better than the horses, owing to the inborn stubbornness in their natures as well as to their coolheadedness. They sat on their haunches and, ears bent forward intensely and fore-feet propped well out in front of them, felt their way down with infinite caution, and no detriment to their dignity. It was a comical sight to see them move along so slowly and seriously, sitting on their haunches, and it looked as though they were balking against gravity.

When "Johnny" reached the bottom, and was proceeding along in a careless manner, he suddenly fell into a deep snow-hole. He must have stayed there for some minutes before we missed him, for on looking around, when about to put on his pack, we espied his nose, ears, and pack-saddle just above the snow. We realized that he must be uncomfortable and hastened to pry him out, which process was effected by grabbing his nose and tail and then his middle and lifting him out. When free from his bondage he walked over to be packed unconcernedly, —plucky little brute that he was,—for he must have been almost frozen to death. All of the animals, maybe without appreciating it mentally, displayed a lot of grit, for none of them balked once through the day.

Now followed as trying an experience as any that had preceded. It was now 5 o'clock, but we still entertained the vain hope of reaching feed that night. The floor of the basin over which we now proceeded was a wicked mixture of rocks and snow, absolutely the worst obstacle that Nature puts in the way of animals in these parts.

There was no way of continually keeping to the snow, and, in passing from the snow to the rocks, the animals would lunge into the caves which always occur at the juncture of rocks and snow. In doing this they gashed their legs frightfully, and only escaped cutting an artery or breaking a leg by a miracle. On one occasion my horse's hindquarters broke through the crust with such

"THE VERY PICTURES OF DEJECTION."

"'JOHNNY' SUDDENLY FELL INTO A DEEP SNOW-HOLE."

violence that the whole pack, saddle and all, went off backwards.

We kept up this hard, slow traveling until night found us on a barren, snow-bound rock island, without a vestige of vegetation. Neither timber nor feed was in sight, and the prospect for the night was miserable for man as well as beast. We turned the animals loose after unpacking them, and, as there was no fuel, went to bed on the smoothest places procurable, taking with us the few dried prunes which we ironically called dinner.

That night was one of sound dreamless slumber despite the rocks and our burning skins. The next morning, when the rest of us awoke, Fairbanks had been down to timber-line for fuel, and the result of his labor was a bright fire, which cast flickering shadows on the still dark rocks and snow. Over this small fire we cooked some hot breakfast and felt much better for it. The effect of a fire and a hot cup of coffee in a cold, dreary place like this is to raise one's spirits immensely. There could not be much joviality in camp that morning, however, for the glare of the snow during the previous day had rendered Kobbe and Halloran snow-blind, and they were suffering much agony from it. During that day and part of the next they could scarcely see, but then the soothing effect of green meadows, and the deep shadows of the trees, and a sky which did not seem like night in comparison with the earth cured them, and their eyes were none the worse for their scorching.

As soon as possible that morning we got the animals down to a little meadow. where we stopped to let all hands recuperate, and talk for a while, in no complimentary way, of Harrison's Pass.

THE ASCENT OF SAN ANTONIO.

By Willoughby Rodman.

The highest mountains of Southern California are Grayback (also known as San Bernardino) and San Gorgonio. These two peaks rise from a common base, and, with that uncertainty which characterizes the nomenclature of this section, the three names given are applied to them indiscriminately.

The higher of these peaks attains an altitude of more than 12,000 feet, and is said to rise higher above the level land immediately surrounding it than any mountain in the world.

To the southeast rises Mt. San Jacinto, an extinct volcano, whose rumblings even to-day cause the Indians to speak of it as the abode of evil spirits. This mountain is said to have the highest vertical rock wall of any mountain in the world.*

But the best-known mountain, the real king of the Sierra Madre Range, is San Antonio, erroneously (and lovingly) called " Old Baldy."

Situated near the center of the complicated system of cañons and ranges comprising the Sierra Madre Range, towering far above its neighbors, " Old Baldy " is the dominant feature of the landscape. It is the first prominent mountain to greet the traveler from the north or

---

* What Southern California lacks in altitude of its mountains is made up by he altitude of its lies.

GENERAL VIEW OF THE CUCAMONGA MOUNTAINS, LOOKING TOWARD NORTH-NORTHEAST, SHOWING THE ROUND HEAD OF "OLD BALDY" AT THE HEAD OF SAN ANTONIO CAÑON. Photo by Mr. G. R. Roundthwaite. Courtesy of U. S. Weather Bureau.

east, and is the most prominent object to the dwellers in the San Gabriel Valley.

It deserves its pet name, for age-long battle with the winds from every quarter has completely denuded of vegetation its hoary summit. For about half the year a cap of snow adorns the crest, while at other times the white rock of which the peaks are composed produces a similar effect.

This mountain is situated near the easterly boundary of Los Angeles County, about fifty miles northeasterly from Los Angeles, and is the culminating point of the second range of the Sierra Madre Mountains, which extend in three parallel ranges between the ocean and the Mojave Desert.

The altitude of San Antonio is not accurately known. Measurements by the county surveyor of Los Angeles County show an altitude of 10,890 feet. The United States Coast and Geodetic Survey record is 10,100 feet, which is probably more nearly correct.

It is visited by a number of persons every year, as the ascent presents no great difficulties, being practicable, on the south and west sides at least, for saddle-animals. The greater number of visitors ascend from the San Gabriel Cañon, returning by the same route, as this is the easiest, though longest, of the approaches. The ascent by the west or south side is perfectly safe, though laborious. The ascent from the north presents some danger.

The writer had the pleasure of making the trip in November, 1903, spending two most enjoyable days en route. The party was composed of six members of the Sierra Club,—Messrs. Force Parker, Clair Tappan, R. B. Dickinson, Ross T. Hickcox, Thornton Kinney, and the writer,—all of whom, except Mr. Tappan, took part in the Kern River outing. Taking the Santa Fe train leaving Los Angeles at 7:30 on the morning of November 7th, we arrived at Uplands, where we left the railway, at four minutes after 9.

From Uplands a ride on a trolley-car soon brought us to the limit of passenger travel, but we begged a ride on a construction-car to the end of the line. Here we were joined by Dr. and Mrs. F. J. Dawson, of Uplands, who were to accompany us to our camping-ground. Our burros were awaiting us, packing was soon completed, and our tramp began. It was a genuine delight to be once more in Sierra Club "uniform," with our faces turned towards the mountains.

We had selected the San Antonio Cañon route, as it requires the least time. The trail through the San Gabriel Cañon passes through grander scenery, and is in most respects more attractive, but it requires several days, and our time was limited.

San Antonio Cañon is entered by a road which passes over a broad mesa, the road dipping considerably as it crosses the spur which forms the cañon's eastern wall. For about eight miles we followed a broad, well-made wagon road, and in consequence did not feel comfortable. Three of us varied the monotony by taking a wrong road and climbing an intervening ridge to regain the path. At the power-house of the Sierra Power Company we paused to inspect the machinery as well as some large trout, the sight of which caused delicious thrills. Ten minutes more on the road, then a sharp pull took us over the "hog-back," a steep rocky ridge which deserves its name.

Soon after this, leaving the road, we continued along the floor of San Antonio Cañon about two and one half miles; then, making a sharp turn, entered Bear Cañon, where a steep, narrow trail made us begin to feel at home. For a short distance the trail follows a brook, and is embowered by overarching trees. Then, leaving the cañon, winding along a mountain-side, a steady climb of about one mile took us out of the timber and brought us to Fern Flats, our camping-place.

It would be difficult to imagine a more dreary or unattractive camping-place than Fern Flats. Bullion Flat at its worst must yield to it. The only reason for its use is, that it is the last place where water can be obtained. It has nothing else to recommend or justify it. Beyond the timber-belt, though below the timber-line, situated near the head of a broad cañon, it is swept by a bitter wind. Fuel is scarce and must be carried some distance. There is not sufficient level ground for sleeping-places, and altogether a prospect is presented which would daunt all but true mountain-lovers. But as all true "High Sierrans" are genuine mountain-lovers, we did not growl overmuch, but proceeded to make the best of it.

First came wood-gathering—long hauls and small profits. But a bright fire and the prospect of an abundant supper eased all our cares, and soon we were partaking of a meal which did not require the keen air of the mountains to make most enjoyable. Mrs. Dawson came to our assistance with some of that automatic (?) buckwheat flour which requires only a suggestion to transform itself into cakes, and which, with maple syrup, was to our meal "like the benediction that follows after prayer." After a perfunctory and not too thorough dishwashing, fresh logs were piled on the fire, pipes were lighted, and we entered into the domain of the blessed.

(Here, at the suggestion of the editors, I omit ten pages on the joys of camp-fires.)

But I must mention one circumstance. By that camp-fire in a windy cañon of the Sierra Madre the Southern California Section of the Sierra Club was born. An organization was completed and work planned. The object of the section is to forward the work of the Sierra Club in Southern California. It is strictly subordinate to the parent club (Sierra Madre?). It will take no action not sanctioned by the directors, and will always work in the name of the club, and for the purpose of extending its influence and furthering its objects.

I shall not at this time trouble the readers of the BULLETIN with an account of the work performed by the section since its organization, but state that we hope in the future to accomplish even more.

At about 11 o'clock we began to crawl into our sleeping-bags. As the night was bitterly cold, some left the fire with regret, and some did not leave it at all, dragging their beds into the very ashes. It seemed to the writer that the temperature was even lower than we found it on the Mt. Whitney trip in July, 1903. During the night water in a cooking utensil froze to the thickness of three quarters of an inch; and a thick frost accumulated on the rubber case of one sleeping-bag.

Breakfast was rather cheerless, on account of the cold, but we prepared to start in good spirits.

At Fern Flats the real climbing begins. The trail from there on is narrow, though distinct and well worn.

For some distance it zigzags up the wall of the cañon, coming out upon the southeast side of San Antonio, among large though scattered pines.

Following the edge of the cañon about half a mile, the trail reaches one of those very long, sharp ridges which form the approaches to the summit. The climbing was steep, but the view more than compensated for our labors.

Our trail followed the edge of the magnificent precipice which forms the mountain's southwest side. In many places the fall is sheer for nearly two thousand feet, and at all places it is precipitous. The granite has become disintegrated, and the cliffs and " slides " are almost snow-white. Stones sent rolling down raise a cloud of white dust. The effect of these white walls and slides is peculiar and striking. Many seeing the mountain for the first time, think its sides are clothed with perpetual snow.

Several of these long ridges, converging, form the summit. These ridges are covered with stunted pines. Near the summit these trees present very curious phenomena. The wind is so strong and blows so persistently as to materially affect their growth. A tree of nearly three feet in diameter will at a distance of about thirty inches above the ground be so bent over as to grow almost parallel with the mountain-side. On the side exposed to the prevailing wind, and on the opposite side, branches are entirely wanting, and those growing on the other sides are generally short and stunted. On a few trees are observed rather long branches which, projecting over the ground, produced the effect of a wide-spreading bush.

Leaving the edge of the south slope, the trail follows

a saddle for about a quarter of a mile, then follows another ridge for a short distance, dipping below its edge. It would be well-nigh impossible to keep to the backbone of the ridge at this place, as the wind sweeps across it with enormous velocity. Except a few small pines, there is no vegetation. The footing is composed of small, loose stones, so hard and so moved about by the wind that in places there is not even a trace of the trail. But there is no danger of straying, as the summit is in sight. For the last half-mile the climb is exceedingly laborious. The ascent is gradual, and the footing sure, but the force of the wind necessitates a constant struggle, sometimes a full stop. Often small quartz pebbles were blown into our faces with great velocity, having the imagined force of a charge of bird-shot. The wind seemed to increase as the summit was approached.

Reaching the top, the writer found Messrs. Parker and Tappan crouched shivering behind the monument of the Coast and Geodetic Survey, and was glad to crawl under their friendly gray blanket. It was only under shelter that one could breathe in comfort. The velocity of the wind we estimated at forty miles an hour.

The view from the summit is grand. It is entirely different from the prospects from the peaks of the Sierra Nevada. There is no circle of snow-capped granite peaks such as makes the view from Brewer or Williamson so wonderful. The eye is not charmed by an apparently endless succession of sierras and peaks, nor by the courses of great cañons. But the view may well be called magnificent, and would repay exertion however violent or hardship however great. San Bernardino (Grayback) and San Gorgonio loom above us. To the south lies the ever beautiful San Gabriel Valley, while westward is the intricate maze of the San Gabriel Cañon. From San Antonio to Mt. Wilson, in the first range, the distance is about twenty miles. Between is the enormous basin drained by the San Gabriel River. This watershed is marked in all directions by a perfect tangle of cañons.

Many of these cañons pass between precipitous walls of great height, and their scenery would prove attractive even to those accustomed to the great cañons of the Sierra Nevada. Many small mountains rise from the basin, but none sufficiently high to obstruct the view. Mts. Wilson, Lowe, and San Gabriel are prominent points of the first range.

Unfortunately, our view was obstructed by clouds and by a thick haze of smoke and dust. On clear days it is possible to obtain views of the Colorado River as far south as Yuma. To the southwest San Diego is visible, while the coast can be traced for a long distance. The islands of San Clemente and Santa Catalina can be distinctly seen, with a great expanse of ocean. To the south and east lie vast stretches of the Mojave and Colorado deserts. It is said that Mt. Whitney is visible, but clouds rendered it impossible for us to determine this matter. Our disappointment was somewhat mitigated by the consideration that, even had the view not been obscured, we could not have fully enjoyed it, on account of the wind, which not only rendered a standing position extremely difficult to maintain, but caused such a flow of tears as to interfere with vision.

Back of the Coast Survey monument some person had made in the loose rock a gravelike excavation about a foot deep, and had constructed along one side a stone breastwork about a foot high. Whether he was prospecting for gold or for a quiet grave I do not know, but I used it as a protected observatory. Lying in the pit, I managed, by peeping through the interstices of the stones, or over its edge, protecting my face with my hands, to obtain several views. Before me was a wide stretch of desert, orange yellow, with dashes of *ecru* and long streaks of gray or white. Directly in front wound the sinuous defile of the Cajon Pass. To the right the enormous mass of the San Bernardino Mountains bulked the horizon, while beyond towered in solitary majesty the beautiful peak of San Jacinto. Although the view was what might be called "fitful," the prospect was magnificent and inspiring. Each of us felt fully repaid for his exertions, and would willingly repeat them for the same reward.

Soon we were assembled, and, as the cold and wind made a long stay impossible, took a hasty luncheon and prepared to descend. We had sent our burros back to the valley, so our downward climb was a knapsack trip. We did not retrace our steps, but followed the easterly ridge, descending into the cañon of Lytle Creek. The first mile of the descent might be called dangerous; and one of weak nerves would find it really appalling. The ridge is very narrow, almost a knife-edge. On one side there is a sheer fall of many hundred feet; on the other the descent is so abrupt that one falling could not recover himself. There is no trail. All there is to do is to keep as close to the edge as one dares. The edge is horizontally serrated,—that is, deeply indented. Those who climbed Mt. Whitney will remember the appearance of its eastern side. The northerly side of San Antonio presents the same features, but the indentations are more numerous and not so deep. It was necessary to keep a sharp lookout to avoid stepping into one of these indentations. The wind-gods, evidently resenting our intrusion upon their domain, and wishing to make our departure as unpleasant as possible, made one last furious assault, almost taking us from our feet. Walking that narrow ridge in the face of such a wind was no easy task. We have heard of people who crawled along the ridge, but we managed to keep our feet.

We kept close to the edge of the ridge for more than a mile, then turned away near the abandoned works of the Agamemnon Mine. For several miles we followed the wagon-road made to be used in connection with the mine, but now abandoned. Soon after it reaches the bed of a small cañon, the road is entirely washed away for some distance, the only footing being loose stones.

Pausing near a stream for the last meal of our outing, we built a rousing camp-fire and attacked our " remnants " with vigor and zest.

We had first thought to cross the ridge which separates Lytle Creek Cañon from the Cajon Pass, spend several hours on the platform of a mountain station, and take a Santa Fe train passing at about 5 o'clock in the morning. But the prospect of sitting on cold, hard planks four or five hours was not alluring, so it was determined to push on to Glen Ranch, which we did, arriving there at 11 o'clock at night, sixteen miles from the summit, twenty-two from our morning camp. Of course, every true mountaineer prefers sleeping on the ground to everything else; but after our tramp we managed to reconcile ourselves to the comfortable beds of Glen

Ranch. Then at 5 in the morning came a sixteen-mile drive to Rialto; the railway; Los Angeles at three minutes after 10; and the end of our outing.

It was not a long jaunt. We met with no adventures, accomplished nothing noteworthy, and our objective point was not one of the grander mountains of the world. But the trip will always be remembered by those who made it. The little taste of camp life, the genuine good-fellowship, and the inspiration of the mountains, made our fifty-hour outing an experience to be remembered with the greatest pleasure.

The trip is one which recommends itself to every member of the Sierra Club. It is thoroughly enjoyable, and more than repays the necessary exertion. It is hoped that many club members will make this trip. And they will please remember that the Southern California Section is entirely at their service.

SIERRA CLUB BULLETIN.

PUBLISHED IN JANUARY AND JUNE OF EACH YEAR.

Published for Members.   Annual Dues, $3.00.

The purposes of the Club are:—"To explore, enjoy, and render accessible the mountain regions of the Pacific Coast; to publish authentic information concerning them; to enlist the support and co-operation of the people and the Government in preserving the forests and other natural features of the Sierra Nevada Mountains."

OFFICERS FOR THE YEAR 1904-1905.

Board of Directors.

Mr. JOHN MUIR . . . . *President*
Mr. ELLIOTT MCALLISTER . . . . *Vice-President*
Mr. J. N. LECONTE . . . . *Treasurer*
Prof. W. R. DUDLEY . . . . *Corresponding Secretary*
Mr. WILLIAM E. COLBY . . . . *Recording Secretary*
   Prof. GEORGE DAVIDSON,   Prof. A. G. MCADIE,
   Mr. J. S. HUTCHINSON, JR.,   Mr. WARREN OLNEY.

Auditing Committee,
Directors McADIE, McALLISTER, and DUDLEY.

Committee on Publications,
Pres. DAVID STARR JORDAN, *Chairman.*

Mr. J. S. HUTCHINSON, Jr.,   Dr. MARSDEN MANSON,
  Editor Sierra Club Bulletin,   Dr. EMMET RIXFORD,
Mr. A. G. EELLS,   Mr. EDWARD T. PARSONS,
Mr. J. S. BUNNELL,   Mr. R. H. F. VARIEL,
Prof. J. H. SENGER,   Mr. TRACY R. KELLEY.

Committee on Admissions,
Directors DUDLEY, OLNEY, and MCALLISTER.

Committee on Parks and Reservations,
Prof. GEORGE DAVIDSON, *Chairman.*

Prof. W. R. DUDLEY,   Pres. DAVID STARR JORDAN,
Mr. J. M. ELLIOTT,   Mr. ABBOT KINNEY.

Committee on Outing and Transportation,
Mr. WM. E. COLBY, *Chairman.*

Mr. J. N. LE CONTE,   Mr. EDWARD T. PARSONS.

SECRETARY'S REPORT.

From May 9, 1903, to May 7, 1904.

At the annual election in April the Directors named on the preceding page were elected to the Board to serve for the year 1904-1905. The officers there named were elected at the first meeting of the new Board.

There were one hundred and ninety-nine new members added to the list during the year, while ninety-eight names were dropped from the list by reason of death, resignation, or non-payment of dues, making a net increase of one hundred and one members for the year. The total membership now numbers seven hundred and sixty-four.

There were certain unusual expenditures during the past year, such as the outlay of one hundred and fifty dollars in the improvement of the Tehipite Trail, the payment of one hundred dollars necessary to complete the Le Conte Memorial Fund, the purchase of Professor Lawson's Geological Bulletin on the Kern Cañon for each member of the Club (which was kindly furnished at actual cost of paper and presswork), also the additional outlay connected with the exchange of publications with the Appalachian Mountain Club, and the increased expense of rent of the club-room in the Mills Building, and the extra cost of the two issues of the BULLETIN which appeared during the year, and which were both of larger size than usual. In spite of all this additional outlay the finances of the Club are in as good condition as ever, and there remains a balance of about six hundred dollars in the treasury after every bill has been paid.

The Le Conte Memorial Lodge in Yosemite Valley has been opened for the summer as a Club headquarters where persons may obtain information regarding the high mountains and how to reach them, and where maps, photographs, and books belonging to the Club can be consulted. As has been the custom in the past, a custodian or caretaker has been selected to take charge of the Lodge during the three months of heaviest travel to Yosemite. Mr. R. L. McWilliams, a recent graduate of the University of California, has been chosen to fill this position, and is in every way qualified to represent the Club.

The Lodge will be formally dedicated on the 3d of July, when the Outing party will have reached the Valley, and thus a large attendance of members of the Club will be rendered possible. The services will be very simple in their nature, and will thus be in entire keeping with the simplicity which characterized Professor Le Conte's life. There will be addresses by those who knew him intimately, a poem written by one of the members will be read, and a bronze tablet, with appropriate inscription indicating the purpose for which the building was erected, will be permanently inserted in one of its walls.

The Outing for this summer will be taken through Yosemite to the Tuolumne Meadows, where a permanent camp of two weeks will be established, and from which place the party will return through Hetch-Hetchy Valley and by way of Lakes Vernon, Laurel, and Eleanor to the Hetch-Hetchy and Yosemite valleys' logging-train, which connects with the main-line railroads. Limiting the party to a number that can be conveniently and satisfactorily handled and provided for will doubtless make this year's Outing the most successful that has been undertaken.

The local walks that have been recently inaugurated by the Club have proved to be a great success, and will tend to build up and strengthen that phase of the Club's life. Seven all-day walks have already been taken to points of interest in Marin and Alameda counties, and have had an average attendance of twenty-five persons. The excursion to Mt. Diablo, taken May 28-30th, proved to be most delightful. Twenty-eight members of the Club spent the night of the 29th on the very summit of the mountain and witnessed a most glorious sunset and sunrise, and were also fortunate in having a full moon to add to the rare scenic effects. Since Admission Day, September 9th, will fall on a Friday this year, it is proposed to take a three-days' excursion, September 9-11th, to the Big Basin Redwoods in Santa Cruz County this fall. The local walks will be discontinued after the middle of June until September 9th, on account of the High Sierra Outing and the vacation period which will intervene.

It is proposed to have a Club pin, which can be made of either oxidized silver or gold from a die which will be a copy of the Club seal, only much reduced in size. Since the price of such pin can be greatly reduced if a sufficient number apply for the same, it is requested that any member who contemplates purchasing one, provided the cost of the same in silver does not exceed one dollar, send his name to the Secretary.

Respectfully submitted,

WM. E. COLBY,
Secretary of the Sierra Club.

HEAD OF CATARACT GULCH.
(LUNCH-PLACE ON FIRST SIERRA CLUB WALK.)

AMONG THE REDWOODS OF SEQUOIA CAÑON.
(ON THE WAY HOME FROM THE FIRST SIERRA CLUB WALK.)
Photos by Antoine Schmitt.

TREASURER'S REPORT.

Owing to the absence of the Treasurer, Mr. J. N. Le Conte, who is at present in the East, the Treasurer's report for the year 1903-1904 will be postponed until the January, 1905, issue of the BULLETIN.—EDITOR.

NOTES AND CORRESPONDENCE.

In addition to longer articles suitable for the body of the magazine, the editor would be glad to receive brief memoranda of all noteworthy trips or explorations, together with brief comment and suggestion on any topics of general interest to the Club. Descriptive or narrative articles, or notes concerning the animals, birds, forests, trails, geology, botany, etc., of the mountains, will be acceptable.

The office of the Sierra Club is at Room 16, Third Floor, Mills Building, San Francisco, where all the maps, photographs, and other records of the Club are kept, and where members are welcome at any time.

The Club would like to purchase additional copies of those numbers of the SIERRA CLUB BULLETIN *which are noted on the back of the cover of this number as being out of print, and we hope any member having extra copies will send them to the Secretary.*

Owing to the fact that the Editor, Mr. J. S. Hutchinson, was called to Alaska on business, and that Professor and Mrs. J. N. Le Conte are in the East, the labors of editing this issue of the BULLETIN devolved upon the Secretary of the Club. Any errors and shortcomings in the editing are due to the lack of time and many difficulties which confronted the Secretary in undertaking the work on such short notice.

APPALACHIAN MOUNTAIN CLUB,
1050 TREMONT BUILDING, BOSTON, May 10, 1904.

TO THE EXCURSION COMMITTEE OF THE SIERRA CLUB,
SAN FRANCISCO, CAL.

Greeting: The Committee on Field Meetings and Excursions of the Appalachian Mountain Club extends, through you, to the members of the Sierra Club, the courtesies of the Committee and a cordial invitation to participate in the Field Meetings, Excursions and Outings of the Appalachian Mountain Club for the season of 1904, upon the same terms and with the same privileges as enjoyed by the members of the Appalachian Mountain Club.

For the Committee on Field Meetings and Excursions,

GEO. W. TAYLOR, *Chairman.*

LONE PINE, INYO CO., CAL., May 17, '04.

PROFESSOR MCADIE, SAN FRANCISCO.

Dear Sir—Your letter safe the other day. Thank you for your help. I shall look forward to the time when I hear from you again. I am very glad to say we have started our subscription to finish the Mount Whitney Trail, and I am glad to say we are getting along very well, but I am afraid we shall need outside help. Independence has promised me $100, and Keeler will help a little, and I think Mr. B. P. Oliver, of 114 Montgomery St., S. F., will help, and his friends. I shall be very glad of your help in speaking to any of your friends interested in the mountains. Perhaps you may induce some of the Sierra Club to help us. Most of the people are poor, and many have offered to work instead of giving money, but we need some money for powder, food, and pack-animals. Last year we borrowed all the tools and cooking outfit. I hope you will try and help us, if it is only a few dollars.

We hope to have the trail completed by the 4th of July, but it depends on the money and the snow, but the snow is very light and soft. We have had some very warm weather lately, and the water from the mountains is coming very fast—much earlier than last year. I am in charge of finishing of the trail, and I am very anxious to get at it. Trusting you will do all you can for us, and some day we may be able to repay you,

Yours truly, G. F. MARSH.

[If any member of the Club desires to subscribe to this fund for completing the trail from Lone Pine to the summit of Mt. Whitney, such subscription forwarded to the Secretary of the Club will be sent to those in charge of the work.—EDITOR.]

STANFORD UNIVERSITY, CAL., April 8, 1904.
MR. WILLIAM E. COLBY, SECRETARY OF THE SIERRA CLUB.

Dear Mr. Colby—I take the liberty of calling your notice to a subject which seems to me to merit emphatic attention from the Sierra Club, and one which might well receive mention before the members at the Saturday meeting. This is the nomenclature of features in the California mountains.

In the first place, and specifically: the Sierra Club should this summer permanently fix the original Indian names, which are so exquisitely appropriate, on the three most striking wonders of the Hetch-Hetchy Valley,—the shower, *Tuccoolala;* the cataract, *Wapama;* and the rock, *Kolana.* (John Muir, California Series 7, Picturesque California.) These have been dubbed in a commonplace fashion by mappers and tourists,—the first "Ribbon Fall" or "The Hetch-Hetchy Bridal Veil," and the second "Hetch-Hetchy Fall,"—or have been left unnamed, while their true, primitive christenings have remained quite in oblivion. "Falls Creek" likewise is an applicant for emendation, and "Mt. Smith," on the crest of the cañon-wall just south of the cascade between the Little Hetch-Hetchy and the Tuolumne Cañon, is obviously a disreputable misnomer, and could easily be altered without the least prejudice to the aspiring scion of the legion of Smiths.

Secondly, and more generally: there are grand natural features throughout the Sierra Nevada, either doubtfully, disgracefully, or doubly named that offer opportunity for the accomplishment of great good by such an organization as the Sierra Club in return for the simple application of a little interested, slightly authoritative attention, now while the range is yet young to the civilized world. As other examples, might be taken Whitney's "Obelisk" in the Merced Group, which assumes priority, I think, over the name "Mt. Clark," now in common vogue,—perhaps too much so for betterment,—and the Indian synonyms for Yosemite points of interest. (Whitney, Geological Survey of California, 1865; and the Yosemite Guide-Book, 1869.)

Why should not the Sierra Club have a committee to investigate such matters, to discover priority in the naming,—or, if need be, as Mr. Gannett has suggested, overlook such priority,—and in general to decide questions of fitness in the application of place names? Such a committee as an organ of the Sierra Club would serve a purpose in this State similar to that of the U. S. Board on Geographic Names, with perhaps a little more legislative in addition to its judicial power, and thus bring man's only addition to Nature's work more in harmony with the refined and sturdy beauty of our "Range of Light."

Please pardon me if my enthusiasm has led me into a discussion which may have already received full consideration from the officers and members of the Sierra Club, and believe me,

Very sincerely your friend, ROBERT ANDERSON.

[The Directors of the Club have some months since appointed a Committee on Names whose duty it is to investigate and act on just such matters as the writer of the foregoing letter has called to our attention. Unfortunately, it is more difficult to change names in the region mentioned by the writer since the geological surveys have already covered that region, but in the Southern Sierra, in the vicinity of the King's River, where the surveys are now being extended, there is greater prospect of doing some good.—EDITOR.]

1001 JACKSON ST., OAKLAND, CAL., May 29, 1904.
To Mr. WM. E. COLBY, SAN FRANCISCO, CAL.

Dear Sir—Permit me to call your attention to the recent loss sustained by Mr. Fiske, the world-renowned photographer of

Yosemite Valley. In the fire that consumed his home and studio Mr. Fiske lost two cameras and lenses worth $600, three quarters of his negatives, and a large part of his stock.

Mr. Fiske is a most superior artist; his beautiful pictures have told the story of Yosemite's grandeur throughout the civilized world.

Mr. Fiske has spent over twenty-five years in Yosemite; he is seventy-five years old; at his age the loss is very discouraging. His pressing need is "to get new cameras, outfit, and supplies to work with."

Mr. Vickery was good enough to suggest that possibly the Sierra Club might assist in replacing the cameras.

If your Honorable Club should take a favorable view of this matter, will you kindly send the check to Geo. Fiske, Yosemite, Cal., and oblige   Very respectfully yours,

(Miss) F. M. HALL.

[The above communication was received too late to bring before a Directors' meeting, and on account of the absence of several of the Directors a meeting cannot be called until after the summer vacation. Any one interested can send any contribution to Mr. Fiske direct as suggested above.—EDITOR.]

1412 SPRUCE STREET, PHILADELPHIA, PA., April 19, 1904.
J. S. HUTCHINSON, JR., ESQ.

My Dear Sir—A note in the SIERRA CLUB BULLETIN (vol. V, No. 1, pp. 78, 79) refers to the highest mountain ascents. May I call your attention to a short article I published in the Bulletin American Geographical Society, New York, January, 1904, discussing the highest mountain ascent, which all the evidence shows was made by Mr. W. W. Graham? I think he ought to have the credit therefor.   Yours very truly,

EDWIN S. BALCH.

[We have examined the Bulletin American Geographical Society, New York, January, 1904, and do not find the article referred to above. Instead we find the following note on page 51: "In the *Scottish Geographical Magazine* for January there is a summary of recent mountain climbing in the northwestern Himalayas, completed during the past season by Dr. and Mrs. Bullock Workman. Dr. Workman reached 23,399 feet on a fixed peak of 24,486 feet, which gives him the world mountaineering record for men, the greatest height before attained being the summit of Aconcagua, 23,083 feet, the highest of the Andes."
—EDITOR.]

ITINERARY FROM BIG TREES TO LAKE ELEANOR.

(FURNISHED BY S. H. SMITH.)

First Day's Walk.—There is a good trail from Big Trees to Squaw Hollow; thence to Beaver Creek, crossing where there is good trout-fishing; thence easterly to Finnesy's, on Griswold Creek. This is a good camping-place with a fine meadow and pasture for stock, and good hunting can be found in the neighborhood.

Second Day's Walk.—The trail thence leads southeasterly to Shumack's Ranch on Skull Creek; thence, across Fisher's Creek, there is a plain trail southerly to Dry Meadow Ranch, and from there to Baker's Crossing. There is good hunting and fishing at Baker's.

Third Day's Walk.—There is a bridge across the Middle Fork of the Stanislaus River, and a trail runs thence due south to South Fork at Cedar Camp, going thence downstream to the bridge, where a direct road leads to Long Barn. Close at hand is a reservoir, just above the bridge, where there is also good fishing.

Fourth Day's Walk.—From Long Barn, following main road to crossing of the North Fork of the Tuolumne, crossing same at Harding's; thence along wagon road, crossing Wright's and Hull's creeks to Lord's, on Rush Creek. From here the trail leads in a southeasterly direction, crossing Two-Mile Creek and the Middle Fork of the Tuolumne River; thence to Rosasco's on Reed Creek, where good camping can be found.

From Rosasco's to Lake Eleanor, the following day, is but a short tramp.

TRIP NO. 2.

Instead of going from Dry Meadows Ranch to Baker's Crossing, go from Dry Meadows to Beardslee's Flat, almost due east, where there is good fishing, camps, etc., if party desires to stay several days. There is a good trail from Beardslee's to Parsons or Strawberry. There are good accommodations at Strawberry, hotel and cabins, and fishing and hunting within a half-day's walk. A good trail leads easterly to Bell Meadows, where there is a good camping-ground. The trail from here is southeasterly to Lily Lake. There is a fairly good trail from Lily Lake east to the crossing of the West Fork of Cherry Creek; from here follow the contour of the country due south to Kibbe Lake. This part of the route is quite rough, but will repay the trampers. Kibbe Lake is on the head-waters of one of the streams feeding Lake Eleanor, and about six miles distant.

ALASKA (Vol. III): *Glaciers and Glaciation.* By Grove Karl Gilbert, Harriman Alaska Expedition. 231 + xii pages. New York: Doubleday, Page & Co. 1904.

To the mountaineer who has climbed among glaciers or in glaciated regions this volume will prove most attractive and readable. It is an account of a reconnaissance of the glaciers and glaciated fiords of the Alaskan coast made in the summer of 1899 by the Harriman expedition. The expedition was fortunate in having with it so able a glacialist as Mr. Gilbert. His record of glacial conditions on the Alaskan coast, while from the nature of the expedition only partial, will prove most valuable both for purposes of comparison with earlier records and with those that may be made in future years. The present waning of the glaciers on that coast, together with the manifold evidence of their former seaward extension, renders the region one of the most promising fields for the study of the causes of glaciation, and numerous observations as to the stages of retreat or advance of the glaciers will form part of the necessary data for that study. The book comprises three chapters. The first deals with existing glaciers, the evidence of their retreat, and other features of interest. The second chapter deals with the Pleistocene glaciation of the region, including a discussion of the morphogeny of the region in preglacial time. The third chapter deals with certain general considerations as to glaciers. The book is profusely illustrated, and the pictures, taken in connection with the characteristically lucid style of the author, contribute greatly to the pleasure of reading. A feature of the illustrations is the preponderance of pen-and-ink sketches made from photographs.

[Dr. Gilbert has kindly presented the Club library with this valuable volume.—EDITOR.]

Indians of the Yosemite. By Galen Clark. 110 + xxviii pages. Yosemite Valley Cal. Price, cloth, $1.00; paper, 50 cents.

Mr. Clark has been a member of the Sierra Club for many years, and during the second year of its establishment he had charge of the headquarters of the Club in the Yosemite Valley.

The book gives an interesting account of the history, customs, and traditions of the Indian tribes which frequent the valley; it contains an appendix of useful information for Yosemite visitors, and has tables of distances to points of interest, and gives the heights of all the Yosemite peaks and waterfalls.

The book is illustrated by Chris. Jorgensen and by halftone reproductions from photographs.

The author was the discoverer of the Mariposa Grove of Big

Trees, and for twenty-four years was the guardian of the Yosemite Valley. Thus he is without a doubt one of the best authorities on the beauties of this wonderful valley and the Indians who inhabited it when he first met them in 1855.

[Mr. Clark has kindly presented the Club Library with a copy of his book.—EDITOR.]

Bulletin of the Geological Society of America.
Domes and Dome Structure of the High Sierra. By Dr. G. K. Gilbert, of the U. S. Geological Survey.

A copy of this was also received too late for review in this issue.

The Alaska Boundary. By Professor George Davidson, President of the Geographical Society of the Pacific, and a Director of the Sierra Club. Published by the Alaska Packers' Association of San Francisco.

A copy of this valuable book was received too late for review in this issue of the BULLETIN.

FORESTRY NOTES.

Edited by Professor William R. Dudley.

AREA OF RESERVES.
The latest report of the Commissioner of the General Land Office states that there are now fifty-three forest reserves in the United States, created by Presidential proclamation, and embracing 62,354,965 acres, 2,179,200 acres having been added to the total area during the year preceding June 30, 1903. The final report on the large areas suspended in 1902 in Northern California from sale and entry has not yet been made public, although a few thousand acres included in this suspension have been already returned to the public domain as unsuitable for forest or irrigation reservations. It is reported that the Pine Mountain and the Santa Ynez reservations in Southern California have been joined by reserved land, and in the future the two will be administered under one head, and under the name of the Santa Barbara Forest Reserve.

MANAGEMENT OF THE RESERVES.
Some years since the BULLETIN explained the organization of the forest-reserve service, under the General Land Office of the Department of the Interior. It still remains much the same, but an important position has been added, that of "Head-Ranger," who directly supervises the field-work of the several rangers of his district. He must have some technical knowledge, particularly of forest trees, surveying, and timber-scaling, and is appointed only after a formal examination. The change has proved to be a good one. These better-informed, more responsible head-rangers have in cases of vacancies been left to perform the duties formerly assigned to supervisors, to the betterment of the service. Time has proven that the forest-ranger system is a good one, if the men are carefully selected on the basis of merit and a knowledge of their duties. They are expected to patrol the forest, occasionally build or repair trails, prevent or extinguish fires, prevent timber depredations, and the pasturage without a permit of domestic flocks and herds.

The higher officers of the service are expected to determine whether a certain reserve is fitted for pasturage, the number of stock it will readily support, and to supervise the permits issued by the General Land Office to such as apply for pasturage. They also sell a small amount of timber, generally of an inferior class. Practically, this covers the required duties, aside from clerical and administrative ones, in the forest-reserve service; and it falls short of forestry because there are no men in the service sufficiently well trained to undertake the real problems of forestry on the large scale the reservations demand.

In view of the fact that attempted legislation providing for the transfer of the reserves to the Bureau of Forestry again failed in the late Congress, it is important for us to know the method and results of the present management of the public forests. Is it reasonably safe from unexpected disasters or from defective methods that will bring the forest reserves into disrepute before a transfer to trained hands can be secured.

According to the theory of the present management, protection from fire and from injurious pasturage are by far the most important duties of the service. Regarding pasturage, the facts are as follows: On July 5, 1900, the Department of the Interior issued an amendment to its "Rules and Regulations Governing Forest Reserves," prohibiting the pasturage of sheep and goats on the public lands in the forest reservations, except in Oregon and Washington, in situations where continuous moisture and abundant rainfalls would allow the grazing of sheep. It also provided for the limited pasturage of sheep and goats in a reserve in any State or Territory where, in the judgment of the Secretary of the Interior, it will not work injury to the reserve or the interests dependent thereon. "The pasturing of livestock other than sheep and goats, will not be prohibited in the forest reserves so long as it appears that injury is not being done the forest growth and water supply and the rights of others are not thereby jeopardized." Subsequent amendments stated that "stock of all kinds will receive preference in the following order, viz.: 1. Stock of residents within the reserve; 2. Stock of persons who own permanent stock ranches within the reserve, but who reside outside; 3. Stock of persons living in the immediate vicinity of the reserve, called neighboring stock; 4. Stock of outsiders who have some equitable claim." Grazing is free, and from these permits the United States derives no revenue. Nineteen hundred and one was the first year of pasturage on the reserves under the permit system. In 1901 and 1902 sheep and goats were allowed to enter eight reserves only, one each in New Mexico, Utah, Oregon, and Wyoming, two in Arizona, and two in Washington, aggregating 16,800,000 acres. In 1901 the number allowed on eight reservations was 1,400,000; the number entering, 1,214,418. In 1902 the number allowed, 1,197,000; the number entering,

1,151,278. In 1903 the number allowed, 887,000; the number entering, 812,828; in portions of five newly created additional reservations in New Mexico, Arizona, Montana, and Wyoming, 601,400 were allowed in 1903, and 600,249 actually entered. It will be observed that no permits are granted for sheep pasturage on any of the California forest reserves. Nevertheless, reserves in several States, including California, have been invaded by herders with large bands, in defiance of the regulations. The cases have been brought into the courts, and the decisions noted in previous numbers of the SIERRA CLUB BULLETIN. In the Act of June 4, 1897, Congress evidently intended to give the Secretary of the Interior authority to punish any violation of the regulations it empowered him to make governing the forest reservations. The judge of the United States District Court, Southern District of California, filed an opinion on November 14, 1900, that the Act of June 4, 1897, "in so far as it declares to be a crime any violation of the rules and regulations thereafter to be made by the Secretary of the Interior for the protection of the forest reservations, is in substance and effect a delegation of legislative power to an administrative officer," and therefore unconstitutional. On the other hand, the United States Department of Justice has rendered two written decisions to exactly the opposite effect. The Department of the Interior has no right of appeal in cases of decisions adverse to the United States, and injunction proceedings against sheep trespasses are slow, and in the great mountainous tracts often exceedingly difficult of execution. Advantage of the situation is taken by the sheepmen, no less than 34,000 sheep trespassing on the Sierra Forest Reserve in June, 1903, according to the complaint of the superintendent. The result is great annoyance and a demoralization of the authority of the Interior Department. Congressional action, making it a criminal offense to pasture stock on a reserve without a permit would be the simple and effective remedy. A bill for the protection of the public forest reserves and national parks passed the House on April 23d, but the Senate has taken no action, so far as can be learned.

In 1901 pasturage of horses and cattle was allowed in thirty-two reserves, permits being given to 277,621 head; in 1902 pasturage was given 357,552 head in thirty-seven reserves; and in 1903 pasturage was given 529,973 head in forty-four reserves. Cattle and horses have been allowed in the eight reserves open to sheep pasturage; also in all the California reservations. The following are the California statistics on this subject. The total amount of the reserves in this State is 8,853,129 acres,—in Northern California, 4,923,535; in Southern California, 3,929,594 acres.

GRAZING OF HORSES AND CATTLE IN CALIFORNIA RESERVES.

	1901.		1902.		1903.	
	No. Allowed.	No. Entering by Permit.	No. Allowed.	No. Entering by Permit.	No. Allowed.	No. Entering.
Northern California	40,500	35,145	53,000	48,144	54,600	......
Southern California	Only Stock in or near Reserves.	5,751	15,150	10,641	13,100	......
Total.....	......	40,896	68,150	58,785	67,700	......

During the present season permits were granted before April first.

Regarding this general question, it will be observed that the Department has taken a most important step in regulating grazing on the forest reserves, according to the number the area will more than readily support without injury to forest cover or the streams. In the California statistics it is evident that the effort is to discriminate in favor of the thinly wooded and almost arid mountains of Southern California. The weak spot is the open defiance in some regions of the regulations rightly limiting grazing, the weakness of the law no doubt being locally increased through the connivance of venal forest rangers. Under the Bureau of Forestry we might expect an immediate change in both respects. The Sierra Club has been very jealous of the Sierra forests. It intends to labor for the transfer of the reserves to the Bureau of Forestry at the next session of Congress, as it has done in the past; and if any one camping in the mountains learns of overgrazing in any locality, or of the dereliction of rangers, he should make it known.

Apparently the United States has a far better system for controlling forest fires within its reserves than exists under any State government. New York has done far more than any other State in acquiring lands avowedly for stream protection. These lie in the Adirondack and Catskill mountains. Several million dollars have been spent, and the State owns 1,163,414 acres in the Adirondack Park alone; but at present it is committed to two things which are absurd, antiquated, and which threaten the very existence of what seemed during the period of legislative appropriation and purchase an enlightened forest policy. It makes no provision for the removal or use of timber in any part of its preserves; it even forbids tree-cutting; and it has no paid patrol to protect its forests from fire. It has fire-wardens, but they are paid only for the time actually spent in fighting fires. The State ignores the fact, well understood in the West, that it is far greater economy to employ a regular patrol to watch for and extinguish fires in their early stage than to pay large bills for fighting forest conflagrations. This is best illustrated by the destructive fires in the Adirondacks in 1903, and a comparison with the forest-reserve fires in California in 1902, the last season for which we have detailed statistics. In the Eastern States a long drouth existed from April 20th to June 8th. During that time fires became frequent, and finally almost uncontrollable in the northern and western parts of the Adirondacks, although all but twelve per cent originated on private lands. This carnival of fire was only ended by the heavy rains which broke the drouth. In an area of about 7,000 square miles, or 4,480,000 acres, 600,000 acres were burned over, involving a cost to the State for fire-fighting alone of $175,000, a direct loss of property of $3,500,000, and a very great but unknown indirect loss in the way of young forest growth, of fish, young animals, birds, etc.* In California, in an area of 8,853,129 acres (the forest reserves), 7,895 acres were burned over in 1902 during the dry season of from four to five months. The extra cost for fighting these fires was $1,080; but add to this the entire salary and expense list of the forest reserve service for that year,—viz., $76,281,— and we have only $77,381. The California drouth is nearly three times as long as that of 1903 in New York, the area under consideration twice as great, but the real cost for fighting fire was a small fraction of the $175,000 paid out in New York. There are times, of course, when serious and costly fires invade the reserves, but nearly always from the outside,—as an instance, the destructive Mt. Wilson fire in Southern California a few years since, started on Baldwin's Santa Anita Ranch. As a rule, every year shows a decrease in acreage and a decrease in number of the real forest fires in the California reserves. This is due to the efficiency of the patrol, the printed warnings of heavy fines, and the careful explanations given campers concerning methods of treating their camp-fires and the effects of destructive fires on the forest. There is no doubt that Californians are better informed about these matters and more careful than formerly; and this education is due chiefly to the forest-reserve regulations, which are based on expert advice from the Government foresters.

* "Forest Fires in the Adirondacks in 1903," by H. M. Suter, U. S. Bureau of Forestry, 1904.

CALIFORNIA'S POLICY APPROVED.
So far as it has gone, California has pursued a wiser course in regard to forestry matters than any other State. It has supported the United States in every movement to preserve the Nation's Sierra forest, and its appropriation of money at the last legislature to aid the Government forester in investigating the forests of California and devising, on the basis of such scientific knowledge, a plan of treatment and a plant of fire-control that shall be the best that science can give us, is everywhere spoken of as the most enlightened policy yet adopted by a State. The special committee of the New York legislature appointed to consider the best method of repairing the disasters of 1903, advises a forestry policy and co-operation with the Bureau of Forestry, after the plan adopted by California. *Forestry and Irrigation* says: "The creation of the Adirondack and Catskill mountain preserves was a long step in advance, but it must be followed by more progress if the work is to be kept abreast of that now inaugurated by California."

CONGRESSIONAL INACTION.
Although a larger number than usual of bills affecting California lands and forests were before Congress, none of importance came up for final action. The old game of "Do nothing the year before a Presidential election" was played. The transfer of the forest reserves to the Bureau of Forestry, the purchase of the Calaveras Groves, the repeal of the Timber and Stone Act, of the Commutation Clause of the Homestead Law, the modification of the Desert Land Law, the protection of the reservations, were all brought before Congress for action, but Congressional leaders bandied them about in committees until it was "time to go home." Every one failed, although it is certain that some of the most important would have passed if they could have been brought to a vote. The Calaveras Grove bill suffered from too many putative relations. The advocates of the great Appalachian Park and the White Mountain Forest Reserve were lying in wait until the energy of the California Club should carry through the Calaveras Grove bill. In that event every effort would have been used to make the latter a precedent. Members of Congress were very well aware of this. The Calaveras Grove question is not in the same class of the others, as a matter of fact. Even if the forests of the Appalachians were all swept away, one century or two would with care restore their pristine greatness and beauty. Not so with the Calaveras Big Trees. The growth of two thousand years would and could never be replaced.

President Roosevelt, in both general and special messages to

Congress, vigorously commended all of the above measures. The Public Lands Commission (Messrs. Pinchot, Newell, and Commissioner Richards of the General Land Office, the ablest and most conscientious students of the questions in the country), in its report to the President, which he transmitted to Congress with letter of approval March 7, 1904, strongly recommends the repeal of the Timber and Stone Act and the distinct modification of the Desert Land Law; it was not prepared to formulate the needed reform in the commutation section of the Homestead Law. It is under cover of these laws that many frauds of land speculators have been attempted and fully consummated during the past five years. It has been done by evading the original intent of the law in ways both legal and illegal. Thousands of acres of timber land have thus passed from Government control into the hands of millionaire investors for a ridiculously small sum, when it was intended that only quarter-sections or thereabouts should go to a single person, for his own domestic and home-building purposes. To show how rapidly the public lands are disappearing, and under what entries, we have compiled a table from the records of the General Land Office, embracing all the chief sources of loss, excepting State and railroad selections. We cannot show, however, what is testified to by others,—that much of this land has passed in large tracts into the hands of the rich, and not into the possession of the small landholder. It will be seen that during the fiscal year closing June 30, 1903, nearly 23,000,000 acres of public land, chiefly west of the one-hundredth meridian, and much of it the timber land of the Pacific Slope, was disposed of. This is more than one third the entire amount now embraced in the forest reservations.

CASH SALES OF PUBLIC LAND IN THE UNITED STATES.
(*By acreage.*)

	1899.	1900.	1901.	1902.	1903.
	Acres.	Acres.	Acres.	Acres.	Acres.
Timber and Stone Entries.	59,019	300,019	396,445	545,253	1,765,222
Mineral Land Entries....	39,752	55,626	67,036	97,657	97,046
Desert Land Entries.....	350,251	590,155	686,382	929,230	1,025,825
Homestead Entries.......	......	8,478,409	9,479,275	14,033,245	11,193,120
Homestead Entries Commuted to Cash........	505,472	552,564	716,661	1,105,850	2,194,991
Total Acreage disposed of under all Entries.......	9,182,413	13,453,887	15,362,796	19,488,535	22,824,299
Excess Over the Previous Year..................	728,517	4,271,474	2,108,908	3,925,739	3,335,764

The amount disposed of in 1898 was 8,453,896 acres, showing that the greatest activity in public-land sales in recent years occured during the fiscal year of 1899-1900, the year when the men of the T. B. Walker and H. H. Yard type were to be met with in Northern California, exploring the forests with troops of timber-cruisers. They came from the exhausted forests of the East. This was the year when the American Forestry Association, at the request of members of the Sierra Club, passed a resolution requesting the creation of a forest reserve to extend from Lake Tahoe around the entire head-waters of the Sacramento Valley. The Sierra Club has never been less than five years ahead of public opinion, but California has moved with almost equal promptness, and we shall eventually see the success of most we ardently desired in forest conservation.

It is apparent from the table that the passage of the National Irrigation Act on June 13, 1902, and anticipation of this event, stimulated excessive activity under the three most defective of our land laws. We have a very grave duty to perform in the light of these statistics. The rights of the men of average property and financial ability seem to be at stake in the West. Laws should not stand which enable one class to overreach another, particularly in the matter of acquiring land, the foundation of a State's prosperity. We can encourage discussion of this subject everywhere; we can advise the Government to liberal suspension or reservation of public land during the current year; we can finally use every means in our power to induce Congress to revise our land laws, at its next session, in accordance with the expert opinion of the Public Lands Commission, and in harmony with the excellent intent of the National Irrigation Act.

SAN FRANCISCO PEAKS, NEAR FLAGSTAFF, ARIZONA. A Delightful Mountain Trip, easily Done in a Day.

From the triple peaks of these mountains, rising 7,000 feet above the surrounding country, and 14,000 feet above sea-level, a magnificent panorama is spread to view, rivaling that from Pike's Peak. From Flagstaff, on the Santa Fe main line, the trip is easily made on horseback in a day, and should be included in every traveler's itinerary. Distance from Flagstaff to base of mountain is ten miles over a good road, thence five miles up the trail, through the forest. Horses, guides, and outfit obtainable at Flagstaff.

PUBLICATIONS OF THE SIERRA CLUB

Number 32

SIERRA CLUB BULLETIN

Vol. V   No. 3

JANUARY, 1905

SAN FRANCISCO, CAL.

1905

SIERRA CLUB BULLETIN

Vol. V. JANUARY, 1905 No. 3

CONTENTS:

	PAGE
FIRST ASCENT: MT. HUMPHREYS . . . *J. S. Hutchinson, Jr.*	153
Plates XXV, XXVI, XXVII.	
ADDRESS AT MEMORIAL EXERCISES . . *Alexander G. Eells*	176
MT. LYELL AND MT. RITTER ASCENTS BY SIERRA CLUB OUTING OF 1904. *Russ Avery*	181
Plate XXVIII.	
A DEER'S BILL OF FARE . . . . . . *Alden Sampson*	194
DOMES AND DOME STRUCTURE OF THE HIGH SIERRA . . . . *G. K. Gilbert*	211
Plates XXIX, XXX, XXXI, XXXII.	
SOME ASPECTS OF A SIERRA CLUB OUTING . . . . *Marion Randall*	221
THE EVOLUTION GROUP OF PEAKS . . *J. N. Le Conte*	229
Plates XXXIII, XXXIV, XXXV.	
ORGANIZATION OF SIERRA CLUB	238
REPORTS:	
Report of the Treasurer	239
Report of the Outing Committee	240
Report of the Custodian of the Le Conte Memorial Lodge (1904)	241
Statement Concerning the Proposed Recession of Yosemite Valley and Mariposa Big Tree Grove by the State of California to the United States . . .	242
Action of the Sierra Club on the Proposed Change of the Boundaries of the Yosemite National Park . . .	250
NOTES AND CORRESPONDENCE	254
BOOK REVIEWS . . . . *W. F. Badè*	262
FORESTRY NOTES . . . . *William R. Dudley*	265

All communications intended for publication by the SIERRA CLUB, and all correspondence concerning such publication, should be addressed to the Editor, Elliott McAllister, 228 Crocker Building, San Francisco, California.

Correspondence concerning the distribution and sale of the publications of the Club, and concerning its business generally, should be addressed to the Secretary of the Sierra Club, Room 16, Third Floor, Mills Building, San Francisco, California.

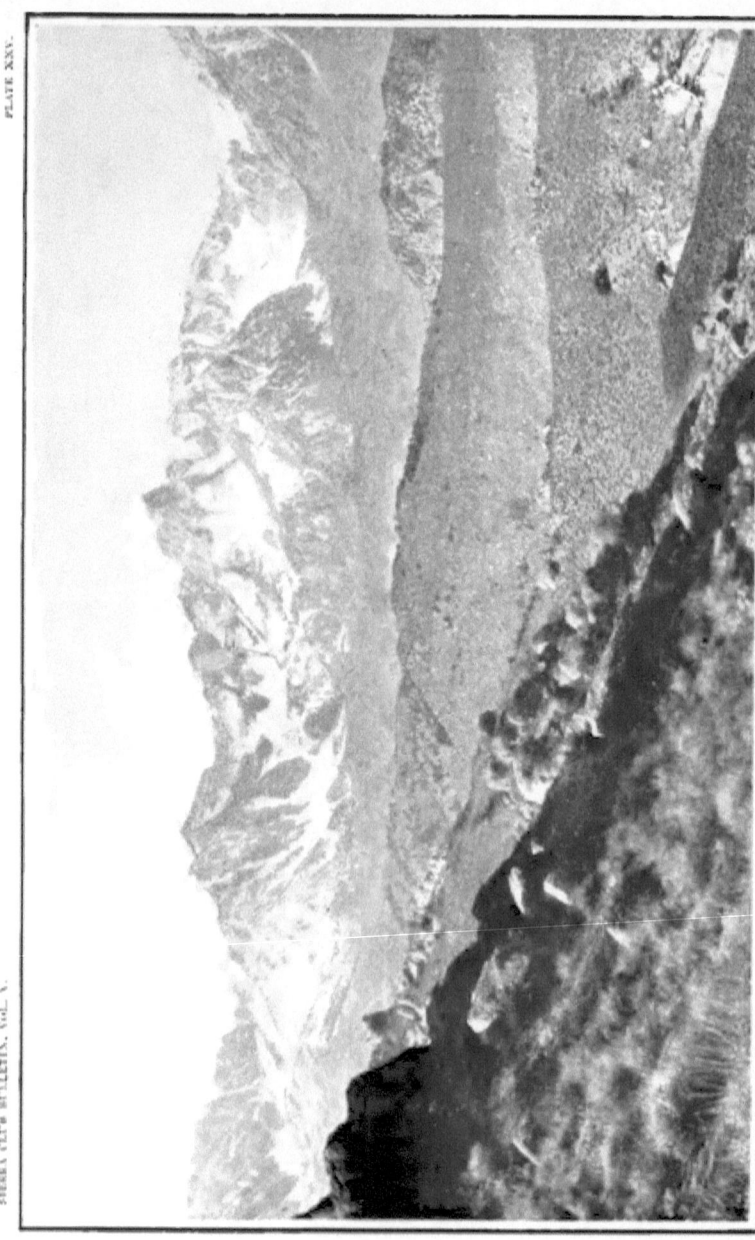

MT. HUMPHREYS FROM THE EAST (14,055 FEET).
From a photograph by A. A. Forbes, Bishop, Cal., 1904.

FIRST ASCENT: MT. HUMPHREYS.

By J. S. Hutchinson, Jr.

Untrodden summits in the Sierra are now very scarce, and the sight of one gives every mountain-climber a thrill of excitement such as comes from no other source. It was such a feeling that came to me in midsummer, 1903, when with Messrs. J. N. Le Conte and J. K. Moffitt, on the North Palisade, we looked far to the northwest across the Goddard Divide and saw looming in the distance, entirely isolated, the rugged, spiry, and unscaled summit of Mt. Humphreys, its eastern and western sides falling in precipices and steep slopes until hidden by the intervening ridge; its whole aspect one of defiance. The fascination of that mountain increased as Mr. Le Conte told us of the attempt which he and Mr. Cory made to reach its summit in 1898.*

Nor was it the unscaled summit of Mt. Humphreys alone that attracted us. We were looking into a rough and rugged wilderness of peaks which "may well be called the heart of the High Sierra," where "the peculiarly savage type of High Sierra scenery seems to reach its culmination,"* "the finest portion of the crest

---

* See Mr. J. N. Le Conte's article, "The Basin of the South Fork of the San Joaquin River," SIERRA CLUB BULLETIN, Vol. II, p. 249.

of the Sierra Nevada Mountains,—their scenic culmination, their final triumph."* If this region was the heart of the High Sierra, then, in truth, the very center of this heart was Mt. Humphreys. Judged from a mountaineering standpoint, it was indeed a most promising country into which we were looking.

As a result of this glimpse into that promised land, the following summer (July 11, 1904) found a party of four—Dr. Charles A. Noble, Mr. Albert W. Whitney, my brother, E. C. Hutchinson, and myself—camped in Lost Valley, or Blaney Meadows, as it is called, on the South Fork of the San Joaquin River. Hither we had come from San Francisco by the most direct route (via Fresno, Shaver Lake, and the Red Mountain Trail). We were bound for Mt. Humphreys.†

Lost Valley is an ideal spot for a permanent camp. It is one of the most beautiful of our high mountain valleys (elevation, 7,650 feet). The meadows are fine; the river broad and majestic; the glaciated cliffs tower high above and almost completely surround the valley. For two days we camped on the west bank of the river. During this time we reconnoitered to the eastward, toward Mt. Humphreys.

Four miles up the cañon of the South Fork, above Lost Valley, a stream comes in from the northeast. This is known to the sheepmen as the "North Branch of the

---

* See Mr. Theodore S. Solomons' article, "A Search for a High Mountain Route," SIERRA CLUB BULLETIN, Vol. I, p. 230.

† The mountain was named, in 1864, by the California Geological Survey party under Professor Brewer, and the name first appears on their map made that year. It also appears on a map entitled "Part of California and Southern Nevada," Sheet No. 65, Geographical Explorations and Surveys west of the 100th Meridian, Expedition of 1871, under command of First Lieutenant Geo. M. Wheeler, Corps of Engineers, under the direction of Brigadier-General A. A. Humphreys, U. S. Army, and on the "Topographical Map of Central California," 1873, J. D. Whitney, Geologist. On these maps, the name is "Humphreys' Peak."

South Fork of the San Joaquin River." It heads at the main crest of the Sierra very near Piute Pass, just south of Mt. Humphreys. From there, after flowing northwesterly for about six miles, it turns abruptly southwesterly and flows five miles into the South Fork. As the name by which this stream is known to the sheepmen is so unsatisfactory, Mr. Le Conte, on his map which is published in this number of the BULLETIN, has changed the name to "Piute Branch," and I shall refer to it hereafter by this new name. Noble and I explored almost to the source of the Piute Branch to determine if our "jacks" could be taken to the base of Mt. Humphreys. We found that it would be possible to do so by traveling on a terribly rough sheep-trail which starts out eastward from Lost Valley, climbs the ridge bounding the South Fork on the east, and follows this ridge southward until it plunges down into the cañon of the Piute Branch; from there on it follows first the north and then the northeast side of the stream to Piute Pass.

On the third day after reaching Lost Valley we moved our camp across the river, fording at a place where the stream was widest and least rocky; but even here the water came high up on the sides of the packs and the animals had great difficulty in keeping their footing on the rough bottom. By the use of long ropes a crossing was made in safety. Here we camped in a grove of cottonwoods, in the midst of a luxuriant garden of lupines, columbines, and alpine lilies. In the middle of the afternoon we were surprised and delighted to have Mr. Le Conte drop into our camp. He and Dr. G. K. Gilbert, with their packer, Osceola Kanawyer, had arrived in the valley the night before, on their way southward from

Yosemite, and were camped half a mile below us. We were pleased to have them join us in our evening meal. While at dinner Dr. Gilbert discovered some perfect bear-marks scratched on the light-gray bark of the cottonwoods near by. Some were made by the bears thrusting their claws into the bark in the act of climbing; others were long parallel scratches made by the bears reaching up to full height and then scratching downward.

When Noble and I returned from our trip up the Piute Branch plans were made to take our jacks up that stream; but as soon, however, as the other party arrived, and we found that they would ascend Evolution Creek* (a stream which enters the South Fork from the east four miles south of the Piute Branch), we planned to accompany them up that stream, and then strike off toward Mt. Humphreys, taking our jacks with us as far as possible and knapsacking it the balance of the way.† This we did, accompanying our friends nearly to the Hermit, where we left them, and our party climbed up the northern wall of the cañon about a thousand feet, by an old steep sheep-trail. This trail brought us to a glacial shelf or plateau which projects out from the ridge which separates Evolution Creek from the Piute Branch. On this shelf are a number of little meadows and tiny lakes. There is one good-sized lake, half a mile long and about a quarter of a mile wide, situated on the very brink of the shelf. On the shores of this lake were patches of bunch-grass in sufficient quantity to supply

---

* Mr. Le Conte has described the trip from Lost Valley to the Hermit in an article which appears in this number of the BULLETIN. In his article he has given the name "Evolution Creek" to the stream, which heretofore has been called the "Middle Branch of the South Fork of the San Joaquin River,"—a very excellent change.

† For map showing our trail and route see Plate XXXIII, opposite page 229.

the jacks for three or four days, and a short distance off were a few straggling, storm-beaten, dwarf pines, which would serve as firewood. The margin of the lake was fringed with the exquisite alpine heather. Here we finally made our camp, at an elevation of about 11,100 feet. The region was destitute of all vegetation excepting the few trees, the grass, and the flowers. The water of the lake was as clear as crystal and of a deep bluish green color. The shore-line was a rocky wall, composed of large boulders. This is a feature characteristic of nearly all high mountain lakes which freeze solid in winter. When a lake of this sort freezes solid, the ice grasps firmly the boulders in the bottom; a thaw then comes, and the ice cracks. Later the cracks fill with water, and, in turn, this water freezes again. The expansion caused by the freezing of the water in the cracks causes the blocks of ice carrying the boulders to be pushed toward the shore, and in the course of many years all the boulders in the lake are deposited around its margin and built up into a kind of wall, projecting considerably above the surface of the water.

No sooner had we arrived at our camping-place than we were visited by numerous little birds of very beautiful plumage. They were about the size of an ordinary English sparrow. The head was of a light ashy color, the back a sooty black, the body a most beautiful cinnamon-brown, while the wings and tail feathers were blackish. A few of the feathers were slightly tipped with white These birds were the gray-crowned finch, or leucosticte. They were very tame and inquisitive, and flitted from rock to rock near by and watched all our camping operations.

The view across the lake, and still farther across

the deep gorge of Evolution Creek, to the mountains bounding that cañon on the south was wonderful. The Hermit thrust its head high above the level of the lake. At times the water was slightly ruffled by the wind, but generally it was smooth and placid, and the reflection of the neighboring bluffs and peaks was perfect. The echoes from the cliffs were clear and distinct and repeated themselves over and over again. This lake was christened by Whitney "Lake Frances."

We made camp about 2 o'clock in the afternoon, and then Whitney and I went exploring up to the ridge lying between our camp and the great basin which bounds Mt. Humphreys on the west, to determine the best course to take on the following morning. Above us in the ridge was a depression, and leading up to it was a little valley. Our course took us up this valley and past numerous little snow-bound and ice-covered lakes and into some rocky talus. On our way up to the ridge we took careful notes, and came to the conclusion that it would be perfectly possible to take animals up as far as the talus slope. From there on it looked as though we could get animals up by building a trail in a few places. We were encouraged by the prospect, but when we reached the ridge all hope of ever getting animals over was shattered, for we stood upon the brink of an immense cirque, or amphitheater, filled with snow and ice, and immediately below us was a precipice of several hundred feet. Some one had been there before, for at this spot there was built a large monument of rough stones. This cirque was one of a chain of cirques which formed the northern face of the ridge. It would be impossible for any one to get across at this place, even without pack-animals, and

MT. HUMPHREYS FROM THE SOUTHWEST.

LAKE FRANCES (ALTITUDE, 11,100 FEET).

From photographs by J. S. Hutchinson, Jr., 1904.

so we explored along the ridge to the rim of the next cirque eastward. Before reaching this we had to ascend a small intervening peak, from the summit of which the whole Humphreys Basin was spread out before us. Such a fascinating scene of desolation I never expect to see again. Nothing but snow and lakes, tiny streams and foaming cascades, glacial erratics and granite bosses, and the whole surrounded by the jagged mountains, and there, alone in solitary grandeur, rose Mt. Humphreys, the king of all the peaks. From the summit of this small peak we skirted along the rim of the cirque for a possible pass, and the prospects were far from bright. However, when almost in despair, we discovered, dropping downward from the rim, a deep chimney. It sloped downward at a steep angle for perhaps six hundred feet, and was filled with a long tongue of snow, which was frozen on its surface. To the left of the chimney rose a high vertical wall, and alongside of the wall the snow had melted away, leaving a passage through which it was just possible for a man to squeeze. We tested this passageway and found that we were able to travel down it. We then retraced our steps hurriedly back to camp.

The next morning we were up very early and, after a hasty breakfast, we made an inventory of the provisions for our knapsack trip. The provisions consisted only of the most substantial and condensed food. We also took two small pails, a tin plate, four cups and four spoons, a fifty-foot rope, the ice-ax, and the camera. Besides these, each of us took a light feather sleeping-bag. We then cached all the balance of our camping outfit, covering all with rubber sheets. The jacks were tethered with long ropes where they could get feed and water. These preparations having been completed, we followed up the little valley where Whitney and I had ascended the day before. The packs were heavy and we moved slowly, stopping frequently to rest. By 10 o'clock we reached the snow-tongue pass (about 12,200 feet), at the head of the snow-tongue which I have already mentioned. Taking off our sleeping-bag rolls, two of them were started down the snow-tongue. They bounded, plunged, and jumped furiously, and finally landed at the top of a rocky buttress which projected out at the foot of the snow-field six hundred feet below us. A third one was then started. Half-way down the slope it struck upon a rocky island which projected up through the snow and burst open like a sausage, scattering cans, bags of coffee, sugar, and sticks of chocolate in all directions over the snow. It was a difficult task to gather up the fragments, for the field was so steep and frozen that it was impossible to move on it without the use of the rope and ice-ax. On the shores of a little lake near the foot of the snow-tongue we stopped for a hasty lunch. This little lake is located in the bottom of the cirque into which we had descended, and for that reason we named it "Cirque Lake." The pass over which we had come we called "Snow-Tongue Pass."

Across the immense granite basin which bounds Mt. Humphreys on the west were seen several tiny groups of dwarf pine, in which a camp could be made, but upon reaching that place it was found that a high bluff rising behind completely shut off our view. As we wished to camp within full sight of the mountain, we decided to seek further. Whitney had gone exploring, and presently returned with the news that he had found a good place, very much nearer the mountain. Following him, we were led to the place which he had selected. It was treeless, with the exception of the dead remains of an old pine near by, but it gave us a splendid view of the mountain. It is always cold in such High Sierra altitudes, and so our camp was located in a little flat-bottomed gully, protected by two walls of granite (elevation, 11,000 feet). Our evening meal was tapioca soup, fried ham, tea, and hardtack.

The sun was low in the western horizon, and his soft light brought out in fine bold relief every crack and crevice in the mighty mountain which arose high above us so near at hand. Long we gazed at it with the glasses to ascertain if there was any way to the summit. Two steep gorges appeared, one starting near the base of the mountain and running obliquely from left to right, striking the crest perhaps a quarter of a mile to the right of the summit; the other one starting in the first gorge, two thirds of the way up from the bottom, and running at right angles to the first obliquely from right to left. This second gorge disappeared behind a sort of buttress, itself a mere knife-edge, which ran out southerly from the main peak almost parallel with the crest. This second gorge was visible for half its length, and the balance of the way it was hidden in the deep shadows cast by the setting sun. Each time the glasses were put down it was with a remark to the effect that if it were at all possible to ascend from this side it could only be through the deep and narrow gorge which runs up the mountain face from right to left and disappears behind the buttress.

The sunset lights on the mountains are always the finest, far surpassing the lights of sunrise. As the sun sinks there is a warm and mellow light cast on the whole landscape, and now the furrowed face of Humphreys looked particularly grand. The contrast of the high lights and the deep shadows was intense. All along the base of the mountain is a succession of talus slopes extending upward five hundred feet. This is of a light gray color, and is formed by the blocks of granite falling from the cliffs high above and sliding down numerous parallel chutes which lead to the top of the talus. The bottoms or floors of these chutes are worn smooth and almost polished by the streams of rock which have dashed through them. From the mouths of the chutes the talus slopes spread out in perfect cones. Above the talus, and extending all across the face of the mountain, is a chocolate-colored band, perhaps fifteen hundred feet in thickness, its upper edge scalloped and fluted like the teeth of a saw. Above this chocolate-colored band is the cap of the mountain, extending upward a thousand feet higher. This cap is of a terra-cotta color. The combination is peculiar and beautiful, and in the rays of the setting sun it was glorious.

The sun set behind the " Pinnacles," a ridge between us and the South Fork, and showed a long line of spires, spikes, blocks, and needles, side by side. The great snow-filled cirques across the cañon took on a vivid pink. The little lakes far below us and the tiny streams reflected the blush of sunset. The mountain shadows gradually faded and the twilight softly stole upon us. The moon, then at its first quarter, soon began to show her light. No sooner was the warm sun gone than the chill of evening settled down. Noble and my brother built a stone wall to protect us from any wind which might blow on us from the west. Whitney made as large a camp-fire as our wood-pile would permit, and I prepared our lunch for the next day. We lit our pipes, sat in the warmth of the genial fire, discussed the day's doings, and took considerable "thought for the morrow," wondering what it "might bring forth." The day had been an energetic one; the morrow might be even more so; and at 8:30 we were ready for our beds.

Near midnight I began to realize that I was in a semiconscious state, and presently awakened with chilly sensations, to find that I was doubled up, hugging myself in a vain effort to keep warm. The fire had burned down to a mass of glowing embers. I hastily arose to rebuild it. The moon had followed the sun and was just setting behind the western mountains. It cast an almost ghostly light over the snow-fields, which appeared like great white sheets laid over the bones of the mountains. The lakes were a mass of molten silver, and the glacial polish was burnished brass. Humphreys was a great black wall close at hand and of immense height. Overhead the myriads of stars twinkled brilliantly. There was no sound except the constant murmur of the little near-by rills. As I looked over this weird scene, from the setting moon to the millions of brilliant stars, and then across the glaciated basin to the snowy peaks, and finally to the great black wall of Humphreys, I felt as never before the force of the words, "The heavens declare the glory of God and the firmament showeth his handiwork." A cold wind had arisen, blowing down from the mountain and across the frozen lakes, bringing with it an unpleasant chill. I threw some logs on to the burning embers, crawled back into my sleeping-bag, and rolled nearer the fire. Three more times during the night some one of us was up to renew the fire. Before long, "morn in the white wake of the morning star came furrowing all the orient with gold."

At 5 o'clock (July 18th) we were up and cooking our frugal morning repast of bacon and coffee, and by 5:30 had packed our lunch, shouldered rope, ice-ax, camera, and field-glasses, pocketed our Sierra Club register, and were on the march toward the mountain. The air was crisp and cold. The sun, although half an hour above the horizon, was hidden from us behind the mighty wall of Humphreys, which was silhouetted black, clear, and sharp against the blazing east,—every pinnacle, every blade, every jagged spur, every sawtooth clear-cut and sharp,—and above all fanlike rays of light shot up into the clear atmosphere. On we went over the granite basin, strewn with glacial erratics, past frozen lakes lying in glacial basins. Every lake had its floating ice and its field of snow. Whatever soil there was, was made soft and spongy by the ice crystals. The traveling was comparatively easy until the talus slope was reached. Here was a lake, larger than the rest, which had to be skirted. Once past this, the ascent of the talus was commenced. The rocks were small and piled so steep that they started with almost every step. Our course took us up this five hundred feet, to the mouth of the gorge which I have already mentioned as running diagonally up the mountain from left to right. Although we had examined the mountain so carefully from a distance, and had mapped out our proper course, yet when actually on its side it was impossible to tell which was the correct gorge. Noble, Whitney, and my brother worked up the steep chimney toward the left, and finally came along a narrow horizontal shelf back to the main gorge, while I tried a chimney to the right, and then worked horizontally to the left, striking the main gorge at about the same elevation as the others. From here on the gorge was very steep and the rocky surface highly polished, either by snow-avalanches or boulders sliding over it. It was difficult traveling, and would have baffled us completely except for the cleavage-planes which ran diagonally across the polished slope.

After an hour of steep climbing we reached the gorge running at right angles to the one we were in. From this place Whitney continued up the first gorge to where it ran out at the knife-edge. On his return he reported that the eastern slope was a sheer polished precipice of several thousand feet. The second gorge, which we had just reached, was almost straight and sloped down to us at an angle of forty-five degrees. It was very narrow and V-shaped, the bottom scarcely ten feet wide. The right-hand wall, forming the knife-edge of the mountain, arose almost vertically above us, perhaps a thousand feet. The left-hand wall, which formed a sort of buttress, which I have already described as extending south from the summit, inclined somewhat from the perpendicular. This wall also was the merest knife-edge, with precipitous sides down to where it joined the main mass of the mountain near us.

The whole mountain—at least the cap of it for a thousand feet down—is composed of terra-cotta-colored granite, cracked and broken into huge blocks by the frost and ice. As we looked up the gorge we saw that the cleavage-planes all ran parallel and dipped down toward the east at an angle of sixty or seventy degrees.

On the cliff to our right were the places from which the huge cubes and parallelograms of granite had broken off, and in the bottom of the gorge were the fallen masses. The loosened blocks on the western wall, which was somewhat inclined, although cracked, broken, and misplaced, still remained approximately in their original positions.

After crossing a snow-field, which was frozen hard, a small shelf was reached, the last level place on the mountain, and from here commenced the final ascent of the gorge. Almost immediately we came upon the same large smooth, polished granite slope which had baffled Messrs. Le Conte and Cory. It formed the bottom of the gorge, and sloped upward for a distance of thirty feet as steep as a cathedral roof. To add to its difficulties, it was completely covered with a thin layer of ice, about a quarter of an inch thick. A single trial of walking on it was enough, for we immediately went tobogganing to its foot. We tried it on all fours, but this was impossible. Finally, to the right was found a tiny rocky chute between this icy granite slope and the eastern wall of the gorge. Up this for ten or fifteen feet I climbed, and here, being blocked by a large boulder, it terminated; but from this point, running off diagonally to the left, there was a tiny cleavage-joint in the granite slab. The nails in my shoes would cling to this as I reclined on my hands, face downward, against the frozen surface. In this way I worked crosswise over the slope and up to the broken cliffs above. Once there, it was an easy matter to reach the top of the boulder which had blocked the tiny chimney. Soon all of us were over this difficulty. Upward we went, clambering over boulders, hands and feet both in constant use. The chute was frequently blocked by the huge slabs and cubes of granite fallen from the cliffs above. In places the blocks had fallen in such a manner as to make caves, the floor of the cave being the bottom of the gorge, the ceiling the under portion of the boulder itself. From the ceiling of one of these caves we found suspended many long icicles the size of broomsticks or larger. These we found to be delightfully refreshing, and quenched our thirst by nibbling on them or else by catching the tiny drops of water which were trickling from their ends. Our altitude was now about 13,500 feet, and I dare say that these icicles in this cave form the highest source of any of the branches of the San Joaquin River. The huge boulders, dropped as they were in this narrow gorge, were a constant source of trial and menace to us. Some of them were unstable, and must be avoided on that account; others were so lodged that they formed little precipices which we must circumvent.

A hundred feet more of climbing and crawling on hands and knees, and the gorge opened up a little. All knew that shortly our fate would be sealed and the worst must be known. At this moment I happened to be ahead. Suddenly, and almost unawares, I came upon the knife-edge of the Sierra crest and looked over into a yawning abyss, down two thousand feet, to a wide-spreading snow-field held in a granite-walled amphitheater. I turned toward the summit above us, but could not see the extreme top, for it was hidden by the wall to our left, which arose two hundred feet above us, still inclined at an angle of seventy degrees. The lower part of the wall to a height of perhaps fifty feet was smooth and unbroken, except for a few crevices and projecting ridges caused by the cleavage of the rock. To ascend this seemed possible, and I called to the others, "I think we can make it." It appeared to be the only way. Without realizing how precipitous the slope was, I started up it, getting here a toehold and there a fingerhold, all the while pressing my body closely against the cliff. In this way I ascended for thirty feet, and then the wall seemed absolutely smooth and unbroken. I gazed to the right and to the left and up above me. All was apparently as smooth as glass. In an unguarded moment I looked downward to see if I could retrace my steps. My first view was through the cleft where the gorge broke through the crest knife-edge almost directly below me and down and down the cliffs and on to the snow. I looked for the tiny ridges in the wall by which I had ascended, but could not see them, so closely was I pressed against the wall to avoid going over backwards. A cold chill crept down my back. My knees began to shake. The alarm, however, was only momentary. I saw the uselessness of fear, turned my face to the wall, and then looked on things above, determined not again to look downward. When I had fairly gathered myself together, I noticed above me about ten feet, and somewhat to the left, that a couple of blocks of granite had been split out, leaving a little pinnacle. If this place could be reached I would have accomplished something, and would have a vantage-ground from which to look for better things. If not to go up higher, I at least could have the rope thrown to me and, with a hitch about the pinnacle, could descend to the gorge again. Finally, off to the left I found a little foothold which had been overlooked before, and somewhat above it a fingerhold. By the use of these and

LOOKING DOWN A GORGE ON MT. HUMPHREYS.
From a photograph by J. S. Hutchinson, Jr., 1904.

a few others which appeared, and by hugging the rock very closely, the pinnacle was finally reached. Above this the inclination of the wall was not so great, and to the left there ran up a number of little parallel chimneys caused by the breaking out of the blocks along the cleavage-planes; but each chimney at some point was blocked with a large cube which had not yet been fully dislodged. It was possible, however, to work from one chimney to another, and thus avoid the obstructions in each move from chimney to chimney, gaining ten or twenty feet in altitude. Presently, after a climb of about two hundred feet from where I had left the others, I reached the knife-edge of the buttress of which I have already spoken. The summit of the mountain was only about twenty feet above this and the way was clear. I then searched around for a better way of ascent. The western wall of the buttress was a sheer drop over five hundred feet to a shelf, and from the shelf there was still another drop to the talus slope. The south side of the buttress was a mere knife-edge, notched throughout with sharp pinnacles. I returned to the eastern side and examined all the little chimneys running down there. All of them before reaching the bottom of the gorge ended, leaving a smooth cliff thirty or forty feet in height.

I returned through the little chimneys by which I had ascended as far down as I could, reaching a point where the wall below the chimney was more inclined than below the other chimneys, and where it was also more broken. At this point the rope was thrown up to me. I made it fast around a projecting rock, and with its aid my brother hauled himself up to my position. We then lowered the rope again for the others to follow, but they—the married men of the party—had been deliberating and holding a council in the interim, and had decided that they had no right to take the risks which appeared necessary to complete the climb. Instead of attempting to follow us, they climbed a prominence which formed the summit of the eastern wall of the gorge. This they said was "Married Men's Peak," and jokingly called themselves "moral heroes."

Finally, at 11 o'clock, my brother and I scrambled on the summit (14,055 feet), and no longer looked on things above, but rather on things beneath—and far beneath. Circling all about us, three thousand feet below us, west of the main crest, lay the great granite amphitheater four miles in diameter, covered with large patches of snow and lakes of various sizes and shapes. Lake Desolation was just below us. This amphitheater is bounded on the south and southwest by the snow-tongue ridge over which we had passed, on the west by the Pinnacles, and on the northwest by a range midway between us and the Abbott group. These form an inner semicircle, beyond which is another concentric one, inclosed by the Evolution Group, the Goddard Divide, the divide between the South Fork of the San Joaquin and the King's River, the Seven Gables, and the Abbott Group, commencing on the south and extending far around to the north. Beyond the Abbott Group lay Red Slate and Red-and-White peaks. To the eastward the mountain dropped off a sheer precipice for two thousand feet or more into a huge snow amphitheater. From there the snow slopes at a steep angle several thousand feet further, and then a rolling volcanic country completes the balance of the distance down to the town of Bishop, more than ten thousand feet below us and about sixteen miles distant. Owen's Valley is laid out in square farms like a checkerboard, and for miles and miles the green alfalfa-fields gave life to what would otherwise have been an almost lifeless scene. To the southward we could see the rugged line of the Palisades. Far below us, both north and south, forming part of the main crest, were several mesas, or tablelands, probably remnants of the old base-level through which the knife-edge and saw-teeth of Humphreys had cut their way.

The summit of Humphreys is not more than eight feet square and contains the same parallel lines of cleavage which I have referred to as existing in the gorge. It is one mass of cracked and broken blocks, thrown loosely together in such a way as to warn one to move cautiously lest the whole top should break off and fall into the great abyss to the eastward. While my brother built a cairn as a last resting-place for our Sierra Club register, I examined very carefully all about the summit for a possible way of ascent other than that by which we had come. The north side was almost sheer for five hundred feet down to the peak on which Le Conte and Cory had climbed. The whole western side was a series of precipices and shelves down to the talus slope, and then on down at a gradual angle to the granite basin. The southern wall, as I have already said, dropped at least a thousand feet to the knife-edge of the main ridge, which then extended on downwards until it connected with Mt. Emerson, near Piute Pass. The drop on the east was the worst of all.

There were no signs of any one having been on the summit of the peak before. Probably no one had ever stood where we then were, unless perhaps during the early Jurassic period, before the mountain was fully sculptured. Then the mariners of that age (if there were any) might have sailed upon the waters of the Pacific close to the base of the mountain, and, there landing, have climbed up its then gently sloping sides. The mountain is very different from most peaks of the Sierra. It stands absolutely remote and alone. The nearest peaks are those of the inner semicircle of which I have spoken, but they do not reach much over 12,500 feet, and from our position appeared low. The nearest peak which approached us in height was Mt. Darwin, eight miles distant.

After an hour spent in viewing the landscape, we signaled to the others, and finally all met at the gorge where we had parted company. The process of descent to this gorge was about the reverse of our upward trip. The rope was in constant use, and we both heaved a sigh of relief when we were safely down. From there on the descent was practically over the same course by which we had ascended. It was much easier, for in many places where in ascending we had climbed on hands and knees now we could make a toboggan-slide of fifteen or twenty feet over a smooth surface or down a gravel chute. It was somewhat hard on portions of our clothing, but we "got there," and that, for the time being, was the main object. The rope was again used several times. The rocks in the steep chute lay so loosely that great care had to be used lest we should start an avalanche. Whitney and Noble went on ahead down one of these chimneys, and were several hundred feet below us. My brother and I moved with the utmost care to avoid setting any stones in motion, but suddenly a number started; these started others, and in a moment a deluge of them was tearing down the chute directly toward those below us. We shouted like mad for Noble and Whitney to get out of the way. They looked back and saw the torrent coming. This chute was bounded on its eastern side by a precipitous wall, in which, near where they were standing, was a deep vertical niche. They rushed for this, and had no sooner concealed themselves than the avalanche went shooting past them. This was a warning, and thenceforth in similar places we all remained close together. In an hour we had reached the top of the talus. Here, by making a slight detour, we reached a snow-field which gave us a toboggan-slide of several hundred feet down to the granite basin. It seemed like an easy matter to cut across this basin directly to our camp, but the similarity of the snow-fields, lakes, and the granite bosses made it like a maze, and even when we were within a short distance of our camp it took us many long minutes of searching to locate it. Soon a drink of some newly brewed tea refreshed us.

We were unanimous that we ought not to remain another night in this exposed place, and so at once shouldered our bundles and descended five hundred feet to the thickest of the several clumps of trees which we had passed the day before. Here, beside an old sheep-corral, we made a more comfortable camp, protected on all sides by the mountain pines, and having here a bountiful supply of wood. Below us was a fine brook, and a plunge in this had the magical effect of making us whole again and putting new life into every fiber, vein, and muscle. What a glorious camp-fire we had that night! How brilliant the moon seemed! How comfortable and cozy seemed our combined kitchen, social hall, and bedroom!

By 4:30 the next morning we were retracing our steps toward our Snow-Tongue Pass. In an hour or so we reached Cirque Lake. Near here, in the snow, we followed for quite a distance some fresh bear-tracks going toward our pass. An hour later we were at the pass, and from there took a last, long, lingering look at Humphreys. On the other side of the pass we saw more bear-tracks going downward in the direction of our Lake Frances camp. What if the jacks and bears had been in mortal conflict! It was with a warm thrill that we came upon the lake, and there, on the opposite shore, saw our four jacks. They actually seemed glad to welcome us back home. The deep emerald waters of the lake were irresistible. In we plunged, only to swim to the shore with teeth chattering, knees shaking, and toes tingling, but again what a resurrection of hopes, joys, and ambitions came from the icy tonic!

On our return trip from Snow-Tongue Pass to Lake Frances, we passed many patches of red snow. A cup of this was melted and filtered through a paper, leaving a decidedly reddish deposit of very fine particles. After returning from our camping trip an examination of these particles under the microscope showed them to be little globules resembling fishes' eggs. Each globule appeared translucent and seemed luminous, as though shining with a light coming from the interior.

After lunch we descended to Evolution Creek. Here at the junction of the trails we found a monument of twelve stones, Le Conte's prearranged message, meaning that he had already descended the cañon. We followed, and the next day joined his party at the Mt. Goddard camp.

The following day we climbed Mt. Goddard, and then on the succeeding day started for King's River Cañon, by way of Collins Meadow, Tehipite Valley, and Simpson Meadow. At Collins Meadow, Whitney and Noble, owing to their limited time, left us and struck out westward by a trail which leads to Trimmer Springs. From there, they had the novel and exciting experience of a midnight flume-ride down to Sanger. Five days later, the rest of us were in our old familiar camping-grounds in King's River Cañon. Here Dr. Gilbert left us to explore the Roaring River country, and the remainder of the party hastened home, and our camping-trip was at an end.

Although the trip was at an end, yet the best of all was still to come—the retrospect. Every such trip as we had just completed has its joys, its pleasures, its excitements; there are the rugged mountains and the snow-filled cirques, the foaming streams and the roaring cascades, the alpine meadows, the wild flowers, and the glorious camp-fires; but there are also the hardships, the trials, the privations,—the lost trail, the straying mule, the drenching rain, the mosquitoes. But, with the retrospect, all is changed; all the trials, all the hardships, all the difficulties have faded into the background, and there is left a perfect and everlasting picture, ever increasing in beauty as the months go by. And now, after half a year has elapsed, and we can get the view of our trip in its proper perspective and can compare it with all the other camping-pictures which live in our memories, I think we can truly say that this last, this view into the Mt. Humphreys region, is one of the choicest treasures.

ADDRESS AT MEMORIAL EXERCISES.*

By Alexander G. Eells.

It has fallen to me to take part to-day, on behalf of the Alumni of the University of California.

To say what the name Le Conte signifies and stands for to me, or to any other of the older graduates, is far beyond my powers of expression. "Dr. John" and "Professor Joe"! The names call up images of the springtime of one's life, with its freshness and vividness, when all was eager anticipation, and a rosy haze veiled the difficulties and dangers—the chivalric period, with its rainbows of promise and its sowing of the seeds of future achievements.

Dr. John I met unawares during my entrance examinations, those days of dread to the stripling applicant for admission from a country school. Restless from nervous apprehension I had wandered to the end of the old "dummy" track toward Oakland, and was sitting at the station, waiting for the car to take me back to Berkeley, when a most kindly old gentleman sat down beside me and drew me into conversation. If he had been my own father, his sympathetic interest could not have been greater, nor his words more full of cheer and encouragement. The incident is amongst the most vivid of my college recollections.

Professor Joe I first met, soon afterwards, at one of the home-gatherings which were common then. I cannot explain the fascination which led me shyly to follow

---

* See page 254—" Notes and Correspondence."—Editor.

him about, to listen whenever he spoke, nor the thrill of his words when he chanced to speak to me—for he neglected no one. No more can I describe or explain the charm of a good woman, but I know that Professor Joe had it; and that with it he had also that nobility of spirit which commands respect, loyalty, and devotion.

It is not so much what he said nor what he taught that lives in my memory. The man impressed himself. My most distinct recollection of his teaching is of the substance of a lecture on the importance of scientific methods —those "tools of thought." The idea was new to me at the time, and striking. Yet that idea seems as little connected with himself as though gleaned from an encyclopedia. In himself, he was far above, and he inspired thoughts far above any mere method,—thoughts for which words are too coarse and too scant. In this was his true greatness; and however valuable his scientific work, it cannot in the mind of any of his one-time students be compared in importance with his personal influence nor with his spiritual radiance.

There are keen and brilliant minds that are yet as distant and as cold as Arcturus with reference to human emotions. Men of science especially are apt to deem it a merit that their thinking is impersonal, uninfluenced by considerations of the consequences to merely human interests. Their admirably logical conclusions are held and taught with a lofty disregard, and sometimes disdain, of the pity of it. They are more interested in the "success" of the operation than in the life of the patient. The student at our colleges, and even the average man of affairs of these days, has his impulses and instincts curbed and his sympathies blunted by certain abstract and wholly unemotional doctrines which are dignified and sanctified with the name of laws—the law of wages, the law of supply and demand, the law of population and subsistence, the law of the survival of the fittest, and the rest. These do credit to the human mind as a thinking machine, an intellectual engine, but are hardly creditable as ideals for an immortal spirit, whose wealth is not in the abundance of the things it possesses here but cannot take into the hereafter.

Fortunate is the institution of learning whose influential teachers are men, rather than dispensers of formulæ; men whose measure of success is the effect upon the character of the student rather than conformity with abstract laws.

Fortunate indeed also are the students whose impelling ideas, however severely scientific, are yet alive, not excavated from books, but throbbing with the human grace of such a teacher as Joseph Le Conte—alive to pity, and to kindness, and to the service of mankind.

Professor Joe was a scientist, but science to him was not merely clods and beasts and laws and logic. Human nature, human ambitions, human affections he rated far above these. For him science was but the stepping-stool for aspirations and for ideals which do not halt at the grave—which indeed can come to full fruition only beyond the grave. He knew well, and he made his hearers know, that scientific methods are only contrivances, man-made artifices, to be made use of where useful; but that to be bound by them is to be enslaved by one's own servants. In the great crises of life it is not any of the "ologies" that save. It is the homely truths consecrated by the experience of the whole race of man, and embodied in the words *mother, sister, wife, children, friends.* Neither the Greek Sage nor the Galilean Prophet taught science.

It is fitting that we should dedicate this memorial in this unpretentious way. It is entirely in keeping with the simple, unaffected character of him to whose memory we do reverence.

Around us are the scenes he loved. Yonder dome holds up its massive head doing honor to his name. To us all the surroundings are enriched by associations derived from him. Like him, they hold themselves grandly superior to the trivialities and the artifices of conventional life, and to its petty distinctions. These mountains are hospitable to all alike. As the President of the Sierra Club puts it, when we come to the mountains we come home—home from the hollow pageants, the narrow conventions, the whited sepulchers—home to the peace and calm of the spirit.

In his autobiography Professor Joe tells us that at one time he thought seriously of joining the ministry; but found his calling elsewhere,—not to his regret,—for, as he says: "One may be a preacher of righteousness in more ways than one." His life-work demonstrates that there is no more effective way than just to be true, stoutly and sturdily true, to one's higher self, to one's ideals. This, after all, is the only way to make those ideals animate and forceful in the practical world. Mere preaching about them cannot give them vitality nor influence, any more than reading about it in a book can impart what Nature has in store for those who set foot upon her mountains.

These sublime surroundings are attuned to what is noblest in us. Through them, voiceless Nature is preaching righteousness. She stands for it stoutly and massively, and she needs no ritual, and she needs no artifice.

So he that hath the sublime in his soul, let him preach righteousness by living it forth in its native simplicity, stoutly and sturdily. He shall awaken a responsive chord in all unperverted natures, and a multitude shall call him blessed.

Let us dedicate this simple lodge to this purpose. to this ministry. Here our beloved teacher came again and again, as one comes home, for cheer and for aid. Hither let us turn as often as we may, not only for what we may gain of good from the sermons in these stones, but still more for the higher, more quickening inspirations from a life true to itself and in touch with Nature.

> "God's truth has many voices; sun and star
> And mountain and the deep that rolls afar
> Speak the great language; and of mightier worth
> The lips and lives of godlike men on earth."

MT. LYELL AND MT. RITTER ASCENTS BY SIERRA CLUB OUTING OF 1904.

BY RUSS AVERY.

MT. LYELL.

Bang! W-o-w! "Everybody get up, get up, get up!" These explosive sounds in the early dawn that have become so familiar to the outing members of the Sierra Club were just as potent at 3 o'clock in the morning at the base camp on Lyell Creek as they were when, for the first time, the cunning cruelty of man inflicted them upon an innocent sleeping humanity.

The startling sound produced by shooting off the giant bomb went crashing among the trees, was hurled from cliff to cliff, and its reverberating echo had barely died in the distance before every tree and rock seemed alive and calling to its neighbor to be up and doing, for "tomorrow" had come—the strenuous day set apart for the climbing of snow-clad Mt. Lyell.

In a few minutes indistinct figures could be seen slipping out of the dark recesses of the forest into the dim light of the camp-fire and forming themselves into animated groups around the steaming kettles and the fragrant coffee-pots. It is said that the imminence of danger and the comradeship of the mountains makes brothers of us all. A cursory view of these shadowy forms confirmed this observation, for all the women in the party, in obedience to the rules of the committee for this day, had eschewed the conventional and cumbersome skirts and arrayed themselves in bloomers or overalls, the sensible costumes of hardy mountaineers.

The informality of breakfast being quickly finished, the party was formed into a circle and told off in three companies with Captains Willoughby Rodman, Duncan McDuffie, and Olcott Haskell in charge thereof, respectively.

At 4:15 o'clock, just as the gray dawn began to light the cañon depths sufficiently to enable us to move with certainty among the rocks and trees, under the able leadership of Mr. E. T. Parsons, we started. We proceeded at first slowly up the steep side of the right-hand cañon-wall and through the forest and over the granite slopes until we reached the basin at the head of the valley we had left. Here our course for half a mile or more over a comparatively level stretch of open country was exceedingly interesting. Before us was the beautiful mass of snow coming far down the mountain-side and feeding the numerous small tributaries to Lyell Creek which we had to ford on inconvenient stepping-stones or leap across where width permitted; to our right were the steep cliffs of this glacial cirque; while to our left the lazy sun was just getting up from his cold couch and beginning to warm himself for the day's routine. As we made frequent stops to rest, we began to take note of our companions. Judging from appearances alone, one would assume that most of the party had slept on the charred embers of the camp-fire and washed their faces with the under-side of a frying-pan; while others had pale and ghostly visages, caused by covering their faces with cold cream and adhesive plasters; and all this care and trouble was taken to avoid blistering of the skin by the reflection of the sun on the snow. All kinds of snow-glasses, hoods, and veils were on exhibition ready for immediate use, while bandanas of variegated colors served to enhance the picturesque effect. Altogether we presented more the appearance of an organized band of gypsy robbers than a respectable party of dignified citizens intent on the serious purpose of scaling a cold and forbidding mountain.

To the most of us the Lyell Glacier was a disappointment. We did not approach it from the right direction to get the best view of its terminal, and we found ourselves traversing its uneven surface before we realized we were near the glacier; and consequently the impression we gained was that of a very large field of snow on a sloping mountain-side with numerous small streams of water flowing from its base. Those of us who started for Ritter the next day gained from the top of the Donohue Pass a much more comprehensive view and a far more accurate impression of its true glacial features. But at best the Lyell is a dying glacier, and is not in the same class with its interesting, picturesque, and progressive neighbor on Mt. Ritter.

The jagged surface of the great snow-field engendered in us all a profound respect. Alternate thawing and freezing, combined with the action of the wind, had made uneven and irregular ridges of snow with knife-edged ice-blades for upper surfaces, and with intervening hollows of from one to four feet in breadth and two to four feet in depth.

Over such a surface our progress for hours was slow and tedious. Three or four stalwart men in the lead took turns in kicking footholds into these slippery edges, and the rest of us followed in single file, each one helping thus to make a better trail for the persons following; but even then, owing to the imperfect vision through unaccustomed snow-glasses, and from many other causes, we were constantly slipping from our insecure footholds and tumbling into the intervening furrows.

As we ascended our course became constantly steeper and more difficult, until the climax was reached in following the last tongue of snow around a ridge of large loose rocks. Here we used a hatchet to cut footholds in the ice, and, after the leaders had safely passed over and occupied comparatively secure positions for bracing themselves among the rocks, a rope was brought into requisition and held taut. Grasping this with our left hands, we crawled one by one around the end of the rock ridge, over the steep edge of the insecure and slippery ice, and on to the loose rocks above.

Great care had to be exercised in clambering over these rocks, as a careless step would start great masses in headlong flight and imperil the lives of those below. It was a great relief to escape the tension of the last half-hour of work and arrive at last upon the summit; and when, at 10 o'clock, the roll was called on Lyell's crest, and it was found that the entire party of fifty-three had reached the top without casualty of any kind, it was a matter of general felicitation.

That the climb was so successful was due to the perfect organization of the party, the precaution of the leaders, and the good sense, endurance, and hardihood of the members. If any of these elements had been eliminated, a large percentage of the party would have seen Lyell's summit only from a long distance off; for the

DESCENT OF MT. LYELL—1904.

ON THE SNOW-TONGUE OF MT. RITTER—1904.

climb up the last few hundred feet was attended with considerable danger and was accomplished with much nervousness and anxiety. But, however great the toil and risk, our troubles were at once dispelled upon reaching the summit by a view of the magnificent alpine panorama. We were in the center of a sea of mountains; wave after wave of mountain ranges extended in all directions in countless recession, the snow-clad peaks forming the foaming crests of the raging billows. Here and there the regularity of the movement seemed broken by opposing winds, and the angry waves, lashed into fury and driven against one another, heaped their waters high in crests of frozen grandeur. Such was the impression given by the steep snows of McClure and the rugged, isolated peaks of Banner and Ritter.

Sheltered among the rocks from the chill winds of such altitudes, we ate our luncheon and enjoyed the inspiring view. At 11 o'clock our attention was attracted by flashes from Lambert's Dome, about twelve miles away, and just across the river from the main camp in the Tuolumne Meadows, where some of our friends had gone and were heliographing to us their greetings. With a small pocket-mirror we answered their congratulations, thus establishing wireless communication on the outposts of civilization.

We signed our names on the Sierra Club register and at 11:30 o'clock began the descent. We left in detached groups, but with one accord avoided the scene of our strenuous labors of the morning, and, by keeping well to the left, in a general northwesterly direction, and following the large and very steep snow-field, we arrived at the base of the mountain without exciting adventure. Those who were going to Ritter remained that night at the base camp, while the others, according to previous arrangement, continued on to the main camp in the meadows, where they arrived that evening footsore, hungry, and weary.

MT. RITTER.

The next day nine members of the Sierra Club left the Lyell base camp and started on a knapsack trip over the Donohue Pass to Mt. Ritter. At the eastern foot of the pass we were surprised to hear voices, and soon we came upon the camp of Mrs. Hoagg's party. They had come up Rush Creek by way of Mono and Silver lakes, and on the day before our meeting had climbed Mt. Ritter from the south.

We arrived early in the afternoon at the upper end of Thousand Island Lake, where we made camp in a clump of twisted tamaracks situated about two hundred feet above the level of the lake. After a hearty dinner, and feeling at peace with the world, we sat on the rocks watching the beautiful effect of the gathering twilight on the rugged side of Mt. Banner. As the devouring shadow of night gradually crept up its precipitous side, it seemed as if the mountain was slowly sinking into the flood of darkness; then came a last pause for a moment, as if the Titan were making a final, desperate struggle to keep his head above the flood, and all was over. Yet, huge and indistinct, the shadowy form with its grizzled fringe of snow stood there in the night rugged, grim, and defiant. In the morning Banner was the first to be wakened by the sunlight; and, like Le Conte Dome in Yosemite, it is at all times the dominant figure in the landscape.

Although the altitude of our camp at Thousand Island Lake was over ten thousand feet, the night was uncomfortably warm, and the mosquitoes were uncommonly neighborly. If we uncovered to keep cool, the mosquitoes kept us awake by their singing and loud demonstrations of affection; if we covered our heads with our blankets to avoid the mosquitoes, we were too warm to sleep. The result was that we passed a very bad night.

We[*] rose early the morning of the 18th of July, and at 4:50 o'clock started toward Ritter. Our course lay to the southward for several hundred yards, then over a large and ancient moraine to the small but beautiful glacial lake at the foot of the snow-field extending westward from the saddle lying between Banner Peak and Ritter. This is one of the prettiest and most interesting lakes seen during the outing. The deep blue of its waters is in marked contrast with the whiteness of the numerous floes of snow and ice that dot its surface, while the reflection of the near-by peaks and rocks reminds one of the fine effects seen in Mirror Lake of the Yosemite. Here also is seen at its best the Ritter Glacier. The thick mass of snow and ice terminates abruptly on the eastern shore, and great blocks break away from the central mass, drop into the lake, and form miniature icebergs.

On the shores of this lake we paused to study care-

---

[*] Before starting from the Lyell base camp we had unanimously chosen Mr. Gould as our leader, and this evening, while around the camp-fire, we completed our organization by casting lots for positions in line. These positions we maintained not only in climbing the mountain, but in making the descent as well. In this way each person took an equal chance with the others in the dangers of the trip, and particularly in the liability to accident from falling rocks started by those who preceded or followed him in the ascent or descent. As thus formed, the party was as follows: Edward B. Gould, Duncan McDuffie, William Frederic Badè, Olcott Haskell, Russ Avery, W. H. Kimball, Willoughby Rodman, Julius Cahn, and Lowell J. Hart.

fully the configuration of the mountain and to plan our attack. It was evident to us all that the only practicable approach would be over the large snow-field to the top of the col between Banner and Ritter, and from there we would have to investigate farther.

The snow afforded much easier traveling than was found in the ascent of Mt. Lyell, as the hummocks were generally neither high nor far apart, and, during our ascent, had not yet been softened by the morning sun. Our progress as far as the saddle was therefore quite rapid and comparatively easy. Here we stopped to take photographs and to study the problem we were about to try to solve.

Ritter Mountain is peculiar in that it has several large ridges of rocks extending far down its northern slope, with long and narrow intervening tongues of snow, many of which terminate abruptly at the feet of insurmountable cliffs. The rocks are very large, unstable, and easily dislodged. The snow is very steep, and when frozen affords difficult footholds; when thawing it is unsafe and is easily started in an avalanche. As it was still early in the morning, and the snow was quite solid, we planned our course up one of the largest of these snow-tongues. As we ascended, the snow-blades became thinner and farther apart and the spaces between them deeper, while at the same time the inclination of the snow-field on the mountain became steeper, the angle ranging, as we estimated, from forty-five to sixty degrees. In some places the snow was as nearly perpendicular as it could well be and still cling to the mountain-side. A photograph taken by Mr. Badè shows this perpendicularity in an excellent manner, the members of the party being almost directly one above another, as if climbing a ladder. We gradually worked to the right, and, leaving the snow-tongue, began climbing over the insecure rocks at its edge. One of the members of the party who had remained behind to get a good photograph of the snow-field, with ourselves in the foreground, came along rapidly to overtake us. When he was still some distance below us and partly hidden from our view by intervening rocks, a stone, which had become loosened by us, started bounding in his direction. All that we could do was to give a cry of warning and await results. His position was interesting and for a few seconds precarious. He could not see what was coming, and, being still in the snow and unable to seek the protection of the rocks, he stood ready to jump to right or left and avoid the threatening danger as best he might. Fortunately the stone passed harmlessly by him.

The rocks became gradually more difficult to climb, until, when we began to think we were almost at the summit, we were confronted by an insurmountable cliff. We then realized that we should have kept farther to the east (to our left) and continued up a snow-tongue that had at first seemed impassable. We could not go on, and none of us wanted to go back; so while we were canvassing the situation our leader began to investigate the possibility of crossing over a very dangerous-looking edge of ice and snow to a rock-ridge beyond. The snow had so thawed away from the rocky cliff on the right that there was a wide and deep crevice intervening, while on the left the snow stood at an angle that was not far from perpendicular, and the top was a mere blade, too thin to give a safe foothold; in addition to which the sun had thawed the whole mass into a treacherous condition. Under these circumstances we very cautiously straddled the difficulty, and breathed more freely when we were again on rocks. Later in the day we viewed this place from below and felt very thankful that we were not compelled to cross it a second time. After a few minutes more of hard work we reached the summit,* having been five hours from our base camp in making the ascent.

The panorama viewed from the top of Ritter is more extended than that seen from Lyell. Looking first to the north, one may see the head-waters of Rush Creek near Donohue Pass, observe much of its course, and see its outlet in the alkaline waters of Lake Mono. The rivulets formed by the melting snows nearer the base of Ritter and Banner flow northward a few hundred yards from the moraine we crossed in the morning and empty into Thousand Island Lake, which in turn is the main source of the Middle Fork of the San Joaquin. Just south of this moraine is the glacial lake previously referred to, and which is one of the uppermost sources of the North Fork of the San Joaquin. The two rivers thus rising within a few inches of each other flow in opposite directions, circle the mountain, and unite their waters several miles to the southward. Farther to the west are the head-waters of the Merced rising from the snows of Lyell.

The well-known mountain peaks to the north are of course Dana and Conness. Lyell and Florence lie to the northwest, but seen from an unfamiliar side are not at first recognized as friends. The South Dome of Yosemite

---

* Mt. Ritter (altitude 13,186 feet) is 96 feet higher than Lyell, 136 feet higher than Dana, and 2,265 feet higher than Hoffman.

is almost as conspicuous here as it is from Lyell. Mt. Clark is to the south of west, while Gray and Red mountains, Merced Peak, Black Peak, Goddard, Humphreys, Red Slate, and, in the distance towards Nevada, the White Mountains, are easily picked out in their order. In fact, snow-capped peaks surround Ritter in every direction, so that one is inclined to unite in the ecstatic descriptions of others who have ascended this mountain and say that the view from Ritter is one of the most sublime to be found anywhere in the High Sierra. The combination of snow, ice, granite, trees, glacial lakes, the Mono Lake and craters, Pumice Valley, the majestic White Mountains of Nevada, the near-by Minarets, and rugged Banner Peak almost within stone's throw, the Coast Range in the dim western haze, and the numberless unnamed peaks and crests to the north and south as far as the eye can see, form a vision never to be forgotten. For two hours we remained on top of the mountain, drinking inspiration from the view, during which time we also managed to do full justice to the usual hearty Sierra Club luncheon.

With a brief account of our ascent we inscribed our names in the Sierra Club register, and on top of the cairn placed the skeleton head of a mazama which Mr. Gould carried up from near Thousand Island Lake for the purpose. Leaving this guardian of the sacred archives, we regretfully turned away from the magnificent view and slowly and cautiously began our descent.

This was no easy task. We followed down a ridge of large and very loose rocks which led in a northeasterly direction to the big snow-field between Banner and Ritter. These rocks would appear from above to be very secure, but when, with too much confidence, one trusted his weight upon them, they would slide from their positions and go crashing down the mountain-side or shoot over a sheer precipice perhaps two thousand feet in depth. We were obliged to exercise the utmost care, testing nearly every rock with foot or hand before daring to rely upon it. We often came to a standstill, and had to explore in various directions before finding a crevice or a ledge that would permit us to continue safely our downward course. When at last we reached the snow,—which had been considerably softened by the sun,—we tobogganed, ran, and rolled down the steep slope until we were once more at the edge of our pretty glacial lake.

We arrived at our base camp at Thousand Island Lake at about 4 o'clock in the afternoon, and, hastily packing our knapsacks, continued on our way for about five miles, camping by the waters of Rush Creek at the eastern foot of Donohue Pass. We were hungry and tired, but good-natured and happy.

For dinner we cooked the remnant of our provisions, except coffee and mush, and soon were enjoying a sleep that dynamite alone could interrupt. The next morning, after a light breakfast and a two hours' tramp, we arrived at the Lyell base camp, cooked a second breakfast out of provisions left there for that purpose, and not long afterwards arrived in the main camp at Tuolumne Meadows fresh and hearty, ready for luncheon and another mountain.

The altitude of Mr. Ritter, as given on the map of J. N. Le Conte, is 13,186 feet. The register-can of the Sierra Club was deposited on the summit July 10, 1897. It contains, in addition to the official register of the club (No. 20A), some interesting memoranda of previous ascents. As these papers are badly weather-worn and faded and the writing is partially obliterated, it may not be inappropriate to give their contents here. The first memorandum is as follows:—

"U. S. Geological Survey. Topographical Survey of Mono Lake Region, —— W. Johnson, topographer. John Miller, assistant. Occupied Mount Ritter Aug. 26th, 1883, with plane-table. Occupied East Ritter, or Banner Peak, same day."

Note two: "Sidney I. Peixotto, 1626 Sutter St., San Francisco; Theodore S. Solomons, 1707 Scott St., San Francisco; Joseph Le Conte, Jr., U. C. '91, Berkeley, ascended July 26, 1892. We came up from Yosemite, Soda Springs, across pass east of Lyell, head-waters of Rush Creek, across divide to lake, head-waters San Joaquin, thence to top of Ritter by way of glacier and wall opposite Banner Peak. Beautiful clear day."

Note three: "Summit of Mount Ritter, Aug. 2d, 1892.—R. M. Price, U. C. '93, Berkeley, Cal.; L. de F. Bartlett, U. C. '93, 1233 St. Charles St., Alameda, Cal. We ascended this peak in 4¾ hours from the head of the large isle-dotted lake or by coming over the glacier to *saddle* between Mount Ritter and Banner Peak, thence scrambling up along the rocks. We reached the lake by following practically the same route as that followed by Messrs. Le Conte, Solomons, and Peixotto. We found the ascent of this peak less difficult than the climbing of a peak to the west of Lyell, which we climbed July 31, 1892.

"R. M. PRICE,
"L. DE F. BARTLETT,
"Sierra Club Tramps."

Note four: "Aug. 20, 1892.—Ascended again, reaching summit at 6 P. M., having come all around the peak, ascending from the south with 8 x 10 camera and plates on my back. THEO. S. SOLOMONS."

A DEER'S BILL OF FARE.

By Alden Sampson.

The summer of 1903 I spent in the forest reserves of the United States, mainly of California, engaged for the Biological Survey of the Department of Agriculture in work for the establishment of game refuges. During days of observation in the saddle, and on foot, and at night by the camp-fire, the subject of a deer's bill of fare often came up for discussion. After repeated conferences with hunters and rangers, the following articles were admitted. As that journey was in a certain sense a voyage of discovery, wherein I was engaged with the study of the general problem of game refuges, unbiased by preconceived theories, so is this list tentative, and includes almost exclusively plants growing in Southern California and in the Sierra Reserve. I would invite criticism from hunters who are able to verify their opinions by the examination of the contents of the stomach of the deer when killed, and would urge all hunters to make a practice of examining and identifying those ingredients. Should this have for result that the hunter thereby gains familiarity with plants, that individual is to be congratulated upon one more card of admission to the delights of the forest.

In forming this list, I have, in almost every instance, tasted the leaves of the plant which is included; by doing this one comes to know with a certain instinctive certainty what a deer would *not* like. The deer have a sensitive and cultivated palate. Their food, if not purified by fire like ours, is still of the cleanest, most appetizing sort, the newest and freshest growth. Their palate is stronger than ours, and they often eat a plant that we cannot quite relish with zest because it has a little too much tang to it, but having tasted many things which I know they eat with pleasure, I should expect to find, in the vast majority of cases, any food which they like not repugnant to our palate if partaken of in reduced strength. So that, in the last analysis, it is largely a question of quantity, not of quality, in which our tastes differ. Their palates do not accept food which we find in small amounts rank and hateful. Whether the deer have a palate more sensitive than ours, or as sensitive, I do not know. Of course, the variety of our food and the range of difference from all sorts of fruits and vegetables to meats and highly flavored sauces, complicated to the extreme degree, and to wines of extraordinary delicacy, a little infinity of items, comprise a vast gamut beyond the possibilities of the deer's bill of fare. But that is not a demonstration that our palate is more sensitive than theirs. If refinement and cultivation consist in the power of perception and discrimination of slight differences, then it may be that the palm must be given to the deer. Their sense of taste is supplemented by the marvelous gift of scent. Their power of scent is incomparably more sensitive and powerful than ours, and these two organs of scent and taste are very closely related. Every one knows from painful personal experience that with a severe cold in the head, which deprives him for the time being of the capacity of smelling anything, the sense of taste also disappears. Even the slight power of scent which man possesses he often impairs by excessive use of tobacco, and thereby as well dulls the sense of taste. The gourmand becomes more and more dependent upon condiments and highly seasoned dishes for his satisfaction; the things which can gratify his cravings become elaborately artificial, and it is almost an axiom that a jaded palate requires a more and more trenchant lash; particularly in hot countries men abuse condiments. I believe that, aided by the power of scent, deer can discriminate between fine shades of difference almost, if not quite, imperceptible to our palates. Their food is not defiled, as much of ours must be, by contact with other individuals of their own species. They gather the finest, freshest, newest growth of herbage, daintily plucking a sprig or a leaf here and there. They are creatures of intelligence and of great zest in living, and their dearest delight is to eat, and to eat the best which the forest affords. Time is no object to them. They give many hours daily to the gratification of their desire for food, whereas humans take an infinity of pains in preparation, and in getting the food to eat, in earning their living, but after all allow but brief time for its enjoyment. As compared with man's hasty and wolflike manner of bolting his food during a few minutes, often in hateful surroundings, three times a day, these dainty creatures are true epicures. They have mastered the difficult and refined art of eating slowly, far more satisfactory than our method, whether health or pleasure be at stake.

Up among the pines and the oaks, in the summer range of the deer, when one looks for a good deer country, he will find it where the buckthorn grows in abundance, the wild lilac and the oak. The deer are fastidious in their choice of viands; any one who thinks that they munch grass like a cow is making the mistake of his life. In the summer they do this hardly more frequently than they regale themselves upon ham sandwiches or chocolate eclaires. Deer will crop the juicy and succulent heads of grass coming into seed, while they are rich and luscious, and they will, with delight, pluck the milky grain of the wild oat as it matures, but their usual food, while it is of great variety, does not chiefly consist of the leaves of grass. They are quite different from antelope, elk, mountain sheep, and the Rocky Mountain goat in this respect. Deer at times, in the winter, doubtless graze like cattle or sheep, but that is a case of "Hobson's choice"; there is little else then upon which they may satisfy the cravings of hunger. In the climate of Southern California the grass is cured standing, and even beneath the snow retains its sweetness like hay; it is hay, and the hillside is Nature's barn, spacious, well ventilated, and safe from destruction even in earthquakes,—only fire imperils the precious supply of food. The conditions under which this crop is cured and held in storage maintain a quality of wildness acceptable to their idea; even if the food itself be tame, at all events it has not been contaminated by touch, as much of our food must necessarily be, but is pure and sweet. In that climate the ripe grass, dry and nutritious, retains its full strength. Besides the standing hay, which the deer eat during the winter, account must be taken of the winter browse, an infinity of little branches, cropped moose-fashion, the tips of fir boughs, spruce, juniper, and pine, withered herbs, and various other unconsidered trifles, taken in lieu of more nutritious diet. Even man loves to chew a straw or the equally nutritious twig, and his power for deriving sustenance from these, in comparison with the deer's, is just about as strong as the relative sense of direction and "locality," as a phrenologist would call it, in the two creatures. Take the carrier pigeon and the deer, on the one hand, and man, reason-guided and stumbling, on the other: what a chasm separates them in the exercise of this wonderful and to us almost inexplicable endowment! In a similar manner, civilized man is one of the weakest of animals in regard to food; until his slave, fire, has half digested it for him, he remains starving in the midst of plenty.

In California the scrub oak always abounds in a good deer range; this is the standby of the deer, and they eat with relish the young growth of all the oak family growing in this part of the world. To begin with there are three species of scrub oak* found in the valleys and on the heights, and in the whole State no less than eleven well-known species, with several obscure additional forms, are found.† Next in the order of their preference comes the California lilac, both the white and the purple varieties; in various sections other names commend themselves. A white lilac (*Ceanothus integerrimus*) is sometimes called deer-brush, significant of the deer's liking for its leaves; also mountain birch, from its delicate form, white tea-tree, presumably because an infusion may be made from its leaves, red-root, soap-bush,—the last very appropriate, since in flower the bush with its white delicate masses of bloom looks like the purest foam. This, however, is not

---
* *Quercus dumosa, Q. vacciniifolia,* and *Q. Breweri.*

† The black or Kellogg's oak, the live oak, the valley oak, the white or Douglas oak, the small desert oak, Engelmann's live oak, the golden-cupped white live oak, the chestnut or tanbark oak farther north and in the Coast Range.

the origin of the name, but the less ethereal circumstance that its flowers may be used as soap.* Other trees besides the oak minister to the wants of the deer; the willow, maple, ash, cottonwood, and wild plum they find agreeable; the leaves of these they eat, and of the wild currant, hazel, elder, tree-mallow, rose-bush, as well as the pleasant-flavored petals of its flowers; the young growth of manzanita, snow-brush, or buckthorn (*Ceanothus cordulatus*), this last a prime favorite,—one finds whole gladefuls of it,—when in fragrant flower sought by all the butterflies and bees of the countryside. This must not be confused with the buckthorn, a much larger bush, tree almost at times, of which they also eat the tender leaves. After much argument *pro* and *con*, I believe it is a fact that, like cattle, sheep, and horses, they eat the leaves of the poison-oak. This I did not myself taste, but several men who are immune to its poison assured me that its flavor is not unpleasant. Deer eat the leaves of the honeysuckle, the peculiar-looking, leafless, delicate, tapering branches of milkweed, the new growth of dwarf white sage, and other varieties of the sage family, huckleberry-leaves, the leaves and green pods of the balloon-plant, the morning-glory and its cousin, the woolly morning-glory, well named from its fuzzy leaves, and on the edge of the desert they eat the plump, juicy leaves of the branching flat cactus, or prickly pear. How they manage to swallow the innumerable needles with which these are covered is a puzzle. Of course, after having been subjected to the

---

* The half-ripe fruit of the buckhorn serves as a similar substitute to remove grease-spots, and there are various other soap-bushes and soap-plants. The zygadene, or death-camass, is one of these, the Spanish bayonet is another, but the best known of all is the tall, wraithlike soap-weed (*Chlorogalum*), its scattered frail branches bearing white starlike flowers which open to herald the evening star.

digestive fluids of the first and second stomachs, and brought up for the final mastication of the cud, these spines are more or less softened and flexible, and are then disposed of with comparative ease before being returned to the third and fourth stomachs for further digestive treatment; it is a complicated process, that of transforming grass into blood.* Also in the desert they eat the mesquite beans, and when ripe revel in the fruit of the prickly pear, as marvelous a distillation of sweets from the awful sterileness of the land as the combs of honey were which Samson found in the carcass of the lion. In the forest deer love the leaves and buds of the tiger-lily,† the sheep-sorrel or wood-sorrel, and the Oregon sorrel, as well as other tart herbs,—for instance, the wild pie-plant (canaigre). They eat acorns, and, in fact, at certain seasons of the year, as well as with Indians, bears, squirrels, chipmunks, the wild pigeon, mountain quail, and woodpeckers, and, I fancy, the fox when very hungry, the wildcat, skunk, and porcupine, acorns are a staple of diet. Deer love all kinds of soft, succulent berries which man finds edible,—strawberries, raspberries, blackberries, currants, blueberries, huckleberries, mulberries, wild currants,—whether black, red, or yellow,—gooseberries, service-berries, elderberries, salal-berries, the Oregon grape when they can get it, the thimble-berry and its relative, the salmon-berry of the north, the berries of the toyon, or Christmas-berry, and also domestic fruits—apples, cherries, apricots, nectarines, plums, pears, peaches, and watermelons, when they can

---

* Donkeys, mules, and horses love the heads of thistles, and I imagine that deer do as well, but have not the requisite evidence.

† *Lilium pardalinum.*

steal them from the garden; wild choke-cherries, the holly-leaved cherry, and, perhaps for tonic variety, the little bitter wild cherry; the hips of rose-bushes, the wild plum, wild grapes, of which there are two varieties, the black and the green, the wild California coffee-berry, and perhaps the bearberry, or killikinick. Cattle, horses, and goats love the lupine, of which there are many varieties; whether or not deer eat these I am not quite certain, but feel a reasonable degree of confidence that they do. They are fond of alfalfa when they can get it, and the leaves of lettuce, beets, turnips, cabbage, chicory, and peas. Green peas and string-beans of course are dear delights. I think that they, as well as humans, eat the humble herb of the garden and farmyard, the world-wide and unflattered pigweed. It is not so generally known as one would expect it to be that the young growth of this plant when boiled makes excellent "greens." When man so employs it he calls it by the more flattering appellation of lamb's-quarter.* Deer eat the leaves of the cascara,† a name certainly advertised sufficiently now to be familiar to all. They eat the tender stalk of the Quixote-plant, which, in full flower, proudly flaunts its cream-white blossoms along the foot-hills, scattered standards of beauty, very striking seen rising high out of the chaparral. This is more commonly known as the yucca, one of several varieties, yet I was corrected by a well-informed ranger for calling it such rather than by the name more usually employed by the Mexicans. Deer love the leaves of the chinquapin and its little

---

* The leaves of the California poppy are used also by the Indians for greens. Does the deer crop these?

† The Mexican cascara sagrada.

triangular nut, also the hazel-nut and the nuts of the various pines when they can get them, of the Coulter, the Sabine or digger pine, the rare Torrey pine, the sugar pine, of the yellow and Jeffrey pines, of the piñon, and the nuts of firs, the cones of which fall to pieces of themselves when the nut is ripe. The berries of the manzanita they partake of as well as men, foxes, coyotes, bears, wildcats, and skunks.* The acid of these dried berries, which remain for months on the bushes in that condition, is admirable for quenching thirst. Many a time have I been grateful to them for that service. Strange as it may seem, these are more efficacious for quenching thirst when one is engaged in strong exercise than water itself. There can be but slight nourishment, only a taste of acid and sugar, in this dried hull of the manzanita-berry, for the withered pulp is no more than that, yet during the starvation months foxes eke out a scanty living on these and on equally dry feed. That is what one gets for being a fox! Yet, if he survives, he maintains superb health, and, if given the chance, would, like all sensible creatures, scorn the most desirable "situation" which would rob him of his freedom and of the fierce delight of winning a livelihood under adverse conditions. This is a faculty requiring skill, determination, and good judgment on the part of the fox, and, like the exercise of any other power, gives its possessor the keenest satisfaction. Here is long life to the likes of him!

Among the grass-seeds in milk which deer like are those of the mountain bunch-grass, the heads of a certain beautiful purple grass, the rich heads of the timothy, and

---

* It is interesting to note that the botanist who gave the scientific name to this plant called it "bear grapes," the Greek *Arctostaphylos*.

the wild blue-grass. They would, I fancy, crop all rich grass-seeds in the milk, since then they are soft and succulent. When the resources of civilization are at command, they find a pleasant change of diet in the green heads of barley, wheat, oats, rye, and buckwheat. Besides the last, there is a plant called wild buckwheat which they affect.* I have the word of John Muir, repeated to me by Ranger Ellis of the Sierra Reserve, that they love the flowers of a little plant of the purslane family, which grows close to the ground almost as flat as a track, in six or eight, or more, delicate purple velvety tufts, and is appropriately called pussy's-paw.

Among the plants which they like is one growing ten or fifteen inches high with the brightest of red flowers, very handsome as seen on the naked gravel among the scattered pines, and irresistibly attractive to humming-birds—the scarlet bugler. They love filaree, Indian lettuce, sweet clover, sour or bear clover, and are fond of the wild cucumber, called by the Mexicans *chilicothe*. They love the suncup, which is one of the little evening primroses, and when feed is scarce the deerweed, or wild broom, the fireweed, with its purple-pink blossoms, a favorite food of that shyest and most elusive creature of the forest, the sewellel, or mountain beaver. They love the blossoms and tender stalks of the soapweed and the leaves of what is called the quinine-bush (*Garrya*),† on account of its medicinal, bitter leaves. When heavy

---

* *Eriogonum fasciculatum.*

† Some botanists place this in the dogwood family; others, more exclusive, in a family by itself. Miss Alice Eastwood, of the California Academy of Sciences, a high authority, says: " I incline to the latter view, for the plants are very different in all respects from any form of dogwood. . . . Some species have very bitter fruit, while others have fruit which is palatable."

with seed in the late summer, a careful observer assures
me that they eat a plant which has no common name, so
far as I know. It grows in gravelly soil, and is from eight
to sixteen inches tall, according to its situation, of a frail
branching nature, very thin and daddy-long-leggish; botanists
know it by a name almost as long as it is, *Gayophytum
ramosissimum*, the "most branchified." There
are many other edible seeds doubtless agreeable to deer;
those of the mock orange, Spanish bayonet, Indian wheat
(one of the sunflowers, also called the compass-plant),
the large vetch,* the pond-lily, and probably others
which the deer know well, and with which I am not
yet familiar. I have admitted nothing to this list until
after careful scrutiny. An intelligent resident of Kern
County, in the southern Sierra Reserve, was comprehensive
in his designation of the deer's proclivities in the matter
of food: "They eat 'most anything that a goat would
eat." But I have grave doubts whether the dainty little
Columbian blacktail would relish the bill-posters and
wind-driven flotsam of the sandlots or of Harlem Heights.
I am indebted to this man for one item of my bill of fare,
identified by the seed-vessels which he gave me, the
short-flowered pentstemon. Like the intelligent man that
he was, my informant had a few of these in his pocket;
their very touch, by mental association, helping him to
tide over a barren hour. The deer love the leaves of this
bush. Every naturalist sympathizes with this mental
trait.

I should like information in regard to the following
items (may they be admitted to the list of food which deer
like?): horse-mint, the close-jointed rush or reed of the

---

* *Vicia giganteo.*

brook with its creeping root-stalk, the shoots of which resemble the long quills of the porcupine; it is one of the horsetail family. There are also sedges with edible roots which I think deer would eat, and they are not averse to digging when occasion demands. For instance, they are so fond of beets, turnips, carrots, and parsnips, that they will dig for them. I have not the evidence at hand, but feel almost sure that they would like the bulbs of the camáss, favorite food of Indians.* Grizzly bears dote on these, and Indians set so great store by them that the Nez Percé war in Idaho was fought for the possession of the grounds where they are found in abundance. As a boy I often ate the new growth of the fern fronds, found in the spring-time in our northern woods. Deer I think would like them.† Among other roots which grow here and which man accepts as food are the wild onion and the bulb of the Washington lily, also the wild hyacinth, the root of the mountain primrose (the *racine amère* of the *voyageurs*), the bulbs of the yellow globe-tulip, and of the green-banded Mariposa lily, by the Indians the most passionately loved of all bulbs that grow. I should expect to find that deer also like these, but have not the requisite evidence that they do.‡ Near Mono Lake, on the desert side of the mountains, grows the bitter-brush, bearing seeds said to be favorite food of cattle and very fattening. The meat of this little nut, which looks like a diminutive

---

* *Camassia esculenta.*

† Bruised fern-roots are recognized Indian food.

‡ Mr. Galen Clark, the *doyen* of the Yosemite guides, told me that near Wawona grew a plant called by the Indians "toonge," which had an edible root like a small sweet potato. This is not found in the Yosemite Valley. Can any one give further information? On the desert side of the Sierra, near Mono Lake, I was told of an edible root, called by the Indians "tubuse," which tastes like milk. Can some one supplement this scanty information?

acorn, is absolutely the most bitter thing I ever tasted, and bitterness has long been accepted as the type of that with which the human palate finds hardest to reconcile itself. I was assured by one hunter that he had often found in the deer's stomach the yellow blossom which, when growing, is of about the size of a half-dollar, of a plant with pungent leaves. It used to be common in Colorado, where the aromatic odor of the drying leaves is a familiar autumnal scent, and recalls many a hunt after deer and elk; it has the unappetizing name of "sneezeweed." To confirm this statement the ranger who contributed it has written, since my return from California, that he killed a deer in the valley of the Big Arroyo, flowing into Kern River, which had the flowers of this plant in its stomach. Do deer like the flower and edible fruit of the wild mahogany?* There is also another so-called mahogany having edible berries, which the Indians and Mexicans are so fond of that they dry and keep them for winter lemonade; and still a third so-called mahogany has twigs of a pleasant birchy flavor, loved as browse by cattle, and it may be by deer. Would they crop the leaves of the domestic parsnip? This has a strong and individual taste.† Do they eat the seeds of a plant which covers wide areas in the Sierra foot-hills, variously known as bear-clover, grouse-brush, and mountain-misery? These seeds are not unpleasant to our palate, but the leaves have a rank tansy-like smell. I do not think deer would eat them, though sheep will do so when sufficiently hungry; but then the

---

* *Cercocarpus betulaefolius.*

† The leaves of the wild parsnip are said to be eaten by horses; whether or not by deer I cannot say. It is reported to be poisonous to sheep and cattle. On this I should like information. The parsley family has a bad reputation; there are said to be poisonous plants among them. Are the roots of any of these poisonous?

unaristocratic sheep is not a deer,—when it comes to a question of the individuality and interest of the two creatures, as well compare a wheelbarrow with the swallow that skims above the surface of a lake, as the stupidly useful sheep with the deer, symbol of free and keen activity in the wild life. An instinct apparently saves the deer from eating the poisonous mountain laurel which causes the death of so many sheep. The deer are old residents here and do not make rash mistakes; they are doubtless protected by instinct developed through long cycles of time and by vicissitudes of every sort. Natural selection with them has developed an infallible instinct, far safer in a case of this sort than man's reason, which has this great limitation and fault, that unless supplemented by wide experience and a strongly retentive memory, it must each time act *ab initio* under the direction of the will, whereas instinct makes its selection automatically, by no effort of the will. The creature's ancestors have equipped him in this admirable way for the struggle of existence. The deer thus rejects instinctively poisons which prove fatal to cattle and sometimes to man. The deer "do not like" them. Sheep, cattle, horses, and man are often tempted. The deer inherit their protective likes and dislikes. This is instinct, which man has exchanged for other powers complicated and far-reaching. It is the exercise of one of these faculties which gives him pleasure in studying a creature so highly organized and so different from himself as the deer. The deer in the gratification of his appetite is as little as possible like the carnivorous animals. They tear and devour their food with a fierce lust which brooks no interference. Until their hunger is appeased they are considerably more dangerous to any one who should attempt to interfere with them than is usually the case. Even man's gentle and faithful parasite, the dog, is wolfish then. How different are the ruminants! One of the processes of their digestion has given the generic name of their tribe to our psychology, so that "to ruminate" and "to reflect" have become synonymous. Let him who doubts the power of a strong and well-regulated digestion to contribute mental poise carefully observe cattle when chewing the cud. Even fierce Texas steers, almost as little civilized as anything that walks, then look quite sentimental, and their eyes have that "mother-look," a far-away, dreamy aspect which reminds one of Buddha and the associations of the lotus-flower. Let not him who has failed to observe this particular phenomenon reject it as fanciful. Only last summer I saw a herd of cattle engaged in the function described, and their look of aloofness and of fine abstraction, as they all stood with their backs to the storm chewing the cud, was most laughable. In their ranks a dignified seriousness prevailed. Boys and girls of our race, and occasionally "grown-ups," betray the rudimentary craving for the cud in the fervor with which they chew spruce gum and various other inferior substitutes. But man has only the faintest conception of what it may be like to chew the cud. The food of the ruminants is then digested to a certain degree, and doubtless is far more grateful to the palate. The fact that it is warm must be in itself a keen delight to a creature whose food as he gathers it is always cold. When the time for chewing the cud comes the deer desires most of all to be unmolested and serene. Even this primary delight is a thing which only an occasional philosopher of the human family achieves. The prophetic soul then broods on things to come. The deer having gathered the carefully selected ingredients of his feast from far and near, may be said at this time to begin to realize the full satisfaction of a delicately selected *menu*. The service rendered to man by fire is no greater than that contributed to the deer's enjoyment by the partial digestion of his food and the marvelous change into something rich and strange. Indians in a crude way pay tribute to this alchemy. Certain tribes of the Southwest carefully save the contents of the deer's stomach and highly esteem this as an article of diet. The long-sustained accomplishment of this function with the deer must give them satisfaction which we can only crudely guess at. With all of man's ingenuity, he has never been able to accomplish this exact sort of sustained pleasure.

Mr. Edison is quoted as saying that all inquisitive and intelligent races and individuals crave a great variety in their food, and that this circumstance affords a good test of mental activity. A stupid person is content with a monotonous diet, getting his satisfaction mainly from the amount consumed; one more quick-witted craves greater range and novelty. Mr. Edison is reported to have expressed the desire "never to see the same dish twice." Applying this test to other representatives of the animal kingdom, we have found that the deer evinces great curiosity and discrimination in regard to the variety of its food. The range of its likes and dislikes is a wide one, and in this respect reveals a creature of versatility. St. Paul found the Athenians always "eager to hear or to tell some new thing"; they also loved novelty and variety. This breadth of interest in the deer, so far as the matter of food is concerned, as compared with the cow's unvarying and monotonous interest in grass, or the porcupine's capacity of being satisfied with pine bark, indicates a mind (as well as stomach) craving diversified ingredients for sustenance. The deer's hobby is food, and it is *quality* primarily rather than *quantity* that gives him delight. This I trust I have to a reasonable degree made evident.

DOMES AND DOME STRUCTURE OF THE HIGH SIERRA.

By G. K. Gilbert.

[Reprinted with permission from Bulletin of the Geological Society of America, February 10, 1904.]

General Character of the Domes.—In the granite areas of the Sierra Nevada are many hills and other summits having the form of domes. A few of the domes are symmetric, with approximately circular or oval bases, but the majority are somewhat one-sided or irregular. Associated with these domelike forms are closely related structures. The granite is divided into curved plates or sheets which wrap around the topographic forms. The removal of one discloses another, and the domes seem at the surface to be composed, like an onion, of enwrapping layers.

Theories of Relation between Structure and Form.— In explanation of these peculiar forms and structures two general theories have been advanced.[*] According to one theory, the separation of the granite into curved plates is an original structure, antedating the sculpture of the country and determining the peculiarities of form. According to the other theory, the structure originated subsequently to the form, and was caused by some reaction from the surface. Visiting the Sierra in the summer of 1903, I had these two theories in mind, and sought for characters by which they might be tested.

---

[*] H. W. Turner gives a digest of opinions, with references, in Proc. Cal. Acad. Sci., 3d ser., Geology, vol. 1, pp. 312-315. To his eumeration may be added Muir (Am. Assoc. Adv. Sci. Proc., vol. 23, pp. 61-62) and Le Conte (Elements of Geology, 4th ed., pp. 283-284), both on the side of original structure.

The dome structure appears not to extend downward and inward indefinitely, but to be limited to a somewhat shallow zone. The opportunities for observing this fact of distribution are not numerous, and, so far as I am aware, are found only on what are called half-domes— that is, domes that have been pared away on one side so as to exhibit the structure in section. The Half-Dome at the head of Yosemite Valley, which has been described by several writers, has been undercut in the development of the glacial trough of Tenaya Creek, so that its northwestern part has fallen away. The curved plates are there seen (figure 1) to occupy a very moderate depth, probably not more than fifty feet, while beneath them the rock is massive, except as vertical shear planes or joints have developed parallel to the flat face.

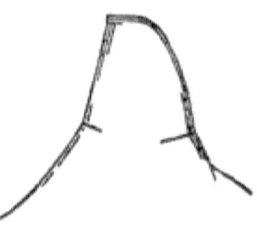

FIGURE 1.—SECTION OF THE HALF-DOME, SHOWING THE RELATION OF THE DOME STRUCTURE TO THE SURFACE AND TO JOINTS.

(The section is at right angles to the side shown in Plate xxx.)

In another instance the estimated depth of the zone of dome structure is about the same, and in a third instance about one hundred feet. This downward limitation of the zone appears to me favorable to the second theory. If the structure were original, one would expect to find it continuing indefinitely downward and inward.

The structure is not restricted to domes. In some districts the walls of cañons, the sides of ridges, and the bottoms of trough valleys are characterized by partings approximately parallel to the surface. (See plate XXXI, figures 1 and 2.) These partings are not ordinary joints, but are distinguished by curvature, and their forms of curvature are always adjusted to the general shapes of the topography. In the last respect they differ greatly from the structures produced by folding of strata. The curves of folded strata are diversely related to topographic features. A syncline may be found in a valley or on a hilltop, and an anticline may have either of these positions; but in dome structure each anticline coincides with a summit and each syncline with a valley. If the dome structure were original, we should expect that it would often be traversed discordantly by superposed drainage and dissection, and the fact of its accordance with features of dissection is therefore unfavorable to the theory that it is an original structure.

Where the granite is divided by a solitary joint into distinct masses, the dome structure of each mass is independent of the structure developed in its neighbor (figure 1). The curves of the dome structure do not cross the joint plane, and are thus shown to be newer than the joint. This phenomenon is not favorable to the view that the structure is original.

These considerations, as they were developed gradually in the field, led me to abandon altogether the hypothesis that the structure was developed either in the original constitution of the granite or at some early stage in its history, and to adopt the alternative view that it followed the production of the principal topographic features and was in some way conditioned by the surface forms.

Relation of Dome Structure to Plane Jointing.—The dome structure appears to have been developed only in massive rock; that is to say, it is not found in rock which is divided by systems of parallel plane joints. Through large areas the granite is divided by such joint systems into angular blocks (plate XXXII, figure 1), and in these areas the peculiar domes do not appear. I thought at one time that the two types of partings might be correlated with certain rock types, but this tentative generalization was afterward completely disproved. There are at least three prominent and broadly exposed types of granite in the Sierra which exhibit dome structure, and each of these is also characterized in some different locality by plane joints. It is easy to understand that the existence of either system of partings within the rock might, by facilitating the relief of strain, prevent the development of the other system, so that their mutual exclusiveness gives no indication of their relative age. But there is independent reason for assigning a greater age to the plane-joint systems. The dome structure, being conditioned by surface forms, is in each locality more recent than the topographic features; but the topographic sculpture is superposed on the systems of plane joints. Minor details of form show the influence of joint structure, but features of the rank of hill and valley are notably independent, their trends making all angles with the strikes of joint systems.

Joints and other division-planes are aids to erosion, whether the process be subaerial or glacial. When in ordinary jointing several sets of division-planes intersect and the rock is separated into blocks, weathering and transportation are both facilitated. In dome structure there is but a single set of division-planes, and the broad rock-plates are almost as resistant as a continuous mass. It results that the granite masses divided only by dome structure tend to survive general degradation, and often to stand forth as prominent hills.

FAIRVIEW DOME.

The Question of Cause.—In the effort to pass from the general phenomena of dome structure to its cause, I have found instruction in a comparison of the disrupting effects of expansion and contraction. When a forest fire sweeps over a rocky hillside the surfaces of rocks are rapidly heated and thereby expanded. The result is a sort of exfoliation. Flakes of rock, broad in comparison with their thickness, break loose and fall away (plate XXXII, figure 2). Thus the effect of surface expansion is to develop partings approximately parallel to the original exterior. The effect of contraction is illustrated by the cooling of a lava stream or dike. The cooling and contraction begin at the surface, and there develop a plexus of cracks, which are propagated downward or inward as cooling proceeds. These cracks are normal to the surface, and they separate the rock into normal columns. Comparing dome structure with these familiar types, it seems evident that it should be ascribed to expansion rather than to contraction, and we are led to inquire what natural process or processes may have expanded the Sierra granite at the surface.

Heating is naturally the first to suggest itself. Diurnal and annual changes of temperature may be dismissed at once, because their influence penetrates but a small distance. Secular changes penetrate farther, and may be quantitatively adequate. Secular warming after glaciation may have been a *vera causa,* but its discussion is complicated by the fact that the dome structure, or at least its principal part, antedated a large amount of glacial erosion. If the structure originated with Pleistocene climatic changes, the changes must have pertained to an early epoch of glaciation.

A second process developing expansive force is weathering, and here again future investigation may discover a true cause; but to cursory and inexpert observation the granites of the Sierra in the glaciated district appear to be unaltered.

A third process—one as to which we have no direct knowledge—is dilatation from unloading. When the granite came into existence by the cooling of the parent magma it was buried under a deep cover of older rock. Because of that cover it was subject to compressive stress, and that compressive stress was of course balanced by internal expansive stress competent to cause actual expansion if the external pressure were removed. As in course of time the load was in fact gradually removed, the compressive stress was diminished and the expansive stress became operative. *Pari passu* with this release of expansive stress there was cooling, and the effect of the cooling was to diminish expansive stress; and the result may have been complicated by other stress factors. So long as the pressure of superjacent material was great, the equilibrium of stresses was approximately adjusted by flowage; but as the descending surface of degradation approached the granite, flowage diminished, and it ultimately ceased. The final adjustment was by change of volume, the change being contraction, if lowering of temperature was a more important factor than relief from load, and expansion, if relief from load was the more important factor. In the latter case (which I regard as the more probable) the parts of the granite successively exposed at the surface were in a condition of potential expansion, or tensile strain, and that strain would be relieved by the separation of layers through the develop-

FIGURE 1.—HALF-DOME AT EAST END OF YOSEMITE VALLEY (SEEN FROM THE SOUTH)

FIGURE 2.—PART OF SOUTHEAST WALL OF LITTLE YOSEMITE VALLEY, SHOWING DOME STRUCTURE.

DOME STRUCTURE IN THE YOSEMITE REGION.

ment of division-planes approximately parallel to the surface.

While it is possible that all these processes are concerned in the production of the structure, I regard it as more probable that some one cause is dominant. The data at hand seem to me not to warrant a confident selection from the three suggested, but if the truth lies among them, there should be little difficulty in obtaining additional facts of crucial character. Certain domes, some of which I saw at a distance, are supposed to be outside the area of Pleistocene glaciation. If they exhibit the characteristic structure, and are really extraglacial, their characters can not plausibly be ascribed to secular changes of climate. It should be possible to determine the relation of weathering to the structure by petrographic study of outer and inner layers at such a locality as that shown in plate XXXI, figure 1, where glacial erosion has exposed a fresh section.

Explanation of Rounding.—The view in plate XXXI, figure 1, was selected as an illustration of dome structure because the plates and partings of the structure are there shown in natural section. In the making of that section the dominant erosional process was glacial attrition or grinding. While this process has been of great importance in the sculpture of the higher parts of the Sierra, it is probably second in rank to glacial plucking or quarrying; and glacial degradation as a whole has been small in comparison with subaerial degradation. In glacial plucking and in most phases of subaerial erosion the most active attack on rock traversed by dome structure is by way of the partings, and the broad outer faces of the granite plates are comparatively unaffected. The removal of the rock is essentially through a process of peeling. One layer at a time is carried away, and the surface at each stage coincides approximately with one of the partings.

Whatever the cause of the dilatation producing the partings, they are formed in succession from without inward. For each one the determining strains are themselves conditioned not only by the form of the outer surface, but by the form of the last-made parting. Parallelism is not perfect, but approximate, and the departures from strict parallelism are of such nature as to reduce or omit angles and other features of irregularity. The inner partings reflect only the general features of the external sculpture. As peeling progresses and the zone of competent strain moves inward, the outer surfaces are successively more and more simple in contour, and the newly developed partings are endowed with still greater simplicity.

Opposed to the rounding process is corrasion. The attrition of a detritus-armed stream or glacier saws through the rock-plates with little regard for the presence or absence of partings. By so doing it creates discordant elements of topography and modifies the conditions under which the expansive strains are developed. In the Sierra the effects of glacial corrasion are at present conspicuous. By the corrasion of the Tenaya trough the base of Half-Dome was sapped, so that a part was sheared off by gravity, producing a vertical flat face (figure 1), in which the structureless nucleus was exposed. In this face the "dome structure" was developed, but, being conditioned by a plane outer surface, the new partings are plane (except at the edges), and thus simulate ordinary plane joints.

FIGURE 1.—HILL SOUTHEAST OF EMERICK LAKE, UPPER MERCED BASIN, SIERRA NEVADA.

FIGURE 2.—A SYNCLINE IN DOME STRUCTURE.
DOME STRUCTURE NEAR EMERICK LAKE.

Explanation of Plates.

Plate XXIX.—*Fairview Dome.*

This dome, sometimes called Tuolumne Monument, is in the Sierra Nevada, west of Tuolumne Meadows. In common with the surrounding country, it is of granite. It stands at the edge of a plateau, its summit being 800 feet above one base and 1,300 feet above the other; it is not above timber-line, but is bare of trees, because in the absence of joints they get no foothold. Pleistocene ice covered it, flowing from right to left and from distance to foreground.

Plate XXX.—*Dome Structure in the Yosemite Region.*

Figure 1.—Half-Dome, at east end of Yosemite Valley, seen from the south; from a photograph by C. D. Walcott.

The view shows the convex side of the dome, in which the structure closely parallels the surface. The height above the nearer base is about 1,500 feet; above the farther base at right 900 feet. The dome was covered by Pleistocene ice, which moved from the right and from the distance. The surface is treeless, because devoid of joints. No rock but granite is visible in the view.

The text contains a cross-profile of the dome.

Figure 2.—Part of the southeast wall of Little Yosemite Valley, showing dome structure.

The rock is granite. The valley is deeply incised in a plateau of relatively mature topography. Pleistocene ice covered everything shown in the view except the distant crest, but the glacial degradation of the upland was slight.

In the upper parts of the cliff the dome structure parallels the surfaces of the upland topography; lower down it parallels the cliff face.

PLATE XXXI.—*Dome Structure near Emerick Lake.*

FIGURE 1.—Hill southeast of Emerick Lake, Upper Merced Basin, Sierra Nevada.

The hill, which is about 250 feet high, is the terminal and culminating points of a long ridge of granite. The dome structure in the ridge is anticlinal, changing in the hill to the inverted canoe form. At the extreme right the convex or anticlinal curvature is seen to merge into a concave or synclinal curvature, better shown in figure 2. The hill was deeply buried by a glacier moving from left to right. Glacial erosion made the rock basin occupied by the lake and excavated the hillside so as to expose the dome structure in partial section.

FIGURE 2.—A Syncline in dome structure.

Emerick Lake (Figure 1) lies out of sight, just beyond the granite slope at right. Its outlet, crossing the sill without notable incision, descends to the foreground at left. Structure and topographic configuration are in harmony. A syncline pitches toward the foreground and also (slightly) toward the lake. At the lip of the lake basin the cross-section is synclinal and the longitudinal section anticlinal.

PLATE XXXII.—*Joint Structure and Fire-Spalling.*

FIGURE 1.—Jointed granite in Kuna Crest, Sierra Nevada.

The granite is traversed by four systems of parallel plane joints. The cliff is at the head of a glacial cirque, and the sloping plain above it belongs to preglacial topography. The general forms of cirque and plain are independent of the attitudes of the joint systems. Compare with Plate XXXI, and observe the contrast between joint structure and dome structure.

FIGURE 2.—Granite boulder from which spalls or flakes have been riven by the heat of forest or meadow fires.

The spall at the left, still standing in position, illustrates the approximate parallelism of fractures thus produced to exterior surface. Probably in this case the strong heat was at the side and local—as the heating would be, for example, if the log at the right should be burned—and the size of the spall was determined by the localization heat.

FIGURE 1.—JOINTED GRANITE IN KUNA CREST, SIERRA NEVADA.

FIGURE 2.—GRANITE BOULDER FROM WHICH SPALLS OR FLAKES HAVE BEEN RIVEN BY THE HEAT OF FOREST OR MEADOW FIRES.

JOINT STRUCTURE AND FIRE-SPALLING.

SOME ASPECTS OF A SIERRA CLUB OUTING.

By Marion Randall.

Mountain trips the world over bear a certain intrinsic resemblance to one another; the lost trail, the bridgeless river, the firm-willed beast of burden, the camp-fire that will not burn,—all these are tribulations to test the qualities of the mountaineer as well in the Cevennes as in the Sierra. But there is one feature of a Sierra Club outing which tends to make it unique, a feature much derided by the doubting Thomas whom you wish to convert, much defended by you if you are a loyal Sierran,—namely, the "crowd."

It sounds rather alarming at first—to camp for a month with a party of one hundred and fifty persons, strangers for the greater part, gathered from all quarters of California and from distant points throughout the world, representatives of every profession, every science, every art, who have only one common bond, the love of nature. They are very queer-looking people too, some of them. They bear a few hallmarks of civilization, it is true; they take off their hats when they speak to you, and smoke pipes and cigarettes; they possess tooth-brushes and mirrors and back-combs,—but you never heard of anything like them in song or story nor saw them upon the stage.

You rashly decide that you don't care very much about making indiscriminate acquaintances. You have a few tried friends in the party, and, though they strongly resemble the other desperadoes, you have a comfortable remembrance that but a few days ago they were orderly and respected citizens, that they still possess bank accounts and have reputations to maintain. But soon you begin to realize that some of these old friends are not quite the companions you would have chosen for the woods. Your friendship is perhaps more superficial than you thought it, or is based upon some common interest which is absent here, and while it costs you something to admit it, they jar upon you. And then you discover that the unshaven gentleman in spotted khaki with a scratch on his nose has seen the same beauty and thought the same thought that you have, and you know he is a kindred soul, though you don't like to acknowledge the kinship.

As day after day passes, and you learn to waive ceremony and accept the easy comradeship of the trail, you find that the bearded ruffian is a learned scientist, the untidy girl in the strange bonnet is an artist of promise, and the neat man in khaki who quotes Shakespeare is one of the packers, and you begin to distrust your powers of discrimination. At last you make the discovery that you yourself look as queer as your neighbor. You are a Sierran by that time, body and soul, ready to find your place in the socialist's Utopia which you inhabit for a few short weeks. You learn to stand in line behind a packer and see him helped first to the dishes of which you mean to partake; and when Charley Tuck, the canny heathen cook, stops his horse beside you as your weary feet plod along the trail, and opening a blackened tin bucket inquires blandly, "You like-a ham-bone?" you accept the offered delicacy with grateful effusiveness.

But, strange to say, even in this democratic society

the aristocrats are sooner or later bound to appear. There is the aristocrat of cleanliness. On the dustiest trail, over the smokiest camp-fire, he is seen always fresh and immaculate. He must have been born clean, for he spends no more time in the washing of face and raiment than the rest of us do, and yet the result is so different! The proverbial leopard who cannot change his spots is bound by no more rigorous law than the aristocrat who cannot acquire any; stainless he is and stainless he remains by no fault—or virtue—of his own, but he is not looked on with favor by the spotted many.

There is the aristocrat of leg and lung, the "hiker," so called, who walks up perpendicular cliffs like a fly, never misses the trail, and always reaches camp first. He is harmless, but is not generally loved, for he is a little overbearing and given to much talking of a certain catalogue of hours and distances which he keeps in his mind and calls his record.

Then there is the aristocrat of good-fellowship. He can hike too, if he wants to, but he knows that one hour of the trail is worth two in camp and that "to travel hopefully is better than to arrive." He may come late into camp, but you may be sure he will come with a smile and be ready on the instant to help cook dinner or to carry half the dunnage-bags to their abiding-places for the night. He will cobble your boots for you, he will mend your clothes, and lend you his blankets when yours are lost; and though he will talk very little about it, his name will be found on the highest peaks and the trout will have reason to remember his rod.

Life in the main camp is a degree more formal than when on the trail. The main camp is a place where

Charley Tuck has stoves on which to cook, where you have a tent in which to dress, and where you get fresh bread instead of galetta. Your days are less strenuous there. Breakfast is obtainable from six until nine, and you do not have to walk abroad unless you wish. Nevertheless, you do not often lunch in camp, for the call of the trail is strong, and the desire to be up and doing leads you daily into the realm of unexplored country which surrounds you.

Dinner is quite a function. It is there, perhaps, that you catch most fully the charm, the picturesqueness, and the jollity of the outing. Behind the long table stand eight girls dressed in the brightest and best their dunnage-bags can offer—shirt-waists fresh from the river, skirts a shade longer and cleaner than the well-worn regimentals, and caps, aprons, and kerchiefs of gaudy bandanas.

Each girl has charge of a kettle and a spoon, and for an hour or more hungry people file past the table for a second, third, even a fourth, helping,—soup, fresh meat, potatoes, bread and butter, rice, tomatoes, pudding, gingerbread, tea and coffee à la tin cow, surely a meal fit for the gods. They think so anyway, these sunburned people in their gay sweaters and bandanas, as, laughing and joking the while, they move along the line, turn from the table with filled plate to join a chosen group of diners on the ground near by, busily wield fork and spoon, and then patiently join the line again for a further supply.

A lazy hour follows until the camp-fire is built and you gather round its circle of red light. The entertainment offered you may be grave or gay, quiet or noisy, but it is never twice alike. Songs, instrumental music, impromptu rhymes, original ballads, and talks on many topics relating to the mountains and the purposes of the club are among the things you hear nightly, and once at least in the course of the trip a grand vaudeville performance calls forth all the talent in camp. These camp-fire gatherings hold a place among your dearest recollections of the summer. The faces that you have seen illumined by the leaping flames can never be indifferent to you, and wheresoever you may meet them, in crowded streets or dingy offices, or in the heat and babble of an afternoon tea, they will bring to you a little thrill of joy as if you caught again a breath from the pines.

Very closely linked with your memory of these general gatherings lies the remembrance of the smaller circle that lingered about the embers of the commissary fire after a day spent in conquering a mountain, or of the little well-guarded fire built nightly within your own precincts by you and your chosen camp-mates, cheerful little altars, whereon the happy fellowship of the day burned to a stronger and closer friendship. Each camping-place of the trip, whether it be occupied for one night or twenty, is arranged after the same general plan: the commissary— kitchen, dining-room, and drawing-room in one—is placed in the center, with the men's camp on one side and the women's on the other. With these boundaries once fixed you are free to make choice of your individual camp. You may elect to camp alone or to join a party of friends; you may choose a site close to the commissary or one on the very outskirts; but if you are wise you will select a spot not too far from the center of things, where, while secluded, you still can catch the glimmer of a dozen clustering fires or hear now and then a merry laugh ring out into the stillness.

One of the charms of the life is its freedom from responsibility. The packing of your dunnage-bag when on the march is the only duty you really have to perform, though some prefer to assume that of washing their clothes (a task generally intrusted to Charley Tuck's brother heathen), but even this becomes almost a social function. By common consent the day after you arrive in camp is devoted to a general washing. Shortly after breakfast the girls return to their camp, and procuring a pile of clothing, go down in groups of three or four to the river. As the morning's programme includes a bath, the favorite costume for laundry work is a bathing suit. It is a pretty though often a humorous sight to see the lassies lined up along the river-bank diligently scrubbing and sousing until the garments have assumed that appearance of uniform griminess which passes in camp for cleanliness.

Short excursions of two or three days duration, lunches and teas with a dozen or more guests are frequent, and are a pleasant element in the social life of the camp. The little picnic parties, where five or six friends elect to spend the day in one another's company, are particularly delightful. You build a fire at lunch-time and have tea or soup or chocolate wherewithal to augment the commissary lunch, and sometimes, if luck attends the fisherman, you have trout.

There seems to be a prevailing impression that the entire club travels day in and day out in one indissoluble "gang." Nothing can be further from the fact, for save when climbing a mountain you travel to suit yourself. You start at whatever hour you wish, walk alone or in company, and spend the whole day or a few hours in covering the distance. It is possible to travel all day without meeting a sign of a fellow Sierran save his footprints in the trail.

And what a spell the forest weaves for you when you are alone! Each turn of the trail has its message. The little woodland creatures, the birds and squirrels and chipmunks, so suspicious of the sound of laughter and voices, look at you with their quick, bright glances and hardly seem to think it worth their while to hide. After all, these are the moments which live. The grandeur of the summit peaks thrills you into awed stillness while your eyes behold it, yet, like remembered music, when the image returns to the mind, something of the stir and the exaltation is irrevocably lost. But the glint of the sun on the river, the meadow knee-deep in flowers of the shooting-star, the creeping shadows and the lingering light in the forest at nightfall,—all these little half-noticed charms of the wayside sink deep into the memory to flash forth again, fresh and undimmed, with a certain haloed brightness.

The Sierra Club has great and noble purposes, for which we honor it, but besides these its name has come to mean an ideal to us. It means comradeship and chivalry, simplicity and joyousness, and the care-free life of the open. You may have marred that ideal often by word or deed, for you are human and must needs carry your follies and weaknesses with you even to the woods; but you must be foolish and weak indeed not to bear home something of the strength and purity and beauty amongst which you have lived.

For a little while you have dwelt close to the heart of things. You have lain down to sleep in a wide chamber walled about by mountains rising darkly against the lesser darkness of the sky, where stars looked down on you between the pines, stars more brilliant than on the frostiest night in the lowland; you have awakened to the laughter of streams and the songs of birds. You have lived day-long amid the majesty of snowy ranges, and in the whispering silences of the forest you have thought to hear the voice of Him who "flies upon the wings of the wind." And these things live with you long after the outing has passed and you are back in the working world, linger even until the growing year once more brings around the vacation days, and you are ready to turn to the hills again, whence comes, not only your help, but your strength, your inspiration, and some of the brightest hours you have ever lived.

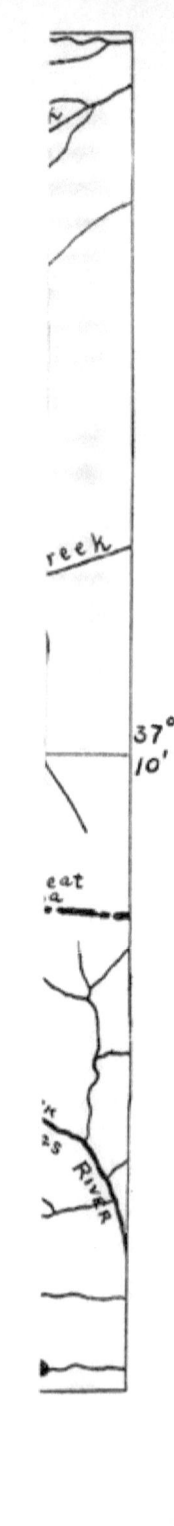

THE EVOLUTION GROUP OF PEAKS.

By J. N. Le Conte.

Hidden away on the northern slope of the Goddard Divide, and in the midst of the wild region which forms the angle between that range and the Main Crest of the Sierra, is an interesting group of peaks and lakes almost unknown to the Sierran traveler. Except for wandering sheepmen, the region was first visited, so far as I know, by Mr. Theodore S. Solomons in 1893. He was so strongly impressed by the beauty and wildness of the scenery, and by the unity, so to speak, of the group of Main Crest peaks, that he named it the Evolution Group, giving to the principal summits the names of the great evolutionists of modern times. But further than a set of notes of his trip left in the library of the Sierra Club he has not published an account of the region, and for that reason I undertake a short description myself, in the hope that others may be led into a region which offers the easiest approach to the giant summits of the Goddard Divide.

The locality named is drained by what is known as the Middle Branch of the South Fork of the San Joaquin River, a name clumsy and objectionable to the last degree. I therefore propose to reject it, the sheepmen to the contrary notwithstanding, and refer to it as Evolution Creek for the present, or till a more suitable name can be decided on by the Sierra Club's committee which has this matter in charge. The junction of Evolution Creek and the South Fork of the San Joaquin is difficult to reach from

HEADWATERS OF THE SOUTH FORK OF THE SAN JOAQUIN RIVER

THE EVOLUTION GROUP OF PEAKS.

By J. N. LeConte.

Hidden away on the northern slope of the Goddard Divide, and in the midst of the wild region which forms the angle between that range and the Main Crest of the Sierra, is an interesting group of peaks and lakes almost unknown to the Sierran traveler. Except for wandering sheepmen, the region was first visited, so far as I know, by Mr. Theodore S. Solomons in 1893. He was so strongly impressed by the beauty and wildness of the scenery, and by the unity, so to speak, of the group of Main Crest peaks, that he named it the Evolution Group, giving to the principal summits the names of the great evolutionists of modern times. But further than a set of notes of his trip left in the library of the Sierra Club he has not published an account of the region, and for that reason I undertake a short description myself, in the hope that others may be led into a region which offers the easiest approach to the giant summits of the Goddard Divide.

The locality named is drained by what is known as the Middle Branch of the South Fork of the San Joaquin River, a name clumsy and objectionable to the last degree. I therefore propose to reject it, the sheepmen to the contrary notwithstanding, and refer to it as Evolution Creek for the present, or till a more suitable name can be decided on by the Sierra Club's committee which has this matter in charge. The junction of Evolution Creek and the South Fork of the San Joaquin is difficult to reach from the south or west on account of the high spurs which surround the head-waters of the latter stream. It is therefore advisable to approach it from the north by following up the South Fork from Blaney Meadows. These meadows, which are the natural starting-point for all trips in the upper San Joaquin Basin, are reached either by the Red Mountain Trail from Pine Ridge, forty miles to the southwest, or by the Miller Trail from the Yosemite region, eighty miles to the north.

It was my good fortune last summer, after attending the dedication of the Sierra Club Lodge in Yosemite Valley, to start on such a trip in company with Dr. G. K. Gilbert, of the United States Geological Survey. We traveled the distance from Yosemite to Fish Camp by stage, and there met our packer and his pack-train all ready for the long journey southward. During the stage journey I was so unfortunate as to lose the box containing my photographic plates, so for what illustrations I offer here I am indebted to my friends. I need not relate the details of the long journey eastward and southward, for these have been already given in a previous article.* Suffice it to say that we followed the regular route by the Beasore and Jackass Meadows to Miller's bridge, then up the valley of the South Fork of the San Joaquin, over Mono and Bear Creek, finally reaching Blaney Meadows on the 13th of July.

Here we met Messrs. James Hutchinson, Edward Hutchinson, Charles Noble, and Albert Whitney, all bent on exploring the region about Mt. Humphreys. As our routes lay in the same direction, it was decided to travel

---

* "The Basin of the South Fork of the San Joaquin River." SIERRA CLUB BULLETIN, Vol. II, p. 249.

together as far as possible. Accordingly, on the morning of the 15th we started up the cañon of the South Fork, and about four miles above reached the north branch of the river, which drains the Humphreys country, and carries nearly half the total volume of the stream. It comes booming across the boulder-strewn flat at the mouth of its cañon, and at first sight appears to be an almost unsurmountable obstacle to further advance. Fortunately there are fragments of a log jam a short distance above, and on this we were enabled to get across. Then a rope was thrown over, and we succeeded in leading our animals through the rough channels.

From this point to the base of Mt. Goddard the San Joaquin Cañon is truly magnificent. It is not as deep as many other of our great river cañons, but it has the peculiarity of lying wholly within the metamorphic rock. The sides are almost perfectly bare, and the many beautiful cascades which pour over them contrast most strikingly with the black walls. The trail from the Blaney Meadows to a point four or five miles above the north branch lies on the eastern side of the stream, and then crosses to the west side by a good ford. At the crossing we stopped for lunch, and then pushed on up the river. A short distance above the ford Evolution Creek enters the cañon by a magnificent fall. There is no well-marked point at which the trail up its cañon branches from the main trail, but by recrossing the South Fork above the junction, and searching along the base of the cliffs, we soon found it starting up at the very base of the fall.

The trail at first is rocky and steep. It has been but little used of late years, and so many trees have fallen across it that traveling is rather slow. As we rose the view across the San Joaquin Cañon became finer. We could see not only to the top of the walls, but far above to the snowy summits which fed the scores of little cascades. Down the cañon we could look for miles, over the country through which we had come, and then up the gorge till it became lost in the wilderness of peaks which form the Goddard Divide. The trail kept close to the stream, and so we climbed past cataract after cataract, till suddenly the floor of our cañon flattened out, and we entered a magnificent glacial valley. This is one of the most perfect examples of a hanging valley that I have ever seen. The floor at its lower end is fully a thousand feet above the San Joaquin Cañon, yet the volume of water it carries is even greater than that of the main stream above their junction. Just above the falls is a large meadow, farther up the customary U-shaped glacial valley covered with timber, and at its head rises a huge flat-topped peak—Mt. Darwin. The meadow is wet and cold,—in other words, it is not the best of camping-places,—but as night was coming on we were forced to "put up" there and make the best of it.

Next morning, after an early breakfast, we took our way up this magnificent valley. A half-mile above camp our scarcely distinguishable trail crossed to the north side of the creek, and continued on that side the remainder of the distance. The traveling was fairly easy, though time was often lost in searching out a route through the confusing *roches moutonnées*. Off to the south could be seen great peaks of the Goddard Group, peaks of black and red slate streaked with snow, and even some with "baby glaciers" at their feet. Standing well out from the south wall some distance above is the Hermit, a

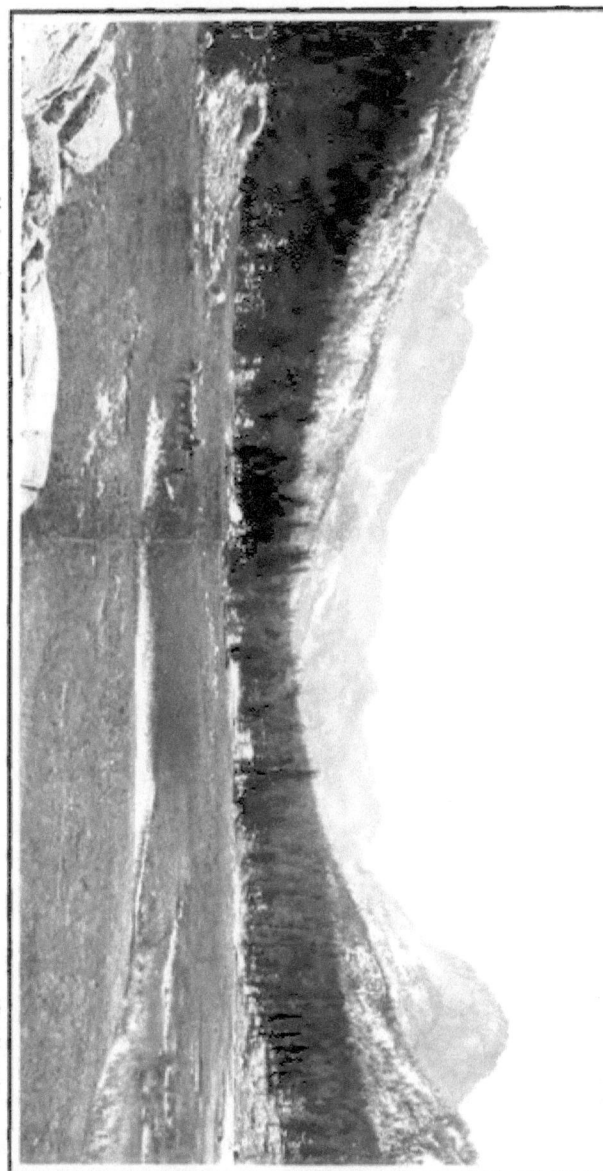

EVOLUTION BASIN.
From photographs by J. S. Hutchinson, Jr., 1904.

wonderful pyramidal rock of clean-cut white granite. Though not quite so large, it reminds one of the East Vidette—that noble monument on King's River. At the head of the cañon, blocking the whole view in that direction, is the colossal Mt. Darwin. Near the head of the cañon our companions, Messrs. Hutchinson, Noble, and Whitney, left us and proceeded by a fairly well-defined trail up the northern side in the direction of Mt. Humphreys, while we went on to the foot of the Hermit and pitched camp.

At this point the valley proper ends in an immense amphitheater, into which streams from all directions tumble in foaming cataracts. The principal one comes down from a shelf at the very foot of Mt. Darwin. Two others enter from either side of the Hermit, while a fourth large one, upon which we were camped, drains the great area to the north of Mt. Darwin. In the afternoon of that same day Dr. Gilbert explored the ridge to the north, and on the following day he and Kanawyer, the packer, climbed a peak back of the Hermit.

On the morning of the 18th, he and I got a fairly early start, determined to explore the head-waters of the main stream. This, as I have said, drops from a shelf at the base of Mt. Darwin, and the first plunge is over smooth glaciated granite at an angle of about forty-five degrees. It was therefore impossible to follow up the stream itself, but fortunately a comparatively easy route was found just to the north. At first we followed an old sheep-trail, but soon abandoned it when it bore off to the northeast. About a thousand feet above camp we reached the level of the shelf, and climbing over a low ridge came suddenly upon the beautiful Evolution Lake and all its magnificent setting of mountains. It was nestled at the very base of Mt. Darwin, whose crags rose almost from the waters' edge four thousand feet toward the blue sky. Immediately above the lake stood two most strikingly gothic peaks,—Mt. Spencer, near at hand, and Mt. Huxley, farther up. The latter is really a wonderfully picturesque piece of mountain sculpture, and though much higher and finer than Mt. Spencer, its much greater distance gives the appearance of two peaks almost exactly alike in height, form, and symmetry.

The view across the lake and back into the well-nigh untrodden region above was certainly enough to thrill the nerves of a Sierra lover. There was so much right at hand to do, and so little time in which to do it, that it was difficult to choose a field for the day. Mt. Darwin, close at hand, was over fourteen thousand feet high, and one of my oldest friends. Mt. Fiske, at or near the junction of the Goddard Divide and the Main Crest, was a point I had always longed to reach, but the Goddard Divide itself offered the most inducements, for, so far as I know, no one had followed the stream to its source and looked down the savage cañons at the head of the Middle Fork of King's River. So bidding good-by to Dr. Gilbert, whose tastes were geological, and who wished to study the wonderful glacial history written about the lake's margin, I struck out alone up the creek, which above this point flows from the south, parallel with the Main Crest. Evolution Lake itself is over a mile in length. It is very irregular in shape, with narrow straits and long peninsulas, and picturesque little islands dotting its surface. At its head is an amphitheater, and the stream tumbles into it by another splendid series of cas-

EVOLUTION LAKE.

From a photograph by T. S. Solomons, 1893.

cades. Here it was desirable to cross the creek and follow the west bank to the next shelf above, where another large lake lies like a jewel in its circular rock setting. Entering this lake from the east is the small stream which issues from between Mts. Spencer and Huxley, and drains the Evolution Group proper. About its head are the Main Crest peaks Haeckel, Wallace, and Fiske, but none can compare with the noble peak (Mt. Huxley) in the foreground about whose base the creek cuts.

Mr. Solomons, as I understand it, went as far as this tributary, and climbed some of the peaks at its head. The region at the head of the main stream he did not explore; so I was particularly anxious to reach if possible the summit of the Goddard Divide. A mile above this lake was another, and farther up still another, each in its miniature amphitheater. Finally I rounded the last spur of Mt. Huxley and entered a great basin at the headwaters. This was walled in on the south by the Goddard Divide, a magnificent range of peaks, covered by an almost unbroken sheet of snow. It curved around to the east also, and finally joined the Main Crest near Mt. Fiske. Off to the west the ridges were low, and over them towered the vast bulk of Mt. Goddard and all the black peaks of its neighborhood. Nearly the whole floor of the basin was covered with snow, except where two large lakes of the deepest indigo-blue, whose unruffled surfaces reflected the snowy peaks about, occupied the central portion. The day was perfect, without a cloud in the sky. I have seldom been so impressed by a mountain scene as by this,—possibly because I was alone, and so far away from the ordinary routes of travel.

On scanning the crest of the Goddard Divide there appeared to be one place far around to the east that looked like a pass. I had observed the creek-bed carefully during the morning's climb, and felt reasonably certain that a burro or sure-footed mule could be brought up this far. If a pass could now be discovered over the Goddard Divide, the problem of reaching the sources of the Middle Fork of King's River would be solved. So I took my way around the shores of these Crystal Lakes, and spent upwards of an hour in working out a way up to the notch. At exactly 12 o'clock the top was reached. The other side, as I had feared, broke down in the savage black gorges of the Middle Fork region, which were choked with snow and frozen lakes far down below. It would certainly be an impossibility to get an animal down anywhere along this part of the divide when the snow was deep, and even late in the season the success of such an undertaking would be very doubtful. Another thing which strengthens my opinion that the place could not be used as a pass is, that no signs of sheep are to be found there.

Far across the Middle Fork basin were piled up the great black peaks, a perfect wilderness which as yet is but imperfectly known. A few miles to the south rose a particularly inviting point, which certainly commands a peerless view. But time forbade an ascent this year, so I named it the Black Giant, and wondered how long it would stand as it has so far stood, an untrodden summit. I remained on the crest an hour, mapped as much of the country as I could, ate lunch, and just before leaving scrambled some distance down the King's River side to get a better look down the cañon. Then I started back, and retraced my steps past the Crystal Lakes, the amphitheater of the Evolution Group, and stopped again at the lower end of the Evolution Lake to take a last look at its magnificent setting. How I missed my camera then!— for the long afternoon shadows streamed back from the jagged spires of Huxley and Spencer, making a perfect subject for a photograph. By 5 o'clock I was back in camp, and shortly afterwards Dr. Gilbert came in. He had spent the day in the amphitheater between the Evolution Peaks.

Next day we said good-by to a camp where every prospect except the mosquito pleases, took our way down Evolution Creek to its junction with the South Fork of the San Joaquin, and up this latter to the base of Mt. Goddard. On the morning of the 20th, Dr. Gilbert and I ascended Mt. Goddard, and renewed our impressions of the Evolution Group from this commanding point. The morning was cloudy, however, and became more so as the day advanced; so we were obliged to descend about noon and return to camp, where we found our companions just returned from a successful ascent of Mt. Humphreys. On the 21st they climbed Mt. Goddard, but fared even worse with the weather than we did, for it stormed furiously on them.

Finally we left the watershed of the San Joaquin on the morning of the 22d, took the Baird trail, and crossed over to the North Fork of King's River by Hell-for-sure Pass. Then we made our way across to the basin of Crown Creek, through Tehipite Valley, and over to the King's River Cañon by way of Granite Basin, following the route previously described.

SIERRA CLUB BULLETIN.

PUBLISHED IN JANUARY AND JUNE OF EACH YEAR.

Published for Members.   Annual Dues, $3.00.

The purposes of the Club are:—"To explore, enjoy, and render accessible the mountain regions of the Pacific Coast; to publish authentic information concerning them; to enlist the support and co-operation of the people and the Government in preserving the forests and other natural features of the Sierra Nevada Mountains."

ORGANIZATION FOR THE YEAR 1904-1905.

Board of Directors.

Mr. JOHN MUIR (Martinez) . . . . *President*
Prof. A. G. MCADIE (Mills Building, S. F.) . . . . . *Vice-President*
Prof. J. N. LE CONTE (Berkeley) . . . . *Treasurer*
Prof. W. R. DUDLEY (Stanford University) . . . . . *Cor. Secretary*
Mr. WILLIAM E. COLBY (Mills Building, S. F.) . . . . . *Secretary*
Prof. GEORGE DAVIDSON (Berkeley).
Mr. J. S. HUTCHINSON, JR. (Claus Spreckels Bldg., S. F.).
Mr. WARREN OLNEY (101 Sansome Street, S. F.).
Mr. EDWARD T. PARSONS (University Club, S. F.).
(Vice Mr. ELLIOTT MCALLISTER, resigned.)

Committee on Publications.

Pres. DAVID STARR JORDAN (Stanford University) . . . *Chairman*
Mr. ELLIOTT MCALLISTER (Crocker Building, S. F.) . . . *Editor*
Prof. WILLIAM FREDERIC BADÈ (Berkeley).
Prof. WM. R. DUDLEY (Stanford University).
Mr. ALEX. G. EELLS (Crocker Building, S. F.).
Mr. E. B. GOULD (Mutual Savings Bank Building, S. F.).
Mr. J. S. HUTCHINSON, JR. (Claus Spreckels Building, S. F.).
Mr. EDWARD T. PARSONS (University Club, S. F.).
Prof. H. W. ROLFE (Stanford University).
Mr. WILLOUGHBY RODMAN (Bryson Block, Los Angeles).

Auditing Committee.

Directors MCADIE, PARSONS, and DUDLEY.

Committee on Admissions.

Directors DUDLEY, OLNEY, and MCADIE.

Committee on Parks and Reservations.

Prof. GEORGE DAVIDSON, *Chairman*.

Prof. W. R. DUDLEY,   Pres. DAVID STARR JORDAN,
Mr. J. M. ELLIOTT,   Mr. ABBOT KINNEY.

Committee on Outing and Transportation.

Mr. WM. E. COLBY, *Chairman*.

Mr. J. N. LE CONTE,   Mr. EDWARD T. PARSONS.

REPORTS.

Report of the Treasurer.

San Francisco, August 17, 1904.

To the Directors of the Sierra Club.

Gentlemen—I beg to submit the following report of the finances of the Sierra Club during the year beginning May 10, 1903, and ending May 9, 1904:—

RECEIPTS.

(From Wm. E. Colby, Secretary.)

From dues, 1903-1904	$1,935.00
From advertisements in Bulletins Nos. 29 and 30	780.00
From special $1.00 assessment for Le Conte Lodge	602.50
From rent of deskroom to Rod and Gun Club	40.00
Sale of publications	6.00
Total receipts from Secretary	$3,363.50
Balance on hand May 10, 1903	614.95
	$3,978.45

EXPENDITURES.

Publications and advertising expenses	$1,466.10
Le Conte Memorial Fund—	
Amount levied by special $1.00 assessment	602.50
Amount voted from Club treasury	100.00
Rent of Room No. 316, Mills Building	300.00
Clerical work and typewriting	201.90
Distribution of publications	192.15
Stamps and stationery	183.80
Trail work on Middle Fork of King's River	150.00
One half salary of Custodian of Yosemite Headquarters	52.50
Printing of circulars	50.50
Public meetings	29.50
Furnishing of room in Mills Building	26.25
Freight on exchanges	17.45
Checks returned	6.00
Advertisements of Sunday walks	3.75
Miscellaneous	15.85
	$3,398.25
Balance on hand May 9, 1904	580.20
	$3,978.45

Very respectfully,

Joseph N. Le Conte,
Treasurer.

Report of the Outing Committee.

The Outing of 1904 will long be remembered as the most successful which the Club has yet undertaken. The number of the party was strictly limited to 150, as it had been found from past experiences that a larger number could not be satisfactorily provided for. The arrangements for transportation and commissary were as perfect as could be desired.

A preliminary camp was established in Yosemite Valley by the Club for two weeks, and many availed themselves of this opportunity to remain in the valley prior to the main Outing. On July 4th and 5th the entire party left Yosemite Valley and traveled to the Tuolumne Meadows, where a camp was established for nearly two weeks. Many interesting side-trips were taken from this permanent camp. Over one hundred of the party climbed Mt. Dana and fifty-three reached the summit of Mt. Lyell. Several ascended Mt. Ritter and visited the Lake Mono region. After breaking the main camp about twenty of the party made the famous knapsack trip down the Tuolumne Cañon to the Hetch Hetchy Valley, where they rejoined the main party, which had also traveled thence over the old Tioga mining road and the Hog Ranch trail. After remaining in Hetch Hetchy for two days the party visited Lake Eleanor on its way to the terminus of the Hetch Hetchy and Yosemite Valley's logging-train, which transported them to the town of Tuolumne, where a train of Pullmans was in waiting to convey them home.

The latter portion of the trip was remarkable because the only means of transportation possible was by pack-train, and the commissary and personal baggage of the entire party had to be packed in that manner over very rough trails during the last week of the outing.

We were very glad to have with us five members of the Appalachian Mountain Club and two members of the Mazama Club.

No accident of a serious nature occurred to detract from the pleasure of the trip.

Though the balance remaining after all disbursements was smaller than in former years, yet the financial arrangements for this Outing were the most satisfactory of any. The Committee have learned from experience that at slight increase of cost the Outing can be rendered much more enjoyable.

The Outing of 1905 inaugurates a departure, in as far as it will be the first one taken outside of California. The announcement of the trip to Mt. Rainier and Paradise Park will accompany this BULLETIN.

WM. E. COLBY,
J. N. LE CONTE,
E. T. PARSONS,
Outing Committee.

Report of the Custodian of the Le Conte Memorial Lodge (1904).

The Le Conte Memorial Lodge was closed on August 18th, having been open during the preceding three months of the summer. The number of visitors to the lodge increased from the time it was opened till about the last of June, when the number was largest. At the latter date the number reached approximately twenty-five daily.

The past summer cannot, however, be taken as giving an accurate idea of the extent to which the lodge will ultimately be used. This is in part due to the fact that, being just completed, its purpose was not even known to residents of the valley. Not being mentioned in the guide-books (in accordance with which the ordinary tourist carefully plans his excursions), no one visited it unless he happened to notice the building in passing. More especially is the number of visitors during the past summer misleading, by reason of the attractions in other parts of the country, which reduced the number of tourists to Yosemite to a point lower than it has been for some years.

Of all who visited the lodge during the summer every one spoke in terms of unbounded admiration, both of the building itself and of the idea of which it is the embodiment.

The style of architecture met with the warmest approval. It was, however, suggested a number of times that the beauty of the interior would be materially enhanced if a style of rustic furniture could be secured more in keeping with the building itself.

The idea of a library was very favorably received. The empty book-shelves suggested the idea to many visitors. Nor were all of them content with merely expressing an opinion on the matter. Already a number of volumes have been received from various persons, while others have promised to send contributions. In fact, if the Club members take an equally active interest in the matter a very good library may be soon gotten together. Also, judging from the favorable responses received from those publishers whom I addressed, the lodge can be further supplied each summer, gratuitously, with the leading magazines, especially those of the Pacific Coast.

The collection of photographs in the lodge was in almost constant demand. The maps were also used to a very considerable extent, especially during the latter part of the season, when campers were most numerous. The supply of maps is, however, rather limited, and not adequate to the demands.

The lot on which the lodge stands was marked out during

the summer, and I understand steps are being taken to erect a stone wall along the boundaries. When this is done and the grounds are properly cleared off and planted with shrubbery the effect will be one of unsurpassed beauty.

Respectfully,
ROBERT L. McWILLIAMS.

STATEMENT CONCERNING THE PROPOSED RECESSION OF YOSEMITE VALLEY AND MARIPOSA BIG TREE GROVE BY THE STATE OF CALIFORNIA TO THE UNITED STATES.

[Prepared by the Secretary of the Sierra Club under the direction of the Board of Directors, and adopted by said Board as its official expression of opinion.]

The Yosemite Valley and the Mariposa Big Tree Grove were granted by Congress, in 1864, to the State *in trust*, "to be held for public use, resort, and recreation." Little was known of the valley at that time and it was many years before it acquired a national reputation. At the present time it is world-famed, and is one of the valuable assets of the nation. Its loss or destruction would affect the entire United States, and every citizen of our country has a direct, vital concern in the welfare of the valley. In 1890 the much larger Yosemite National Park was created by Congress. This latter park includes in its very heart and surrounds on all sides the State Park.

There has thus been created an *imperium in imperio* which has already given rise to much friction. This deplorable state of affairs was emphasized about a year ago, when a fire was permitted to burn some of the finest timber along both sides of the northern boundary of the State Park. Both State and Federal officials insisted that the fire was outside of their respective jurisdictions. The Federal Government will always be hampered in its administration of the National Park as long as the State Park is under separate management. In order to reach the surrounding country its guardians must pass through the State Park, which is the natural base of operations for that whole surrounding region, and yet the Federal Government can maintain no permanent camp and base of supplies in Yosemite Valley because of the State control.

With these conditions existing, Congress is loath to make appropriations for the construction of extensive improvements which would really result in the improvement of State property at national expense. As a result, all the roads entering the National and State parks are private toll-roads, and tribute is levied on every visitor to this region. This condition of affairs is most unfortunate, and would have been remedied long ago but for the existing state of dual government.

But once reinvest the United States with authority over this heart and center of the National Park and headquarters will be established in the valley proper. A system of telephone lines will be constructed radiating from this natural center and extending to all portions of the territory embraced in the present State and National parks. This will insure an effective system of fire protection and will increase the efficiency of the patrol and policing of the park many times. We have assurance that this will be done from President Roosevelt himself, also from the Federal Commission recently appointed to investigate conditions there, and from various other Federal officials.

Major John Bigelow, Jr., Superintendent of Yosemite National Park, in his recent annual report recommends:—

> First:—The acquisition by the United States Government of Yosemite Valley, now owned by the State of California.
>
> Second:—The purchase of toll-roads in the park leading to the valley.
>
> Third:—The purchase by the Government of certain patented lands which are scattered over the park and constitute a considerable part of its area.
>
> "The first of these measures," says Major Bigelow, "is believed to be necessary to secure from Congress an appropriation adequate to the improvement of roads and trails and of the park generally. It is a palpable anomaly for the valley to be under State government and the ground around it under the National Government. The valley would be rendered more attractive, and therefore financially more productive to the State, under National than it is under State government. The acquisition of the valley by the National Government is a matter, to be sure, in which the initiative must be taken by the State government, but I have good reasons to believe the idea that the National Government should own the valley has for some time been gaining in favor with the people of California."

2. The State is unable to properly care for Yosemite Valley.

Though the park has been under the control of the State for upwards of forty years, yet even the main stage roads on the floor of the valley leading to the village are in a deplorable condition. The accommodations provided for visitors have been inadequate for years. In the summer of 1903 the State Commissioners of the valley were, by reason of the congestion in accommodations provided for visitors, compelled to notify the various transportation companies not to allow any more tourists to enter the valley until the overcrowded conditions were relieved.

The State Commissioners have done as well as could be expected. They receive no salary. All the time they give to the affairs of Yosemite Valley must be sacrificed from the time devoted to their regular vocations. Very few have had any previous experience which would specially fit them for the discharge of their peculiar and onerous duties. The paltry ten or fifteen thousand dollars annually at their disposal is entirely inadequate for the needs of the park. It is with difficulty that even this amount is "squeezed out" of the State treasury. The State Commissioners are entitled to praise for what they have accomplished in the face of such adverse conditions.

3. In marked contrast to all this is the management of the Yellowstone National Park by the Federal Government.

The Yellowstone is in charge of Federal engineers and army officers, who have received a life training to qualify them to perform their duties. They all receive salaries, and devote their entire time to the care and management of the park. During the three years 1901-1903 Congress appropriated nearly seven hundred thousand dollars for the care and maintenance of the Yellowstone. The best of skilled engineers are employed in the construction of the roads and trails of the Yellowstone, and they are kept in perfect repair. The roads are broad highways, with steel and concrete bridges.

The hotels of the Yellowstone are large, commodious establishments, first-class in every respect, and with ample accommodation for its visitors.

4. State pride and sentiment is the strongest argument that has been advanced against this proposed change. But when analyzed it is found to be an entire misconception. If anything, sentiment should be all the other way. The Yosemite Valley is the property of the United States, and it has all along been the owner of the paramount title. It has, by Congressional act, allowed the State to take possession under a trust merely. To recede the valley only means to terminate the trust. The United States will not take the valley away nor close it up; but, on the contrary, will render it in every way more accessible and more enjoyable to visit, by reason of better accommodation for visitors. This sentimental argument savors too much of the "dog in the manger" policy to be considered seriously.

5. Our honored President, John Muir, who has devoted his life of activity to the best interests of our forests and natural scenery, has strongly advocated this proposed change for years. In a letter to the Acting Governor written last July he says:—

"The Yosemite Valley, in the heart of the park, and essentially a part of it, should, I think, be ceded to the Federal

Government and put under one management, thus insuring great improvement in present conditions through increased appropriations for roads, trails, and expert work on the valley floor, etc., thus increasing and facilitating travel, to the advantage of the entire country."—*Sacramento Union, July 16, 1904.*

6. President Roosevelt favors the recession. In an article entitled "Wilderness Reserves," written for the Forest and Stream Publishing Company shortly after his Western trip in 1903, reprinted in *Forestry and Irrigation* for July, 1904, he says:—

"As to the Yosemite Valley, if the people of California desire it, as many of them certainly do, it should also be taken by the National Government to be kept as a national park."

And in his recent message to Congress he makes the unqualified statement that, "the national park system should include the Yosemite and as many as possible of the groves of giant trees in California."

7. The Native Sons are strongly in favor of the recession. Grand President McNoble made this recommendation the strongest feature of his annual report.

8. A committee of the State Board of Trade reports that

". . . the board has been impressed by the arguments made by the Native Sons of the Golden West in favor of recession to the Federal Government and the incorporation of the valley and Big Tree Grove with existing national park and forest reservations; also, that such recession will put an end to the inconvenience and risks of a divided jurisdiction now existing by reason of the State control of the valley and the Big Tree Grove, while each is surrounded by Federal reservations under the jurisdiction of the United States."—*San Francisco Call, Sept. 14, 1904.*

9. The Board of Directors of the Sierra Club, by a unanimous vote, authorized the appointment of this committee to urge such action.

10. The California Water and Forest Association adopted the following resolution at its annual convention on December 2, 1904:—

"*Resolved,* That the proposition to cede the Yosemite Valley back to the United States Government should receive the earnest consideration of the Legislature, to the end that more commodious accommodations may be provided for making such valley accessible to the general public, and we recommend such transfer."

11. The San Francisco Chamber of Commerce, that of Oakland and other cities, and many other influential bodies have also favored the recession.

12. The various newspapers throughout the State have almost without exception indorsed the proposed change in editorial comment. Not one dissenting opinion has come to our notice. Since these comments outline some of the arguments to be given in favor of the proposed change, and since they voice in a degree the sentiment of the people on the question, extracts from a few of these expressions of opinion are given in the Appendix hereto.

13. In conclusion, the past has demonstrated that the Yosemite Valley is of a national character, and every citizen of the United States is vitally interested in its welfare. The State assumed the burden of caring for it, and has expended its money for the benefit of every citizen of the United States. Forty years has proven that the State cannot afford to appropriate out of the funds at its disposal a sufficient amount to adequately care for this National Park. California has vital interests which concern her alone. She has forests to protect from fire; she has flood-water problems; she has a State Redwood Park; she has multitudinous interests which demand the expenditure of her own money. She can obtain no funds elsewhere for this work, for her citizens only are vitally affected by such expenditures. Her funds even now are far short of being adequate to meet the growing necessities of this great State. The Yosemite Valley requires the expenditure of at least one hundred thousand dollars every year for its proper care and management. A hotel is absolutely required to be constructed in the valley at a cost of at least two hundred thousand dollars. The State cannot afford to appropriate this amount.

But the United States is amply able to do this, and will, if given the opportunity. Therefore, the Yosemite Valley and Mariposa Big Tree Grove should be receded to the United States, and thereby become a part of the National Park, to which it naturally belongs. The result would be the improvement of the valley and National Park by the construction of the best of roads, bridges, and trails. Ample hotel accommodations of the best quality would be provided. A telephone system for the entire park to guard against forest fires would be inaugurated. The patrol system of the National Park would be rendered far more effective and the valley itself placed under the same system, so that perfect order would prevail, no matter how great the number of visitors. The toll-road system would be abolished, and in all probability a splendid boulevard constructed up the Merced Cañon, which would reduce the time and expense of travel one half and greatly increase the comfort. This would attract immense numbers of tourists from all parts of the world who are now deterred by the arduous nature of the trip and the lack of accommodation.

Each of these tourists would not only learn something of our great State, but would spend money in it. Few of us even begin to dream of the wealth that will some day be poured into California by the multitude of travelers who will annually come to enjoy our unparalleled scenic attractions. We want to hasten that day, and we trust that the members of the State Legislature will do their part in aiding to bring about this result by receding the Yosemite Valley and the Mariposa Grove of Big Trees to the National Government.

Respectfully submitted.   JOHN MUIR, *President*,
WM. E. COLBY, *Secretary*,
GEORGE DAVIDSON,
WM. R. DUDLEY,
J. S. HUTCHINSON, JR.,
J. N. LE CONTE,
A. G. MCADIE,
ELLIOTT MCALLISTER,
WARREN OLNEY,
*Board of Directors
of the Sierra Club.*

[APPENDIX.]

The Yosemite Valley is a wonder of nature of really national magnitude, and, like the Yellowstone Park, more fitly cared for by the nation than by any State. It also happens that the valley is actually inclosed within a much larger national park, and that conflicts of jurisdiction, involving serious results, have already occurred. The entire area of both parks constitutes one natural administrative unit, and it is believed that there is a growing feeling in Congress that such an arrangement should be made.—*San Francisco Chronicle, Aug. 21, 1904.*

If the reports from the mountains last summer were true, there is danger in divided jurisdiction, for it was said that when the most destructive fire that ever visited the vicinity of the valley was raging, the State Superintendent of the valley and the Military Superintendent of the park stood for days disputing whether the fire was on Federal or State territory, until it gained such headway that their combined forces could not master it until it had destroyed the fine forest extending from the Wawona Road to Glacier Point. A single jurisdiction would render such a catastrophe from such a cause impossible.—*San Francisco Call, Nov. 18, 1903.*

Major Chittenden, U. S. A., Chairman of the Federal Commission appointed to investigate and report on matters pertaining to the Yosemite National Park, said that in case the valley was ceded to the United States, and that the Government would agree to assume the care and management of the valley, a fort would be erected in the valley and a system of permanent telephone stations established to give proper protection to the forests from fire.—*San Francisco Examiner, July 16, 1904.*

It would be better for Yosemite if it were in the hands of the Federal Government. The Interior Department has control of the great Yosemite reserve encircling the valley for miles in all directions, and could, without extra expense, supervise the valley as well. Yosemite Valley really belongs to the United States. It should be looked upon as a possession of all the people, and should be made more easily accessible to all. It should receive the attention that the Federal Government could give it. More money would be expended upon it, more care devoted to it, and the expenses of visitors should be greatly reduced. It would become what it should be—a people's park.—*Oakland Enquirer, July 28, 1904.*

The failure of the State to provide for the proper accommodation of visitors to the valley has provoked a wide-spread demand that the reservation be receded to the Federal Government. Should the recession be made, there is no doubt that Congress would speedily provide the necessary accommodations as well as the other facilities to enable sight-seers to visit the valley and its surroundings under the most favorable conditions. The valley should be managed in the interest of the public to whom it belongs, and the convenience of the public should be the first consideration in making improvements.—*Oakland Tribune, Sept. 14, 1904.*

State pride may prevent the Legislature taking any such action, but there is no question that it ought to be done. The present system of divided jurisdiction paralyzes all effort for the satisfactory administration of this greatest of natural wonders. Since it is out of the question for the nation to cede the park to the State, the State ought to cede the valley to the nation.—*Fresno Republican, July 16, 1904.*

Under the absolute control of the United States Government the valley would have the best of care; money for every needed improvement would be forthcoming; it would be carefully policed, and the chances for graft or political jobs would be reduced to a minimum. The citizens of California would enjoy every right in the valley that liberal but well-enforced regulations would permit. It would be "our" valley still. Uncle Sam could not run away with it, and he would certainly be a careful and at the same time indulgent guardian. The fact that the Government is willing to accept the trust is fortunate, and those who appreciate the situation will doubtless hope to see favorable action by the next Legislature on Muir's proposal.—*Stockton Record, July 12, 1904.*

Up to this time State management has been reasonably efficient, but in State hands the administration of the park must always more or less be involved in politics, whereas the Government would be able to administer it through the army precisely as it administers the National Park in the Yellowstone country.—*Sacramento Union, April 22, 1902.*

There is a strong probability that the Yosemite Valley will be receded to the Federal Government by the State of California in the near future. Such a move would probably tend to a greater improvement of the park, as the expenses connected with keeping the great natural wonder open to the public are considerable and can be better sustained by Uncle Sam than the State of California. It would also tend to a quick abolition of toll-roads, make a trip to the valley fraught with less expense to travelers and in the reach of almost every one.—*The New Era, Tuolumne, Cal., May 7, 1904.*

The only arguments that have been presented opposing the transfer are along the line of State pride. When this is analyzed, however, it does not appear justifiable. The park must necessarily remain forever in California, and the retention of title by the State means merely the inadequate continuance of a struggle to meet the obligations demanded by the magnitude of the situation and the traveling public. Public opinion largely favors the transfer.—*Los Angeles Times, Nov. 9, 1904.*

Yosemite is one of California's best assets. Every visitor it attracts from abroad is a source of profit to the people of this State, consequently the more sight-seers for the valley the more profit to Californians. The Government will do what the State has neglected to do, and do it better.— *Oakland Tribune, Nov. 26, 1904.*

"WHEREAS, The Yosemite Valley and the Mariposa Big Tree Grove are among the scenic wonders of the world, and the pride not only of California but of the whole Union; and

"WHEREAS, Their proper maintenance and improvement imposes upon the people of California a burden which, in view of the fact that said valley and grove are national exhibits, should be borne by the National Government; and

"WHEREAS, We believe that the National Government is alone able to undertake the expenditures necessary to properly improve said valley and grove by providing easy means of access, well-planned roads, trails, and other attractive features;

"*Resolved,* That the Board of Directors of the Chamber of Commerce of Santa Barbara County hereby desires to go on record as favoring the recession to the National Government of the Yosemite Valley and the Mariposa Grove, to the end that these natural wonders may receive the improvements which they deserve and the consequent attention from the world that they merit."—*Santa Barbara Press, Dec. 3, 1904.*

It is rumored that, moved by the admirable conduct and supervision of the Yosemite National Park, the State of California is likely, at the approaching session of its Legislature, to recede to the United States the smaller Yosemite grant of 1864, which is in the park but not of it. It is absurd and wasteful that there should be two jurisdictions within one boundary, and the people of California are to be congratulated on the prospect of this wise consummation, which Congress should facilitate by a prompt acceptance of the duty of caring for the whole of the Yosemite Wonderland.—*Century Magazine, December, 1904.*

The superintendent of the Yosemite National Park recommends that the Federal Government "acquire" the Yosemite Valley, which it once gave to the State of California. It is to be hoped that this most desirable end may be accomplished at the coming session of the California Legislature. The reasons for this course are abundant and conclusive. In the first place it is really, as its name implies, a "National" and not a State park. Its natural wonders are national in their magnitude, national in their interest, and national in the scale of expenditure required to make them accessible and protect them from impairment. They should be national, also, in their custody. This sentimental view would perhaps not be altogether conclusive were California rich enough to incur the expenditure involved in the ownership and protection of the park. Unfortunately this State is not rich enough, and practical considerations coincide with the sentimental in requiring that this wonderful valley be restored to the nation, which alone is able to care for it. From all sides come imperative demands for largely increased expenditures on the park with which this State is positively unable to comply. For the next quarter of a century the State will be compelled to tax itself to the full limit of endurance for purposes essential to our material prosperity or for the fulfillment of moral obligations which must take precedence even of so noble an object as the Yosemite Valley. We have recently acquired a State park in the Big Basin of Santa Cruz County, and the forest fires of last summer admonished us that if we are to preserve that magnificent body of timber for the enjoyment of future generations we must incur heavy expense in protecting it from fire. The State, in fact, cannot afford for the present to expend any more money on parks than it will be absolutely compelled to expend to prevent the destruction by fire of the forests of the Big Basin. The Federal Government should, and probably will, if desired, assume charge of the Yosemite Park as it has of the Yellowstone Park, and the legislation required for that purpose by our Legislature should be enacted at the coming session.—*San Francisco Chronicle, Nov. 28, 1904.*

ACTION OF THE SIERRA CLUB ON THE PROPOSED CHANGE OF BOUNDARIES OF THE YOSEMITE NATIONAL PARK.

SAN FRANCISCO, CAL., August 23, 1904.

TO THE HONORABLE BOARD OF COMMISSIONERS APPOINTED TO INVESTIGATE AND REPORT ON THE BOUNDARIES OF THE YOSEMITE NATIONAL PARK.

At a recent meeting of the Board of Directors of the Sierra Club, the undersigned committee was appointed to communicate to your Honorable Commission the views of the board regarding any proposed change of boundaries of the Yosemite National Park.

I. With relation to the western boundary of the park, while we regret the necessity of reducing the area of the park at all, yet, influenced by the fact that there are such a large number of private holdings, we are therefore not opposed to having Townships 2, 3, and 4 South, Range 19 East, withdrawn from the park and added to the Sierra Forest Reserve.

To withdraw any larger area either to the east or north of the three townships mentioned would, we believe, be too great an encroachment upon the wonderful scenic features, for the preservation of which the park was created.

II. We strongly recommend that the northern and southern boundaries of the park be left unchanged (other than the slight change on the southern boundary which would be occasioned by the withdrawal of Township 4 South, Range 19 East, already mentioned).

There is no territory adjacent to either of these boundaries which does not include remarkable scenic features or afford protection to such. Of course we would favor any extension along these boundaries.

III. In relation to the eastern boundary of the park, we not only recommend that no territory be withdrawn adjacent to such boundary, but we also strongly urge the addition of the following territory to the present area of the park: The west one half (½) of Township 1 North, Range 25 East; all of Township 2 South, Range 26 East; and the west one half (½) of Township 4 South, Range 27 East.

We make this latter recommendation for the following reasons: The park is not sufficiently protected on the east along the territory mentioned from the invasions of sheep and other private interests, the territory mentioned includes very few private holdings, and finally it embraces many scenic features of such importance and of so remarkable a nature that they should be made a part of the National Park.

Respectfully submitted.

      (Signed) JOHN MUIR,
             J. N. LE CONTE,
             WM. E. COLBY,
Committee on Yosemite National Park Boundary.

       SAN FRANCISCO, CAL., August 28, 1904.
MAJOR CHITTENDEN, Palace Hotel, City.

Dear Sir—I herewith inclose a copy of the resolutions, or, rather, recommendations, of the Board of Directors of the Sierra Club relative to the boundaries of the Yosemite National Park. The original will doubtless reach you to-morrow.

In explanation of our attitude regarding the eastern boundary of the park, and our suggestion that the territory be increased in that direction rather than diminished, I will give some of the details which influenced us in arriving at the conclusions we did.

We feel that the grandest scenery in the whole park (excepting the Yosemite and Hetch-Hetchy valleys) is to be found in the Tuolumne Meadows and vicinity,—in fact, all along the eastern border of the park. It is this portion of the park which will become almost as famous as the two valleys named, and, excepting the scenery of the two valleys named, the western portion of the park contains nothing that can begin to compare with the magnificence and grandeur of the eastern portion. Professor Joseph Le Conte, in his "Journal of Ramblings in the High Sierra," John Muir in the *Century Magazine* for September, 1890, (Vol. XVIII, pp. 663-667,) and in his other writings, and the report of the Commission on Roads in Yosemite, Fifty-sixth Congress (Senate Document No. 155), all agree that this portion of the park is a perfect "paradise" as far as scenic features and camping attractions are concerned. Naturally, therefore, our Club is deeply interested in its preservation and in safeguarding it as completely as possible.

We have felt that this eastern boundary has in the past been too poorly protected. The meadows on the east approach so close to the park boundary (in one instance, at Tioga Pass, the meadow is even continuous with the meadow that extends within the park) that it is a simple matter for bands of sheep to slip over the boundary unseen, as happened many times during this last summer when our Club was in the meadows. We had thought that if the boundary were extended farther east in the places suggested in our report, that it would bring this finest region of the park nearer its heart, where it would be afforded better protection. Sheep-herders and trespassers would have to travel some distance in order to reach these beautiful spots, and their presence detected before they could reach them, even if they would dare to enter within the boundaries so far and place their flocks in such open jeopardy.

You will also note that we have included much fine scenery in our proposed additions to the park, which is of such an attractive nature that it can well be included in the wonders and scenic features already within the park boundaries.

Regarding the mining phase of the eastern boundary question, I wish there were some way of adjusting it. While there are many claims, yet they can only cover a small area of the territory,—and would it not be possible to allow their owners to retain and work them, under restrictions, of course? Would it not be better to suffer some small detraction of this nature than to cut off the area contemplated and the magnificent scenery it embraces, and thus lose it to the park entirely? Having had a large experience with mines and mining,—for I have made the branch of the law relating to mines a specialty, which I have followed for some years,—I feel that very few of these claims will ever be exploited to any extent. It seems too bad that all this fine territory should be excluded simply to get rid of this mining question.

I have written the above merely by way of explanation of our present attitude relative to the eastern boundary. We all felt so strongly on the subject that I deemed it of sufficient importance to elucidate and give our reasons more in detail.

We shall gladly render any aid within our power or give you such information as we possess in relation to any matters affecting the park, if you will but kindly call them to our attention.

Very truly yours,
(Signed) WM. E. COLBY,
Secretary of Sierra Club.

SAN FRANCISCO, CAL., September 7, 1904.
MAJOR H. M. CHITTENDEN, Palace Hotel, City.

Dear Sir—Upon a further consideration of the proposed change in the eastern boundary of the Yosemite National Park, I feel at liberty to advise you that our Club would not be opposed to a change of the boundary of the National Park which would be defined by the main crest of the Sierra, as you had suggested to me would be the report of the commission, provided that simultaneously with such change at least one tier of townships fronting all along on this proposed eastern boundary be included in an extension of the forest reserve. We feel that something is necessary along this eastern boundary of the park to act as a buffer against invasion, and if the plan suggested can be carried out it would probably be as effective a protection of the vital portions of the park as we could expect.

Very truly yours,
(Signed)   WM. E. COLBY,
Secretary of Sierra Club.

NOTES AND CORRESPONDENCE.

In addition to longer articles suitable for the body of the magazine, the editor would be glad to receive brief memoranda of all noteworthy trips or explorations, together with brief comment and suggestion on any topics of general interest to the Club. Descriptive or narrative articles, or notes concerning the animals, birds, forests, trails, geology, botany, etc., of the mountains, will be acceptable.

The office of the Sierra Club is at Room 16, Third Floor, Mills Building, San Francisco, where all the maps, photographs, and other records of the Club are kept, and where members are welcome at any time.

The Club would like to purchase additional copies of those numbers of the SIERRA CLUB BULLETIN *which are noted on the back of the cover of this number as being out of print, and we hope any member having extra copies will send them to the Secretary.*

DEDICATION OF LE CONTE MEMORIAL LODGE.

The Le Conte Memorial Lodge in Yosemite Valley was dedicated by the Sierra Club July 3, 1904. There was a large attendance of Sierra Club members, owing to the fact that Yosemite Valley had been selected as the gathering-place for the 1904 Outing. The dedication exercises were simple, but very impressive. Wm. E. Colby, the Secretary of the Club, presided, in the absence of the President and Vice-President. Rev. C. T. Brown, of San Diego, gave the invocation. Professor A. C. Lawson, who succeeded Professor Le Conte as head of the Geological Department of the University of California, Mr. Alexander G. Eells, President of the Alumni Association, and Dr. G. K. Gilbert, of the U. S. Geological Survey, each delivered an address. Mr. Willoughby Rodman read a poem written for the occasion, and Miss Caroline Little sang Tennyson's "Splendor Falls on Castle Walls." Miss Harriet Monroe, of Chicago, read an original quatrain. Rev. Joseph Clemens pronounced the benediction. The exercises closed with the singing of "The Star-Spangled Banner." A bronze tablet appropriately inscribed was inserted in the walls of the building.

Professor Gilbert writes concerning the names of the rivers of the Sierras as follows:—

WASHINGTON, D. C., October 24, 1904.
SECRETARY SIERRA CLUB, SAN FRANCISCO, CAL.

Dear Sir—The members of the Sierra Club are well acquainted with the inconvenience of the system of naming which obtains for the primary and secondary branches of the rivers draining the Sierra. The main streams were long ago named where they issue from the foothills. Tributaries of the third rank have been named and are being named as creeks, but divisions of the first and second rank are called forks, or forks and branches; and this system leads to such infelicities as the North Branch of the Middle Fork of the San Joaquin, for example. It seems to me desirable that individual names be substituted for many of the present descriptive names of forks and branches, and a system of individual names would doubtless grow up by slow accretion if no convention is attempted; but as a system of natural growth is likely to result in the adoption of many undesirable names, it seems to me better to have a considerable number of carefully selected names introduced by a competent organization. For this purpose it seems that the Sierra Club is best qualified. The only other organization which occurs to me as at all suitable is the United States Geological Survey, but that organization has wisely adopted the general policy of recording names in use and of proposing new ones only in cases of absolute necessity. You can readily understand that if it undertook the reorganization of nomenclature, it would be sure to rouse antagonism and its efforts would be defeated. Moreover, its knowledge of the range of local appropriate names cannot possibly be so full as that of a local organization like the Sierra Club.

I venture, therefore, to propose to the officers of the Sierra Club that the nomenclature of the rivers of the Sierra be deliberately and carefully considered, with the view to thorough revision.

It is proper to add that no future time would be so opportune as the present. Detailed mapping is in progress, and if the map-makers can have a good set of names to incorporate the result would be accomplished without friction or inconvenience.

I am, very truly yours,

G. K. GILBERT.

[It may be noted that, pursuant to this idea, Mr. Le Conte in his article in the present number has selected the name Evolution Creek for the Middle Branch of the South Fork of the San Joaquin River, and in his map of that region, also printed with this number, he has selected the name Piute Branch for the North Branch of the South Fork of the San Joaquin River.—EDITOR.]

ZAMBOANGA, P. I., May 17, 1904.

SECRETARY SIERRA CLUB, SAN FRANCISCO.

Dear Sir—I am returning from this trip to Mt. Apo before receiving the Club cylinder, but expect to visit it again in the fall.

I have been twice to the summit. I may plant the cylinder on Mt. Banajao, almost equally high, in the mean time and send for another.

Apo is not as high as its reputation. My aneroid readings ranged from 9,100 to 9,480 feet, the lower figure being nearer correct. The first ascent was made by two German naturalists, Koch and Schadenberg, February 22, 1882. Subsequent ascents were by an Englishman, Burke, in 1884; by Lieutenant Thomas and three other Americans, in 1900; and by two teachers, De Vore and Hoover, in 1903. Lieutenant Thomas copied the earlier signatures, and brought down the original as a proof of the ascent. Apo is reputed to be a volcano, but it is not as good a cone as Mt. Lassen; and the top, instead of a well-formed crater, is a small moor. The flora is limited and its affinities northern. My ascents were April 20 and 23, 1904.

This much may be of interest to the Club. I do not care to send more, as anything on the subject is foreign to the scope of the BULLETIN, as Mr. Hutchinson defined it to me last summer. The January BULLETIN has not been forwarded to me. Please change my address to Manila.

Sincerely yours,
EDWIN BINGHAM COPELAND.

ZAMBOANGA, P. I., November 10, 1904.
SECRETARY OF THE SIERRA CLUB, SAN FRANCISCO.

Dear Sir—The cylinder you sent me was deposited on the summit of Mt. Apo October 24th. The altitude is probably about 9,400 feet. My aneroid measurements are rather less, but Major Mearns' figures are a little higher. I have been up but three times, and am told he made six ascents in the course of about a month's work on the fauna.

The panorama is:—
    About N. E., Mt. Roosevelt. (I did not see it this trip.)
    N. 75° E., Davao.
    N. 120° E., Malalag, a very picturesque coast.
    S., Sarangani Bay.
    S. 15° E., Matutan.
    W., Cottabato.

Roosevelt is a peak of a great mountain called appropriately "The Punch Bowl"; another is known locally as McKinley; but as that name is in better use in Alaska, the whole mountain here may better be called Roosevelt. It is rather under nine thousand feet high and wooded to the top. Matutan is a very perfect volcanic cone, which I would estimate at seven thousand feet. It is near the head of Sarangani Bay, from which an army party is said to have started to ascend it, but to have been driven back by leeches, from a region where the subterranean rumbling was deafening.

You already have the record of ascents of Apo up to the time of my former visit. Major Edgar A. Mearns, accompanied by Fletcher L. Keller, visited the summit June 28th, their first time. And parties of soldiers from Davao made ascents September 25th and October 5th. Mr. and Mrs. Knudtson, of Cagayan de Misamis, went up as far as the sulphur vents, where also ended the "unica expedicion Español" in 1880.

Very truly yours,
EDWIN BINGHAM COPELAND.
Bureau of Government Laboratories, Manila.

It has been brought to the attention of officers of the Sierra Club that a certain firm in Southern California has been advertising "Sierra Club Mountaineering Boots." This was an unwarranted use of our corporate name. The firm, on having their attention called to the matter, said that it was an oversight on their part, and have agreed to discontinue the use of our name. The Directors have expressed a determination never to allow the Club's name to be used by others. Business houses desiring to get their wares before the membership of the Sierra Club, and before mountaineers throughout the country, are permitted to use the advertising columns of the BULLETIN after the correctness and qualities of their offerings have been approved. In this way our members have a proper protection against imposition, and our advertisers have a reasonable assurance of the Club's patronage.

PARTIAL BIBLIOGRAPHY, KERN RIVER OUTING OF 1903.

Sunset for October, 1903: An article by Victor F. Henderson.
Sunset for June, 1904: An article by E. T. Parsons.
Overland for January, 1904: An article by Miss Josephine Colby.
San Francisco Chronicle of September 6, 1903: Paper by E. T. Parsons.
San Francisco Examiner of September 6, 1903: Paper by Asahel Curtis.
San Francisco Bulletin of September 6, 1903: Paper by Hartly F. Peart.
Portland Oregonian of September 6, 1903: Paper by Miss Ella E. McBride.

PARTIAL BIBLIOGRAPHY, TUOLUMNE OUTING OF 1904.

San Francisco Chronicle of September 14, 1904: Paper by E. T. Parsons.

San Francisco Bulletin of September 14, 1904: Paper by Hartly F. Peart.

Santa Cruz Surf of October 6, 1904: Paper by Hartly F. Peart.

Watsonville Register of September 10, 1904: Article by J. E. Gardner.

San Luis Obispo Morning Tribune of September 13, 1904: Paper by J. E. Gardner.

Los Angeles Express of July 18-22, August 17, 1904: Papers by Willoughby Rodman.

Los Angeles Times of September 18, 1904: Paper by Claire S. Tappan.

Portland Oregonian of September 4, 1904: Paper by Miss Ella E. McBride.

The Keystone of South Carolina: Article by Miss Marion Randall.

Out West (Mountaineering Number), March, 1905: Articles by Willoughby Rodman, Prof. Wm. Frederic Badè, Miss Marion Randall, and E. T. Parsons.

Other papers to appear later will be noted in the June BULLETIN.

A PACK TRAIL ON MT. WHITNEY.

The following from the *Monthly Weather Review* of September, 1904, is of interest to the members of the Sierra Club. Under date of August 1, 1904, Professor McAdie writes:—

I am anxious to expose a minimum thermometer on the summit of Mt. Whitney, so that the lowest temperature during the coming winter at this great elevation may be obtained. It will be remembered that some experiments were made in the winters of 1897-98 and 1898-99 at Mt. Lyell, elevation 13,040 feet. The minimum temperatures recorded during the two seasons were respectively $-25.3°$ C. and $-27.6°$ C. These were not the lowest temperatures recorded elsewhere in California during those winters.

It is thought we should make every effort to utilize the opportunity for study of atmospheric conditions in these high levels in view of the importance of the data in connection with new theories of formation and structure of cyclones and anti-cyclones.

I inclose copy of a letter received from Mr. G. F. Marsh, Lone Pine, Cal., relative to the completion of a pack trail to the summit of Mt. Whitney. This is a matter of some importance, as it will now be possible during July and August to send supplies to the summit of Mt. Whitney, elevation 14,515 feet, and so far as known the highest point in the United States, excluding Alaska.

Regarding the completion of the trail, Mr. Marsh (under date of July 22, 1904) writes to Professor McAdie:—

> I am very glad to inform you that we completed the pack trail to the summit of Mt. Whitney last Sunday, the 18th. We had three pack-trains loaded with wood, and one saddle-horse. We had a large fire at night, and fireworks which were plainly seen at Lone Pine, who responded with a large fire and fireworks.
>
> We had an ideal day to finish the trail. The weather was perfect. We were so anxious to get to the top that we never noticed the altitude. Most of the time it was bitter cold and windy. We were all fearfully sunburned; our faces were a sight and our lips almost black; but we would not give in. The pack-train had no difficulty at all in climbing the mountain. The trail is in good shape and parties are going over it every day. We shall try to find some means of keeping the trail in good repair.
>
> I think the trail will be open until about Christmas unless early storms come, but it would not be safe to say this, as we do not know how early the snow will come this year. Last year there was very little snow. But I think parties will be safe until the end of October.

In a subsequent letter Mr. Marsh refers to a snowstorm on August 1st that compelled a party to turn back within a half-mile of the monument. "The mountains are covered with a light snow now, but it melts quickly."

On October 10th Mr. W. E. Bonnett, Assistant Observer at Independence, Cal., attempted to reach the summit of Mt. Whitney for the purpose of installing maximum and minimum thermometers. He was accompanied by a guide, with a pack animal and saddle animal. At an altitude of 10,000 feet snow began to fall. They proceeded about 1,000 feet further, when the high wind and dense snow, which was fast blotting out the trail, compelled them to turn back.

On July 26th, eight days after the completion of the trail, one man was killed by lightning at the summit during a sudden snowstorm, and two of his companions were rendered unconscious. The Redland *Facts* records a similar occurrence on July 24th on Mt. San Gorgonio, at an elevation of 9,500 feet, the first case of the kind in the history of the county. Referring to these fatalities, Professor McAdie says:—

> The accidents have a scientific interest in that there are but few records of deaths by lightning in this State. But it should be noted that comparatively few people have been exposed to storms at high elevations. Mr. Byrd Surby was killed on the summit of Mt. Whitney, within fifty feet of the monument. It was snowing at the time of the accident. It is probably not well known that the variations in the electrical potential of the air during a snowstorm are almost as rapid and as great as those prevailing during a thunderstorm. In this present case

I am inclined to think that the electrical disturbance was not localized, but simply incidental to a disturbed field which extended well over the High Sierra, Inyo, Panamint, and Telescope ranges. Also the San Bernardino Range, and probably the mountains of Arizona. This condition lasted perhaps a fortnight.

RESOLUTIONS ADOPTED BY THE EIGHTH INTERNATIONAL GEOGRAPHIC CONGRESS, SEPTEMBER 13, 1904, AND PUBLISHED AT ITS REQUEST.

Rules for Geographic Names.—Local names are as far as possible to be preserved not only in those regions where already established, but also in wild regions. They should on this account be determined with all the accuracy possible.

Where local names do not exist or cannot be discovered the names applied by the first discoverer should be used until further investigation. The arbitrary altering of historical, long-existent names, well known not only in common use but also in science, is to be regarded as extremely unadvisable, and every means should be employed to resist such alterations. Inappropriate and fantastical names are to be replaced, as far as possible, by local and more appropriate names.

The above rules are not to be rigorously construed, yet they should be followed to a greater extent than heretofore by travelers and in scientific works. Their publication in periodicals as the opinion of the Congress will probably prove of great weight. Although in recent years many official systems of determination of geographic names have been enunciated, we have still evidence of the very slight influence which the wishes of the International Geographic Congresses exert over the decision of the official authorities.

To this geographical societies are urged to give wide publicity.

Introduction of the Fractional Scales of Maps.—The Seventh International Geographic Congress expressed the urgent wish that upon all charts, including those published by those lands still employing the English and Russian systems of measurement, along with the scale of geographic coordinance, that the scale of reduction should be expressed in the usual fractional form, $1:x$, and that the latter be added to all lists of charts covering land and sea, and requests the executive committee of the Congress to bring this decision to the attention of all governments, geographical societies, and establishments engaged in the publication of charts.

The advantage to be derived from the support of this resolution, which has its origin with the editor of Peterman's Mittheilungen, and the extensive dissemination of the resolution, is at once evident. In English publications a custom has arisen of adding a statement of the ratio 1 : x to the usually employed x miles to one inch. In America the custom has arisen of going even a step beyond this,—namely, the addition of the ratio of reduction has led to the direct application of the decimal system in the units of measure adopted upon the charts.

To this geographical societies are urged to give wide publicity.

The Decimal System.—The Seventh International Geographic Congress expressed itself in favor of a uniform system in all geographical researches and discussions, and it recommends for this purpose the employment of the metric system of weights and measures, as also the employment of the centigrade thermometric scale.

It is moreover highly desirable that there should always be added to statements of the Fahrenheit and the Reaumur scales their equivalent upon the scale of Celsius.

Similar is this question of the metric system, which reaches even more deeply than the former into the well-established customs of daily life, and has proved not without value in promoting international uniformity and simplicity. Although the metric system of weights and measures has made slow progress, and this alone through the portals of scientific work, its application to geophysics and geography has already made a fair beginning. In England a special organization, entitled the Decimal Association, has taken charge of the matter. The Commonwealth of Australia has intrusted the subject to a commission. We are without knowledge of the efforts in this direction thus far made in Russia.

To this geographical societies are urged to give wide publicity.

Standard Time.—Resolved, in view of the fact that a large majority of the nations of the world have already adopted systems of standard time based upon the Meridian of Greenwich as prime meridian, that this Congress is in favor of the universal adoption of the Meridian of Greenwich as the basis of all systems of standard time.

Publication of Photographs.—It is suggested by the lantern-slides shown by Mr. Siebers and by the photographs of Mr. Willis that it is desirable that in those and the cases of other exploring travelers photographs of geographical significance might be published and accompanied by short explanatory notes, so that they may form collections of representative physical features of different parts of the world.

BOOK REVIEWS.

Edited by William Frederic Badè.

"Birds of California." Easily foremost among the books that have come to the reviewer's table is Irene Grosvenor Wheelock's *Birds of California*.* Many will remember her admirable book, "Nestlings of Forest and Marsh," brought out by the same publishing-house two years ago. In it the author amply demonstrated her capacity for original observation by making a number of independent contributions to our knowledge of avian feeding habits. The same painstaking work has gone into this new product of her pen. The extent to which she has followed up her earlier observations is indicated by a statement in the preface "that the young of all macroshires, woodpeckers, perching birds, cuckoos, kingfishers, most birds of prey, and many seabirds are fed by regurgitation from the time of hatching through a period varying in extent from three days to four weeks, according to the species." If further observation bears out her conclusion, it will mean a considerable departure from current ornithological doctrine on this subject. But whoever chooses to indict Mrs. Wheelock for heresy will have to bring facts and not unsupported statements.

The scope of the book is indicated in the fact that it contains descriptions of more than three hundred common birds of California and adjacent islands. There are ten full-page plates and seventy-eight excellent drawings in the text by Bruce Horsfall. In the arrangement the author has followed the plan made popular by Neltje Blantchan, of substituting general divisions of habitat and color for a technical key. For purposes of ready identification this plan possesses unsurpassed advantages. The untechnical bird-lover especially will find this arrangement convenient. The individual biographies with which the author follows up the more salient scientific facts given for each species are models of easy and graceful writing. They betray at once the workmanship of a keen and loving observer who knows how to convey interesting information with economy of words and a peculiarly charming style. Adverting to the popular belief

---

* *Birds of California*: an introduction to more than three hundred common birds of the State and adjacent islands; with a supplementary list of rare migrants, accidental visitants, and hypothetical subspecies. By Irene Grosvenor Wheelock. 12mo. 578 pp. $2.50 net. A. C. McClurg & Co., Chicago. 1904.

that the burrowing-owl foregathers on friendly terms with prairie-dogs and rattlesnakes, she writes: "The owls hunt among the burrows for young mammals, and the offspring of the 'dogs' are doubtless a choice tidbit; the snakes crawl from hole to hole for the same purpose, but include owl-eggs and nestlings in their menu. So far as I have been able to observe, the 'dogs' are in terror from them both, but the sudden advent of a human intruder causes the three enemies to pop suddenly down the same hole with surprising unanimity."

Californians have long been interested in their native birds. The Cooper Ornithological Club is one of the most active in the country. But all signs indicate that we are on the eve of a more wide-spread awakening of popular interest in our feathered neighbors. The rapid rise of local Audubon Societies and Outdoor Art Clubs is part of the general movement in a State where Nature never locks the door against the student at any time of the year. Mrs. Wheelock's book not only comes opportunely, but comes with the *eclat* of real merit. It takes its place beside the more technical work of Mrs. Bailey as the best general introduction to the birds of California that has yet appeared. It only remains to add that the publishers deserve no little credit for the mechanical perfection they have given the book. Bound in flexible black leather and printed in clear large type on excellent paper, it is as tempting to the hand as it is pleasing to the eye.

"THE ROMANCE OF PISCATOR." Dedicated "to every one who has heard the Siren song of the reel," *The Romance of Piscator* * makes its strongest appeal to the disciples of Isaak Walton. But a charming, though somewhat jerky, love-story which threads its way through many piscatorial adventures bids for appreciation among a larger circle of readers. Perhaps it is inevitable that a successful fisherman's story should be somewhat jerky and improbable; it is in the nature of the sport, and does not seriously detract from the reader's interest in the rapid movement of the story. It is apparent that the author is a true son of the rod and the reel. He knows the woods, the river, and the trout-pools not from hearsay, but from experience. Hence, in spite of evident shortcomings of the story, no woodsman can read the book without feeling again the thrill of long-remembered strikes, when the gray hackle danced temptingly down over the white riffles. And even the most ingrained Walton will find an added element of interest

---

* *The Romance of Piscator.* By HENRY WYSHAM LANIER. With frontispiece. 227 pp. $1.25. 1904. Henry Holt & Co., New York.

in the bewitching, tantalizing, elusive girl who, after a great show of coyness, succeeds in landing Piscator with as much skill as ever he displayed in landing a savage six-pounder. To be sure the Peri says "Fancy!" and travels with "luggage," and consequently does things in an un-American way. But she is lovable and—real? There is room for suspicion that the story but thinly veils what often is stranger and better than fiction, and that the beautiful woman who looks out from the vignette tailpiece is the reality.

"FERGY THE GUIDE." From the same publishing-house we have received *Fergy the Guide*,* by H. S. Canfield. The subtitle fairly describes the book as a collection of "moral and instructive lies about beasts, birds, and fishes," with this exception, that the lies are neither moral nor instructive. But any one who is looking for what Kipling would call "unmitigated misstatements" will find them here in profusion. Among the products of Fergy's imagination are porcupines that shoot quills at a target, a muskallonge that drinks whisky and swims amuck, a malodorous quadruped that imitates chickens and kills them by the hundred, a monstrous woodpecker, and a woodchuck orchestra. One cannot help wishing that Fergy had mingled a little more wit with his loquacity. If he is not allowed to do all the talking he will prove good company at an evening camp-fire. One might, in David Harum's phrase, say of *Fergy the Guide:* "If one likes that kind of thing, that's the kind of thing he would like."

"THE PASSING SHOW." Among those who added to the comradeship and good cheer of last summer's outing was Miss Harriet Monroe, of Chicago. Her "Ballad of Ritter Mountain" helped to make the last camp-fire at Lake Eleanor especially memorable. Although her recent book does not deal with outdoor life, we gladly make unsolicited mention of it here on behalf of her many friends in the Sierra Club who will find in *The Passing Show* † an interesting quintet of modern plays in verse. They are choice and serious in form and thought.

---

* *Fergy the Guide,* and his moral and instructive lies about beasts, birds, and fishes. By H. S. CANFIELD. With illustrations by Albert D. Blashfield. 12mo. 342 pp. $1.50. 1904. Henry Holt & Co., New York.

† *The Passing Show:* five modern plays in verse. By HARRIET MONROE. 125 pp. Houghton, Mifflin & Co., Boston and New York.

FORESTRY NOTES.

EDITED BY PROFESSOR WILLIAM R. DUDLEY.

THE GREAT FOREST FIRE. The week from Sunday, September 4, to September 11, 1904, was a week of the highest temperature and of the most extensive and disastrous forest fires on record in the Santa Cruz Mountain region. On Wednesday and Thursday, the hottest days, the thermometers registered from 106 to 110 degrees Fahrenheit in many places. No forest fires existed on Saturday, the 3d; on Sunday one appeared on the side of Ben Lomond Mountain, west of Ben Lomond; on Monday a fire broke out on Zeyante Creek; on Tuesday a fire started above the electric-power works on Big Creek, spread with great rapidity, and burned to death one man; on Wednesday fires broke out in all directions above Santa Cruz and Soquel, but the greatest of all near the mills at the head of Pescadero Creek. The latter spread southward for nearly ten miles, entered the California Redwood Park Wednesday night, and by the Monday following, when it was under control, had burned over one third the State's lands, many miles of private property, consumed perhaps a half-dozen homes, including one valuable summer residence, and had made all the roads in that part of the county impassable. Eye-witnesses viewing the basin of San Lorenzo River and its tributaries and the Ben Lomond and Butano ridges on Thursday night represent the scene as appalling. The writer, pursuing his way toward the park on horseback, on half of Friday night, saw the silhouettes of the great redwoods and Douglas spruces on the Butano Ridge miles to the southwest one by one burst into flames that shot to the tops like a flash. The trees then disappeared in the lurid smoke or stood as columns of fire. The air was clear to the north, and the appearance of the great volumes of smoke and flame rolling up from the forests of the ridge was like the eruption of a volcano at night.

Fortunately the State park suffered less than many other virgin tracts of timber in that region. By strenuous efforts the warden and the fire-fighters confined the fire largely to the cut-over and chaparral—the "thrown in" portions of the purchase. The beautiful forest about the Governor's camp and the larger and more valuable part of the park west of the East Waddell remains untouched by fire. Most of the redwoods which were defoliated by the fire will recover their original appearance after the lapse of ten to twenty years, and the burned area can be brought in time back to its former condition, probably much improved if sufficient appropriations are available. But the simple cost of fighting to restrain this fire has cost the State above one thousand four hundred dollars. It would have cost two thousand dollars but for the generous donation of the Southern Pacific Company of the services of its employees, amounting to about five hundred dollars, and the free use of their time given by the thirteen Stanford students, who spent two days and three nights in this business. The State's appropriation for the park for 1904-1905, aside from the Warden's salary, is three thousand five hundred dollars.

The lessons of this fire are pointed and plain. Until the State has efficient forestry and forest-fire laws supported by public opinion it should purchase no more forest land for parks. When the "hot spells" come in August or September, with the wind northeast, and the consequent absence of dampening sea-fogs at night, lumbermen should be required to suppress all fires and watch their property closely, and the State should increase its patrol service sufficiently to discover and suppress in the first stage any outbreak of fire in the mountains. The ranchmen and the owners of summer homes in the mountains are of as much importance as permanent property-holders as the lumbermen, and the law should not fail to protect them.

THE STATE FOREST BILL. This bill has been "prepared by the Bureau of Forestry of the United States Department of Agriculture, in co-operation with the State of California, in accordance with an act of the California Legislature, approved March 16, 1903, which provided for the formulation of a State forest policy." It is "An Act to provide for the protection and management of forest land within the State of California," and will be introduced into the present Legislature. It provides for a State Board of Forestry, consisting of the Governor, the Secretary of State, the Attorney-General, and the State Forester, to be appointed under this law, which shall manage all State Parks and woodlands, and have the power of enforcing all forestry laws on private lands. It provides for co-operative work with counties, towns, or private parties interested in forest lands; for a corps of assistants and their duties; for special assistance by citizens; for fire patrol; for prosecutions and penalties; for restrictions in the use of fire, of engines, etc., in forest lands during the dry season; for clearing along roads and railroads; and finally it provides that moneys paid into the State treasury for penalties shall be held for forest protection.

In the main it appears to be a good law. It is weakest in the most important provisions, fire patrol and restraint on the present methods of lumbering in the dry season. It is thought, however, that the great expense involved in better provisions and present public sentiment do not warrant an ideal law in these directions. An excellent feature is the evident intention to keep the service free from politics. Criticism has been made on section eleven, concerning "assistance and compensation of citizens in fighting fires," which provides that "fire-wardens shall have authority to call on able-bodied citizens, between the ages of sixteen and fifty years, for assistance in putting out fire," and that "compensation for services in fighting fire shall be at the rate of twenty cents per hour." It is argued that this will induce irresponsible parties to set fires, notwithstanding the heavy penalties involved, in order that they may obtain wages for perhaps trivial labor. The writer believes the point well taken. He would modify this provision, would make the fire-patrol much more strict, perfect the plans for *preventing* fire, and simplify the machinery for putting out big fires. Indeed, a great forest fire cannot be controlled by men unaided by favorable atmospheric conditions. He would call attention to another weakness; the State may find itself under this law paying for the firefighting on the lands of great timber-owners, when the latter should be made to patrol their land and suppress their own fires.

It may be said that the Sierra Club ardently desires a good forestry law; and these suggestions are made not as against the law, but to meet objections, and therefore bring to its support as much public opinion as possible. A forestry law along the simplest lines is very much better at this time than no law, and the support of right public sentiment is the best of all.

YOSEMITE PARK. A bill passed the Senate on December 12th, and the House on December 19th, cutting off a large amount of land from the Yosemite National Park, returning it to the Sierra Forest Reserve. It was done to promote mining, and particularly the interests of two small railroads which desire to build electric and other lines into or near Yosemite Valley. The bill cut off considerable groves of sugar pines surrounding both the Tuolumne and Mariposa big trees, besides excluding some big trees from the park. It entirely ignored the report of a commission appointed last year to readjust the lines of the park; and for that reason the President has declared his intention to veto the bill unless it is reconsidered and passed according to the recommendations of the commission. The latter is composed of Major H. M. Chittenden, United States Army Engineer; R. B. Marshall, United States Geological Survey; and Frank Bond, Chief of Drafting Division of the General Land Office. The members are entirely impartial and the best possible choice; R. B. Marshall has been in charge of the Geological Survey's mapping of the Yosemite region for some years, and is perfectly familiar with its topography and forests. The matter may be considered quite safe with President Roosevelt.

It may here be remarked that when the bill for the establishment of a national park at the Vancouver Pinnacles in San Benito County comes before Congress, as it is likely to do this winter, it will be acted on by Congress and the President in accordance with an expert report from the United States Department of Agriculture. The examination and report were made at the suggestion of two members of the Sierra Club.

YOSEMITE VALLEY. The proposed recession of Yosemite Valley to the United States and the incorporation of it with the Yosemite Park surrounding it are likely to meet with opposition, possibly with defeat. Final action in the matter hinges on the attitude of the State Legislature, members of Congress having declared their intention of being guided by the recommendation of the Legislature. Already violent partizanship has been shown by certain newspapers, and the subject seems likely to leave the domain of common sense. Recession to the United States, and a termination of the trust on the part of the State, is very desirable, and has been unanimously approved by the Directors of the Sierra Club. In opposition to it, the emotion chiefly appealed to is that of "State pride." This might be reasonable if the pride of the State for its noblest single scene could be injured by the proposed transfer of management. Few travelers and visitors, however, know or care whether it is administered by the State, the United States, or a private individual, so long as it is preserved in a condition suitable to its natural grandeur. That it is in *California*, everybody knows and remembers, and that to see it one must come to California. The United States, if possessor of it, would be a shadow as compared with California in the recollection of any visitor. Friends of recession should remember to always insist that the present means of approach are poor and entirely inadequate; that the State will not build good roads over lands it has no title to; that no individual will build good and free roads; that the United States, not owning the valley, has no interest in building good roads to it; that if the United States is put in possession of the valley it will probably make appropriations for the adequate accommodation of travel on a scale similar to those for the Yellowstone National Park, and far greater than this State can ever make.

PUBLIC LAND FRAUDS. As evidence of the difficulty encountered in prosecuting offenders against the public-land laws, we have the fact that no conviction has yet been secured of either Benson or Hyde, although President Roosevelt's administration has been resolutely engaged for considerably above a year upon these matters. It has been more fortunate in Oregon; four minor parties—Puter, McKinley, Tarpley, and Mrs. Watson—having suffered conviction, and in this downfall the first-named confessed to facts which led to the indictment of two important personages—United States Senator John H. Mitchell, of Oregon, and former Commissioner of Public Lands Binger Hermann, now a Representative in Congress. The cases will not be decided for some time, but the courage and impartiality of the Administration in bringing to judgment members of its own political party is beyond praise. Rumors of extensive frauds in Idaho and Montana are now current, and the Department of Justice is about to begin investigation.

AMERICAN FORESTRY CONGRESS. A congress of five hundred delegates, the first of its kind, bringing together the forestry, lumber, grazing, mining, and irrigation interests, under the leadership of forestry, was held January 2-6, 1905. The very unusual honor of an address by the President of the United States was conferred upon it, while his Secretary of Agriculture presided over its deliberations, and many distinguished men attended its sessions. The range of subjects under discussion was wide, but the evident aim of the congress was to bring all the varied interests into co-operation and make forestry methods and work helpful and practical to many business interests and a part of the life of the nation. Secretary Wilson said it was desired that forestry should not be considered outside of general industrial life, or a purely Governmental enterprise. The President's address was one of his best and most effective. It deserves to be read as a whole, but perhaps the following quotation will give the central idea of the speech: " The great significance of this congress comes from the fact that henceforth the movement for the conservative use of the forest is to come mainly from within, not from without; from the men who are actively interested in the use of the forest in one way or another, even more than from those whose interest is philanthropic and general. The difference means to a large extent the difference between mere agitation and actual execution." This is what we have looked forward to—namely, the time when public sentiment in favor of a rational treatment of the forests shall be thoroughly awakened, and the great industries which depend on the forests shall come to be as much their true friends as the philanthropist. The President in this speech as well as in his annual message continues to urge the transfer of the care of the forest reserves from the Land Office to the Bureau of Forestry; and it seems to us that this event, when it comes, will mark rather than the Forestry Congress the practical ascendancy in this country of true forestry. It will exert a tremendous influence on the attitude of the dependent industries.

PUBLICATIONS OF THE SIERRA CLUB

Number 33

SIERRA CLUB BULLETIN

Vol. V   No. 4

JUNE, 1905

SAN FRANCISCO, CAL.

1905

SIERRA CLUB BULLETIN

Vol. V. JUNE, 1905 No. 4

CONTENTS:

THE GRADE PROFILE IN ALPINE GLACIAL EROSION . . . . *Willard D. Johnson*	PAGE 271

Plates XXXVI, XXXVII, XXXVIII, XXXIX.

SYSTEMATIC ASYMMETRY OF CREST-LINES IN THE HIGH SIERRA OF CALIFORNIA . . . . *G. K. Gilbert* 279
 Plates XL, XLI, XLII, XLIII.

THE TUOLUMNE CAÑON . . . . *Wm. Frederic Badè*. 287
 Plates XLIV, XLV.

INSCRIPTION FOR THE LECONTE MEMORIAL . . . . *Harriet Monroe*. . . 296

OVER HARRISON'S PASS FROM THE NORTH WITH A PACK-TRAIN . . . *Force Parker* 297
 Plates XLVI, XLVII.

CALIFORNIA FORESTRY LAW (1905) 303

ORGANIZATION OF SIERRA CLUB 310

REPORTS:
 Report of the Secretary 311
 Report of the Treasurer 313

NOTES AND CORRESPONDENCE 314

BOOK REVIEWS . . . . *Wm. Frederic Badè*. 322

FORESTRY NOTES . . . . *William R. Dudley*. 325

All communications intended for publication by the SIERRA CLUB, and all correspondence concerning such publication, should be addressed to the Editor, Elliott McAllister, 228 Crocker Building, San Francisco, California.

Correspondence concerning the distribution and sale of the publications of the Club, and concerning its business generally, should be addressed to the Secretary of the Sierra Club, Room 316, Third Floor, Mills Building, San Francisco, California.

CIRQUE BOWL AND GLACIER.

Head-wall 1,000 feet above glacier in center of picture. Distance from wall to lake in foreground, three quarters of a mile.
From a photograph by N. H. Darton, U. S. Geological Survey.

THE GRADE PROFILE IN ALPINE GLACIAL EROSION.*

By Willard D. Johnson.

It was early asserted of the cañons of the Sierra Nevada that they are essentially the products of glacial erosion. A continuous glacier mass, or ice-cap, was supposed to have covered the summit region of the range, with individual glacier tongues channeling its flanks to the foothills, on the broad western flank descending close to sea-level. These cañons, except as to their lower and older parts, were described as U-troughs. There was no mention, however, of distinctive character in their longitudinal profiles.

My own acquaintance with the phenomena of Pleistocene glaciation of the alpine type had its beginning in the High Sierra, in 1883. At this later date prevailing opinion apparently leaned to quite the opposite view,—that glacial occupation, even here, had been relatively protective of the preglacial topography. It was shown that the earlier announcement had been without sufficient warrant. It appeared that glacier extension on the west had fallen notably short of the range-foot. There was

---

* Read at the International Congress of Arts and Science, St. Louis, Sept. 21, 1904. Reprinted, with changes by the author, from the *Journal of Geology*, October-November, 1904.

a disposition to believe that preglacial forms, including the great cañons, had been merely swept clean of decay products and talus, and sound bed-rock smoothed and polished. Of the class of features to which I have to refer as anomalies of grade, only isolated, striking examples received attention; and these were given place in a catalogue of wonders, without attempt at correlation or explanatory description. In the general denial of quantitative efficiency in glacial erosion they were left unconsidered.

As a maker of topographic maps, I had the topographer's familiarity with the erosion aspects of mountains, though of unglaciated mountains only. By fortunate field association I had acquired as well something of the inquisitiveness of the physiographer as to the origin and development of topographic forms. Yet the scheme of degradation disclosed from the widely commanding summit of Mt. Lyell—the first station occupied in my work of survey in the High Sierra—was one for which I had in no way been prepared. In its dominant characters of ground-plan and grades it was unintelligible. Stream erosion was plainly to be excluded. It is no less clear to me now than upon that first comprehensive view from Lyell that the development of such characters by the agency of running water is theoretically impossible.

Most conspicuously in evidence were remnants of an old topography. These were tabular and high-walled, though on closer examination their seemingly flat surfaces proved to be variously graded. Of inconsiderable area, even collectively, they were none the less striking.*

---

* The Dana, Gibbs, and Koip crests, to the northeast of Mt. Lyell, are good examples. In the Bighorn Mountains, in Wyoming, they are larger and more connected.

ARC OF THE CIRQUE WALL EXCEEDING A SEMICIRCLE.

From lake-end at right, in foreground, to head-wall, one mile of continuous lake. Height of wall, 1,700 feet; of cliff at right, 1,200 feet.

They occurred as elements of the widely meandering divide, or of its principal spurs, and never as minor elevations in the basins thus inclosed. In their outlines, in plan, there was presented a pattern of innumerable cirques, as a rule intersecting, and of approximately equal radii though unequal lengths of arc. Often enough to suggest a tendency, this length of arc approached, or even a little exceeded, the half-circle. In such exceptional cases flat-topped arms of the upland on either side made gently graded descent, ending in rounded shoulders still overlooking the basins. These sharp outlines were suggestive of nothing so much as the scattered remnants of a sheet of dough on the biscuit-board, after the biscuit-tin has done its work. The cirque walls, obviously, were walls of sapping and recession. And in a measure, therefore, the greater arcs, thus scalloped in detail, inclosing the basins, were arcs of recession also.

The tables rarely occurred wide apart, but in clusters or short chains. The cirques also were noticeably clustered, alternately, on opposite sides of the divide, and the tabular survivals of the old surface were commonly confined to these sections of the divide, between its more pronounced meanders. Where the old surfaces were grouped, a broadly domed divide as a rule was traceable across them; but detached, they presented as many differently inclined single planes.

In the early development of bad-land forms out of a soft plain there is scalloping in plan, though in less clean arcs than the cirques exhibit. But one characteristic feature of the cirque, regarded as a hollow, had no analogue in these accepted type-forms of running-water erosion—on early and strong grades. The cirque hollow was a true amphitheater; its walls, or precipitous slopes, descended, not to a funnel-point, but to a floor, approximately level. And the breadth of the amphitheater on its floor commonly exceeded even the imposing measure of its depth.

The basins about which the cirques were ranged as alcoves, each contained a central draining cañon. In each, tributary cañons, starting at the cirques, converged toward this central cañon-head, rapidly shallowing and entering at high levels.* It is this point of drainage convergence in the basin which more properly corresponds, perhaps, to the funnel-point of the miniature bad-land form.

Within the basins,—that of the Tuolumne, which I had followed to Lyell, and others subsequently visited,—all surfaces were glaciated, exhibiting abundant polish, striæ, and moutonnée details. Only the crests, with their occasional tabular elements, were free from these evidences. Postulating glaciation, the serrate ridges and the high tables alone had been emergent from the Pleistocene ice; the basins had been "névé fields"; and the central cañons, channel troughs of glacial escape.

Migration of the divides by cirque-wall recession, with accompanying degradation of a thousand feet or more, was to be inferred; but, on the other hand, were the central cañons of the basins wholly preglacial, and merely cleared out?

The troughs at their heads were abruptly deep, often profoundly deep. To notable distances their floors, start-

---

* Such a cañon head, central to a meander arc of the divide, is developed in type form in the basin of the Merced, five miles southwest of Lyell.

PLATE XXXVIII.

A STEP IN THE GRADE PROFILE.

ing full width, were level, holding fiord lakes; or else, more commonly, they had been aggraded to ribbon meadows, on which their streams meandered. Figuratively, I characterized them as valleys down at the heel. But at points far apart compensation of grade was had in steps. Here the draining stream often dropped in a thin sheet, without notch of its own making, or spread in braided cascades. Appeal to rock structure as a determining factor in the development by running water of horizontal elements of such magnitude in the long profile would be futile. The rock of the basins about Mt. Lyell was granitic. Its only large structures were joints—if possible faulting might be disregarded. The joint systems were of all strikes and dips; and some were horizontal. But the preglacial streams responded to such controls in the same manner that present streams do; and the present streams were not at grade. At the foot of each step was an alluvial cone and a wash-plain. The streams were engaged in filling. But, obviously, in many instances, they had before them an immense task of grade adjustment; and the measure of that task was the measure only in part of the glacial degradation.

On the tread of the steps descending to the trough head, where the beginnings of post-glacial refilling were less appreciable, there was persistent occurrence of reversed grades. In such cases the long floor was ponded backward from the polished brink of a cross-cliff, or cascade descent. In the cirques frequently rock-basin lakes lay deep against the curving talus of the head-wall, visibly shallowing forward. There seemed to be revealed a tendency of the ice-stream vigorously to sink its valley at the head, where its feeding snows gather most deeply;

and, as in specific instances the distribution of tributary streams suggested, to sink it again wherever the entrance of a tributary tended to deepen it locally. At least it was apparent that forward grade of bed is not essential to glacier motion.

Mt. Lyell in plan was a four-rayed star of thin arêtes. A small glacier occupied the cirque-basin, or amphitheater, facing northward; and three other amphitheaters, empty of ice, opened severally east and west and south. There was no vestige of an upland surface. It was hardly to be doubted, however, that a stage of plateau wasting had recently been closed here also, and the stage of sinking initiated. Elsewhere combs and spires associated with the tables, though invariably falling short of their high levels, were recognizable as evanescent final forms in the transition from a stream-modeled upland, mantled with residual gravel, to a relative lowland of glacial truncation displaying only sound, bare rock. The old surface had not been worn down; it had been cut away. Sapping and rude planation had been the process —in the summit area, back from the channel-trough heads. On that hypothesis the anomalous topography of wide floors and upright forms in great variety at once became interpretable. Its unit in plan was the geometrical figure of the cirque. And the glacier makes the cirque.

Among the schrunds of various systems sharply lining the Lyell glacier the great arc of the open "bergschrund," a little out upon the ice, closely paralleled the arc of the wall. It seemed possible that the bergschrund penetrated to the wall-foot, along the line of its floor, and that sapping there resulted from some special action to which this

THE BERGSCHRUND.

Height from schrund to flat upland, about 800 feet. Notch in skyline, point of inosculation with opposing cirque beyond, and beginning of thin arête.

From a photograph by N. H. Darton, U. S. Geological Survey.

exceptional opening gave rise. With the aid of all hands from camp, therefore, a descent and direct observation was undertaken. The schrund opened to the wall, and then continued, with rock on one side, for twenty or thirty feet deeper. The total depth was estimated to be one hundred and fifty feet. At bottom, the width between walls ranged from five to ten feet. The floor, so far as followed,—perhaps one hundred feet,—was approximately level, though made up of fallen masses of rock and ice. Observation was conducted with the aid of a sputtering candle, in a rain from the dripping walls. This water seemed to result from local melting; there was no stream entering at the surface. The rock of the wall face was much riven, though undecayed. Disrupted masses were in all stages of dislodgment. Some were to be seen incorporated in the glacier wall at its foot. Open seams in the rock-wall were partly filled with films or plates of ice, thinned by melting, and removable. Icicles of great size were abundant, and the rock fragments of the floor were ice-coated. To venture an inference from a single observation at a single point, the bergschrund foot is a line of frost-weathering, relatively vigorous, because freezing and thawing, there, alternate at short intervals, as compared with the annual intervals outside; and of quarrying, because the glacier acts as the efficient agent of removal. I have failed of opportunity to repeat and extend these early observations, and the hypothesis in explanation is slightly supported; but independently of explanation, the fact of sapping and recession in this summit region seems to be unmistakably attested by the sharply delimited plateaus, their connecting thin arêtes, and the rude platform from which they rise. On the evidence of these same characters it is apparent no less that the process was rapid and its period short.

But head-wall sapping, with planation, is only one process. Scour is another; and scour acts vertically. The greater basins, doubtless preglacial in their outlines on the range flanks, have been expanded over the summit region, and the wide-open, shallow troughs there are essentially the products of glacial erosion, by head-wall recession; and they are the measure of that erosion only in part. The central cañons, on the other hand, as channel troughs of glaciation are doubtless preglacial as to their courses. And in their central parts they may have been deep. But in their upper parts, on the evidence of their grade profiles, they are to be regarded, in the main, as products of glacial erosion also.

The sensibly level elements in these profiles, their great length often, and the common occurrence of grade reversal in the more exposed floors above the trunk-cañon head, seem to imply that the glacier advances from the bottom, escaping from under its own weight; that its lines of flow gradually rise, seeking to equalize depth and load, because ablation planes away and thins the forward part; and that, correspondingly, along the bed, both pressure and velocity, and therefore erosive vigor, diminish.

EASTWARD FROM MT. CONNESS.

In the foreground is the upper edge of a small glacier with its head cliff and bergschrund. Farther away the descending continuation of the same cliff springs from a schrund line, the exact position of which is masked by a lingering snow-drift.

SYSTEMATIC ASYMMETRY OF CREST-LINES IN THE HIGH SIERRA OF CALIFORNIA.*

By G. K. Gilbert.

The substance of the present paper was communicated to the Section of Physiography of the Congress of Arts and Science at St. Louis last September. The section had just listened to Mr. Johnson's paper on "The Grade Profile in Alpine Glacial Erosion." Mr. Johnson stated that since his first observations in the Sierra in 1883 his ideas as to the explanation of the phenomena had undergone development, and he regretted that he had been unable to revisit the region for purposes of verification. It was therefore a matter of gratification that I was able to supplement his presentation by the statement that during two seasons of exploration in the glaciated district of the Sierra I had found his hypothesis of cirque development by glacial sapping of the utmost utility in the explanation of the topography. It happened also that its utility was illustrated in my discussion of the origin of the special features to which my own communication referred.

In the higher part of the Sierra Nevada the glacial cirque is a conspicuous feature of the topography. Each main crest of the great mountain mass, as a rule, is bordered on each side by a row of cirques facing outward. Separating the cirques on the same side of the main ridge are subordinate ridges or spurs. Gradually

---

* Reprinted from the *Journal of Geology*, Vol. XII, pp. 579-585.

the cirques unite to form glacial troughs, and these troughs are separated, at a somewhat lower level, by ridges constituting subordinate features of the range. Some of the ridges between cirques and between troughs are equally steep on both sides of their crest-lines, but many—a large minority—are notably steeper on one side than on the other, and this asymmetry of cross-profile is definitely related to the cardinal points. Ridges trending east and west are steeper on the north side than on the south, those trending north and south are steeper on the east side, and those trending northwest and southeast are steeper on the northeast side. In general, the gentler slope has the grade of a steep roof, and it is often clothed by rock fragments approximately *in situ*. Ordinarily it is too steep for the horse, but is readily scaled by the mountaineer. As a rule, the steeper slope either is constituted by, or else includes, an abrupt cliff which at most points cannot be climbed. Figure 1 of Plate XLI shows a group of high ridges in which the steeper faces are turned to the north, and Figure 2 a group in which they are turned to the northeast.

These slopes are not controlled by rock structure. The principal rock is granite, and this granite is in large part structureless. Where it is traversed by joint systems the details of sculpture are greatly influenced by the joints, but the trend and slope of the greater features are independent of the joints.

A little reflection shows that the distribution of steep slopes is correlated with the alimentation of Pleistocene glaciers. The southward slopes of the east-west ridges, because turned toward the sun, lost more snow by melting and evaporation than did the northward slopes, and a

FIG. 1.—EASTWARD FROM MT. GARDINER.
Compare the southward (right) slopes with the north-facing cliffs.
From a photograph by J. N. Le Conte.

FIG. 2.—SOUTHEASTWARD FROM ALTA MEADOWS.
Compare the northeast-facing walls of the high glaciated valleys with their southwest-facing walls.

smaller fraction of the snowfall they received remained to nourish glaciers. Thus the glaciers resting against the southward slopes were comparatively ill-fed, and the glaciers of the northward slopes were comparatively wellfed. The north-south ridges may be assumed to have been swept, then as now, by dominant westerly winds, which carried much snow from the westward slopes over the crests to the eastward slopes, where it accumulated; and thus the glaciers resting against the eastward slopes were better nourished than those of the westward. These peculiarities of snow distribution may be readily observed at the present time. If one stands, late in summer, upon a peak in the midst of the glaciated district and looks toward the east or north, he sees bare rock, with only here and there a small remnant of snow; but if he turns toward the west or south, he looks upon a patchwork of snow and rock in which the predominance of the rock may not at once be apparent. Figure 2 of Plate XLII illustrates the relations of surviving snow-banks in early summer to northward and southward slopes.

It can hardly be doubted that the distribution of Pleistocene snow deposition stands in causal relation with the distribution of asymmetry in the crest-lines of the minor ridges. And it is in explanation of this relation that I avail myself of Johnson's hypothesis. Each glacier which receives more snow on one side than on the other adjusts its cross-profile to a condition of equilibrium by moving away from the region of greater supply to the region of lesser supply. This lateral motion is of course combined with the general, and more rapid, forward motion of the glacier, but it is nevertheless competent to produce at the side of the glacier phenomena quite similar to those at the head. Figure 1 shows diagrammatically the ground plan of a glacier flowing northward. The greatest snow accumulation is in the cirque, *AA*, where precipitation is at a maximum, where depletion through solar influences is at a minimum, and where circling cliffs protect against removal by the wind. There is great accumulation also along the west margin, *BB*, where the snow drifted by the westerly winds comes to rest in the shelter of the west wall of the glacier trough. Along the eastern border, *CC*, the snow deposit is comparatively small, because of exposure to the westerly winds. The resulting lines of ice-flow are as drawn. Moving directly away from the walls of the cirque, the glacier makes and annually renews the bergschrund *ab*. Moving obliquely away from the west wall of the trough, the glacier similarly produces the minor bergschrund *bc*, and this minor bergschrund leads to sapping and the production of a cliff, just as the major bergschrund causes the cirque cliff. Thus the west wall of the trough is kept steep, and is thereby contrasted not only with the east

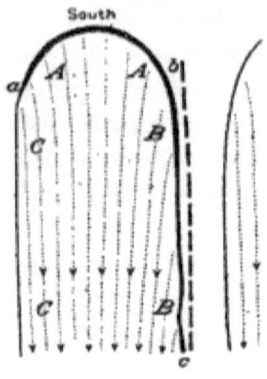
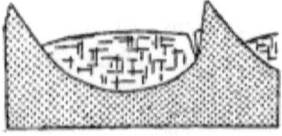

FIG. 1.—Diagrammatic ground plan and section of a glacier.

The heavy line *abc* marks the position of the bergschrund. Dotted lines show direction of ice flow. The broken line marks the crest of the spur separating the glacier from its neighbor on the west.

FIG. 1.—NEAR MT. MCCLURE.
Spur between two glacial amphitheaters, showing schrund line.

FIG. 2.—WESTWARD FROM MT. HOFFMAN.
Compare the glacial topography of the north (right) face of ridge, with the nonglacial profiles toward the south.
From a photograph by A. C. Lawson.

wall of the same trough, but with the east wall of the adjacent trough, so that the rock crest between the two troughs is not symmetric.

Usually in viewing a cirque it is possible to trace about its wall a somewhat definite line separating a cliff or steeper slope above from a gentler, usually scalable, slope below. This line I conceive to mark the base of the bergschrund at a late stage in the excavation of the cirque basin. I have called it in my notes "the schrund line." It can usually be traced for some little distance beyond the cirque, and sometimes for several miles on one wall or other of the glacier trough. Advancing along the trough wall, it descends gradually with a slope which may be assumed to represent the gradient of the ice surface, that surface having been somewhat higher than the schrund line. Its expression outside a cirque may be seen in the lower figure of Plate XLI and the upper figures of Plates XLII and XLIII.

At a somewhat lower level than that to which the preceding paragraphs apply, the Pleistocene glaciers occupied a smaller share of the surface, and there are considerable unglaciated areas. The photographs shown in Plate XLIII were made in this region. The upper view is westward up the trough of a glacier. Beyond the head of this trough is another glacier trough descending westward, and the dividing ridge was partly destroyed by the head-erosion of the glaciers, so that the typical amphitheater is not shown. The south wall of the trough is steep, and shows distinct evidence of sapping. The cliff at top, being composed of thoroughly jointed granite, does not stand vertical, and the fragments recently fallen from it have built a talus which conceals the schrund line.

But it is evident that here the sapping action at the schrund line was more active than the glacial erosion lower down on the slope, so as to create a sort of shoulder or terrace near that level. Stating the interpretation in another way, the excessive alimentation along the south wall of the glacier was here developing a branch gla and a tributary cirque. This cirque was eating its way back into the ridge bounding the glacier. On the opposite side of the ridge, shown in the lower view, are gentle slopes, largely of preglacial origin, but there are also faintly developed cirques, from which small ice-streams flowed toward the south.

At still lower levels are many ridges along which Pleistocene glaciers were developed on one side only—the north or northeast side, so far as observed. The south and southwest slopes retain the preglacial facies, and retain also the actual preglacial topography, except for such equable reduction of surface as may have been accomplished by aqueous and atmospheric agencies. The direction of ice movement in such cases was not parallel to the ridge axis, but approximately normal to it. The glacial excavation did not always take the character of a series of cirques, but sometimes produced a continuous cliff, running with moderate undulation parallel to the ridge axis.

I have no photograph representing this topographic type in its purity. Figure 2 of Plate XLII, exhibiting a ridge of greater altitude, serves to show a somewhat similar cliff, wrought by glacial head-erosion, but imperfectly divided into cirques, and culminating in a crest from which nonglacial profiles descend in the opposite direction. But the example differs from the type in the

FIG. 1.—NORTH SIDE OF GOAT CREST.
The view is from Kid Peak, and looks westward along the crest.

FIG. 2.—SOUTH SIDE OF GOAT CREST.
The view is from Buck Peak, and looks northeastward. Kid Peak is at the extreme right. The bare spots under the crest are shallow cirques.

stronger expression of the ice-work, in the comparatively high grade of the nonglacial profiles, and in the fact that those profiles, as seen in the photograph, conceal south-facing cirques of some magnitude.

The asymmetry of these lower ridges is more pronounced than that of any others, because instead of contrasting two phases of glacial erosion they contrast glacial with nonglacial. It is worthy of note also, though not strictly germane to my subject, that the contrast in sculpture of the two ridge slopes serves to compare the efficiency of subaërial degradation with that of one phase of glacial degradation. The glaciers of these low ridges, being able to develop only on the slopes most favorable for snow accumulation, marked the lower limit of névé conditions and were the feeblest of all the Sierra glaciers.

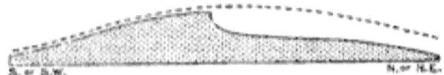

Fig. 2.—Diagrammatic cross-section of a ridge glaciated on one side only, with hypothetic profile (broken line) of preglacial surface.

Their lives must have been short, for they could exist only when glacial conditions were at or near a maximum; they began long after and ceased long before the glaciers of the higher districts. The topographic features they produced were subject to the dulling influence of atmospheric and aqueous attack during both interglacial and postglacial times. And yet the degradation they accomplished was far greater than that of nonglacial agents working on the opposite sides of the same ridges—agents working not only during the same time, but during all interglacial epochs and during postglacial time. It is true that we cannot measure the nonglacial work, which consisted of a general reduction of surface without notable change of form; but whatever the amount, we may assume that it would have been the same on both slopes of the same ridge, had there been no glaciers. The visible ice-made hollows therefore represent the local excess of glacial over nonglacial degradation.

THE TUOLUMNE CAÑON.

By William Frederic Badè.

In the heart of the Sierra, more than eight thousand five hundred feet (about 2,616 meters) above the level of the Pacific, lies a truly alpine valley familiar to every mountaineer who has visited the regions north of Yosemite. It is vain now to regret the association of the word "meadows" with the romantic Indian name Tuolumne. The hunters and prospectors who valued a valley chiefly as an oasis for pack-animals were first at the christening and have succeeded in attaching the name of a common drudge to a queen of the Sierras. Many are the little rivers that know the way to this valley. They are mad little rivers, full of song and fury. Though often hidden in deep gorges, mostly carved through solid granite, they always are heard, now leaping a precipice with shouts of thunder, now singing the joys of a gentler career amid ferns and pines. All of them are true Jordans,—"descenders,"—but fortunately none of them, like the Kern, are found dead at the end. Long ago the valley was a famous hunting-ground of the Mono Indians, whose shapely obsidian arrows still dot the ground where in other days they bit the sod. Its upper end, where the Dana and Lyell Forks unite to form the Tuolumne, is an ideal camping-ground. Last summer the Sierra Club chose it a second time as its rendezvous and sent out thence its climbing parties to Dana, Lyell, and Ritter. These mountains, together with Gibbs, Unicorn, Cathedral, and Conness, form the valley's nearer or remoter periphery, an imposing circle of snowy summits. In the valley, also, the snow lingers far into the summer, but a multitudinous procession of showy spring flowers is constantly treading on the edge of the snow-banks, pushing them up the pine-clad slopes to their last impregnable strongholds. Thence sally forth the six or seven glacier-born streams that join the Tuolumne in and below the Meadows. They make of it a turbulent river that even late in the summer would be dangerous, if not quite impossible, to ford on its foamy speedways.

Immediately below the Meadows the river plunges into a cañon that deserves to be counted among the greatest natural wonders on earth. For a long time it was considered impassable. In places the walls rise in almost vertical precipices to a height of more than five thousand feet. Though the cañon is scarcely more than thirty miles long, the fall of the river within that distance amounts to five thousand two hundred feet. It would be hard to imagine a wilder career for a river than that upon which the Tuolumne enters during this part of its course. Captain Clarence King, after a futile attempt to follow it through the cañon, is said to have pronounced such an undertaking impossible for any "creature without wings." But a few adventurous explorers have traversed it since then, and on the 20th of last July (1904) a party of fourteen men, organized by E. T. Parsons, started on a successful knapsack trip through the cañon. Fortunately all were picked mountaineers, inured to the wilds, for it proved a strenuous four days' trip full of adventure as well as indescribably magnificent scenery. The writer found opportunity to make only a few general notes on the flora and fauna. Both are extremely interesting, and so rich and varied that it would require months to make anything like an exhaustive study of its animal life, to say nothing of the vegetation. The general trend of the cañon is a little north of west. This fact entails a great variety of light effects during the course of the day. The width of the cañon varies constantly, sometimes narrowing to little more than a hundred feet of churning water, sometimes widening to a quarter of a mile of forest and blooming meadow. It should be noted also that the course of the river is much more contorted than the geological survey map would lead one to suppose.

With provisions for four or five days in our knapsacks we left the main party at the Tuolumne Meadows and followed the south side of the river to the entrance of the cañon. The rough work began soon after we reached the point where Conness Creek enters from the north. Below the wonderful White Cascades, beside a magnificent trout-pool that furnished a palatable contribution to our menu, we ate our first luncheon. That afternoon we encountered earthquake taluses overgrown with extraordinarily dense thickets and made comparatively little headway. Opposite the entrance of Return Creek cañon the granite walls are very steep, with numerous abutments resembling giant towers in relief that lead the eye to dizzy altitudes. It was no doubt partially due to the extreme height of these stupendous cañon walls that we seemed unable to get past the entrance of Return Creek. At every turn of the narrow stream-bed the beetling parapets were still looming above us. A never-to-be-forgotten night overtook our party on the edge of a series of magnificent, abruptly descending granite terraces over which the river plunged seven or eight hundred feet into unseen depths, a furious mass of roaring foam and spray. Under some daring pines at the edge of the precipice we built our camp-fires and cooked our evening meal. A few minutes' use of rod and reel again sufficed to add to our menu a delicious *entrée* of trout. Surroundings more abysmally grand it would have been hard to imagine. The sunset glow on the heights above, the witchery of the firelight on pines and rocks, the reverberating thunder of the river's batteries, the white glimmer of endless falls far down the cañōn, the brilliance of the stars, the flutter and scream of wild creatures terrestrial and aerial, the far-flung shadows of lowering cliffs gliding through every gamut of form under the light of the rising moon—these and many other assets, in extraordinary measure, were among the features of that indescribable night. One can only imagine what re-enforcement the imagination of Dante might have gained from the contemplation of scenes like these. But it was not difficult to think of the somber bard treading the giant stairways in the footsteps of Virgil. Yet a voice of antiquity a hundred thousand times remoter than that of Dante or Virgil was speaking in the roar of water that rose from the gorge—the voice of the river grinding and chiseling still deeper the chasm at which it had labored for ages.

The writer is penning these words in one of the most picturesque* parts of the Old World, where at morn and eve

---

* The Upper Rhine.

ONE OF THE FALLS.
(Probably the Tuolumne Falls. See BULLETIN, Vol. I, p. 202.)

A SERIES OF CASCADES.
From photographs by the author.

> "The splendor falls on castle walls,
> And snowy summits old in story."

But these skies, always overladen with moisture, do not furnish material for such gorgeous tapestries as the sun weaves at dawn and sunset on the crests of the Sierra Nevada. Nor have any ruins of the castled Rhine, perched never so loftily, appealed to my mind and imagination with the sublime grandeur of Tuolumne Castle. Perhaps these comparisons are too subjective. Let them serve merely to emphasize from another point of view the stupendous height and massiveness of the Tuolumne's rock fastnesses. Like those of the Grand Cañon of the Colorado, their appeal to the imagination is absolute without the legendary glory of dead robber barons. It is to be hoped that our Government will some time build a trail through this wonderland so that it may be made accessible to those who cannot heed the call of the wild when it leads through and over such obstacles as we encountered on our further progress through the cañon. These obstacles, while not formidable to a seasoned mountaineer, bar out every one who, besides experience in climbing, does not possess a large measure of health and endurance. What the character of the difficulties is has been sufficiently described by R. M. Price in a previous number of the SIERRA CLUB BULLETIN.* The writer, therefore, does not deem it necessary to traverse this ground again.

The second day we passed through what is probably the wildest and deepest part of the cañon. The river now had gone stark mad. One who has not seen the Tuolumne during this part of its course would hardly

---
* Vol. I., No. 6.

deem a river capable of such acrobatic feats, such headlong abandon. Its behavior is in large measure due to the unique character of the stream-bed, composed of smooth, polished granite, and often inclined at an angle of fifty-five degrees. With the friction reduced to a minimum, the water responds to the pull of gravity with an almost incredible momentum. Occasionally the stream in its descent dashes into a depression shaped like the bowl of a gigantic spoon, and on emerging soars heavenward in a majestic white column of spray. Here it resembles a great brilliantly white apron flapping in the breeze, there it is some foam-born goddess of the Sierran wilderness seeking to disengage herself from a thousand yards of filmy lace. In one place a number of smaller spoon-like depressions on the surface of a sharply inclined plane produce the effect of half a dozen beautiful ever-changing fountains that seem to shoot up through the swiftly gliding waters. The writer, with the approval of our party, would suggest the name "Fountain Cascade" for this unique phenomenon. In some of the longer cascades the speed of the water, occasioned by the conditions described above, leads to other spectacular phenomena rarely or never seen elsewhere. Thus it happens not infrequently that the flying current impinges against a giant boulder tossed into the channel by an earthquake, or against some well-buttressed ledge that successfully resists the impact of the river. The collision resembles nothing so much as an enormous explosion covered by a pall of misty smoke through which bombs of spray and fantastic water-wheels are hurled with titanic energy. Even the rainbows spanning the tumult in brilliant segments seem to break with every

COLONIES OF TREES HAVE ESTABLISHED THEMSELVES.

FOREST, CLIFFS, AND CASCADES.

new shock of the rushing waters. The writer must confess to a great curiosity to see the river at such points in early spring, when it carries a double volume of water. The spectacle must be awe-inspiring in the extreme.

To those of us who thought the cañon more or less devoid of vegetation the experiences of these days brought much enlightenment. While in many places it is a deep boulder-choked gorge of bare granite, we found small forested areas throughout its course. Wherever erosion, glacial or post-glacial, has widened the floor of the cañon and permitted the accumulation of alluvium colonies of trees have established themselves. Many of these miniature forests are wondrously beautiful in their setting of lofty cliffs and snowy cascades. Most of them have remained untouched by fire. Straight tapering boles of mighty sugar and yellow pines reach far up into the noonday twilight that reigns under their feathery arches. In the upper reaches of the cañon the make-up of the tree societies is about the same as in Yosemite. The sugar pine, yellow pine, spruce, and incense cedar are the social magnates. Long stretches of the river's margin were found lined with dense hedges of azalea (*Azalea occidentalis*), whose magnificent bouquets of creamy, fragrant blossoms are a delight to the wayfarer and at least a partial compensation for the difficulties encountered in penetrating the thickets. The densest chaparral we encountered was a succession of azalea thickets in a part of the cañon known as Pate Valley. This is a very considerable expansion of the river gorge where Piute Creek enters from the north. In order to reach the river it was at times necessary to crawl through the thickets on hands and feet. The floor of the valley is comparatively flat and covered for a mile or more with an almost pure growth of young incense cedar. Of the many exquisitely beautiful heathworts that flourish in the Sierra Nevada the cañon exhibits a richly varied assortment, and in the grottoes about the falls and among the giant boulders along the river's edge the bryologist doubtless would find an equally choice assortment of mosses and liverworts. We had to keep going so constantly that it was impossible to make any detailed observations.

There were plenty of fresh and well-trodden deer-paths. A number of herds must manage to make a prosperous living in the cañon. One morning early, in a dense thicket of incense cedar, the writer chanced upon a deer-yard—a place where for months they had been accustomed to gather and rest during the day. Two fine specimens were in possession. Evidently expecting some of their own kind, they tarried until they saw me emerging from the thicket, when they were off like arrows from the bow. It seemed only too evident in Pate Valley that would-be sportsmen, in spite of wardens and regulations, sometimes make murderous descents on them. During the night we spent in this valley, a bear, attracted no doubt by the smell of bacon, paid us a friendly visit. When, awakened by the breaking of twigs, two of us sat up, he departed with a precipitateness that left nothing to be desired. Undoubtedly this part of the cañon is a rendezvous also for bears and cougars. The evidences of their presence were never hard to find, although they themselves managed to keep out of sight, forewarned by our necessarily somewhat noisy progress through the cañon. Coyotes were neither heard nor seen on this trip, but at Lake Tioga they made night hideous with their blood-freezing howls.

As might be expected, the cañon is a good breeding-place for rattlesnakes. We encountered a large number. Most of them seemed shy and disinclined to give warning until attacked. I secured one specimen, a diamond rattler, with eleven rattles and one button. This *Crotalus* was the only one that disputed the right of way with me.

On approaching the upper Hetch-Hetchy Valley, during the fourth day's climb, the vegetation of the cañon changed considerably. There was a large intermixture of scrubby oak, and open places frequently were covered with *Rhus*. We had descended from an altitude of eight thousand five hundred feet to an altitude of four thousand, and were entering upon the zone of foothill vegetation. The water of the river also had grown warmer and had lost something of its crystal clearness. Trout seemed to be less abundant and less inclined to take the fly. The river, checking the headlong momentum of its plunges over a thousand falls, began to loiter in immense pools that might have been taken for lakes. Enormous specimens of the California black oak, worthy of the traditions of Dodona, spread their shapely crowns against the horizon. On the sides of the cañon wherever taluses afforded a foothold, the goldcup oak in scattered groves reared its noble arches.

In the gloaming of the fourth day we reached the Hetch-Hetchy Valley and heard that the main party of the Sierra Club had just arrived and was encamping half a mile farther down the river, where we found a friendly reception that next morning. Relieved of anxiety about provisions, we made another meal of what we had left and slept the sleep of exhaustion and contentment under a large oak that in all the long years of its life probably never spread its boughs over such a party.

Our clothing was mostly shreds, and our shoes, in not a few cases, had to be excused from further service. But we had conquered the cañon, hitherto traversed by only a few hardy explorers, and had brought with us a rich store of memories; for our thoughts will long revert to these days of climbing over rocks and earthquake taluses, past beetle-browed cliffs and spray-beaten precipices; to pictures of meadows, riotous with bloom and deeply set in granite frames; to starry nights in woodlands so beautiful that the wanderer longs to linger there and forget the great busy world so far away.

INSCRIPTION FOR THE LECONTE MEMORIAL

Dedicated July 3, 1904.

Here, traveler, pause upon thine upward way,
Enter and rest, and search thy soul to-day.
High are the mountains where thy feet would fare —
Let wisdom lead, that peace may bless thee there.

— HARRIET MONROE.

KERN RIVER AND KAWEAH PEAKS, LOOKING SOUTH FROM HARRISON'S PASS, JULY 24, 1902.

From a photograph by Dr. J. H. Johnson.

OVER HARRISON'S PASS FROM THE NORTH WITH A PACK-TRAIN.

By Force Parker.

Harrison's Pass is about 13,000 feet in altitude—the highest pass in the United States. It opens north and south on the King's-Kern Divide,—that is, on the range separating the more beautiful valley of the King's River from the grander cañon of the Kern.

Were the trail passable in the true sense, the pass would be to mountain-lovers what the Panama Canal will be to commerce. It would save the long hot detour of many days over the Kearsarge Pass and the broiling sun of the Owen's Valley, or the other long roundabout trip by way of the Giant Forest, by which last route the traveler may have come into the mountains.

In July, 1902, Dr. J. H. Johnson and I had been camping for three days at Lake Reflection on the King's River side of the pass. We had been in the mountains for six weeks; provisions were running short, and we were anxious to get over into the Kern Valley on the way home. There were rumors that the Pass could be crossed with safety only on the snow, which becomes soft and treacherous in midsummer. But the Doctor was obdurate and I curious; so we decided to try the pass.

The pass must be about six or eight rocky, steep, and winding miles from Lake Reflection, and the way is an undefined and scattered sheep-trail, which we had to rebuild and repair as we went along. We had five horses, and there were but two of us; so we were accordingly careful. The trail proper runs from East Lake, which is below Lake Reflection on the South Fork of Bubb's Creek; but instead of going back to East Lake, which is where the Mt. Brewer division of the Sierra Club established Camp Le Conte on the 1902 outing, we cut across the ridge, which is very steep and rocky and without sign of trail. We started shortly after sunrise, and getting into the cañon leading to the pass we worked our horses on up the mountain meadows and beside several beautiful small lakes. In one place we crossed boulders under which we could hear the water roaring and rumbling in the caverns beneath; but we could not reach it or even see it.

Finally, at 1:20 o'clock in the afternoon we stood on the snow-fields gazing up the shale slide leading to the gap of the Pass. It is called a pass; but, as has been said, it will be useful only when the Government has placed a derrick there.

We had intended to camp for the night at the last meadow below, but in our enthusiasm had passed it by mistake, and having come up a difficult and dangerous defile we resolved to push on rather than go back to the meadow. There is neither wood nor horse-feed at the foot of the Pass.

It was the middle of July and the middle of the day. The snow was soft and deep; and although we proceeded with great caution and made many tests of its sustaining power, several animals had floundered in the snow and we were compelled to unpack them and dig them out. This was all at the foot as we approached the shale slide leading to the Pass. At its very foot our best riding-animal, a beautiful creature, went through the snow with her front feet at the edge of a snow-basin some six feet deep, and turning a three-quarters somersault came to a stop in its bottom with her feet in the air. Her body fitted the basin so tightly that although she beat the air with her feet and threw up clouds of snow in her struggles to get out it was of no avail. She was "hard a-ground." Whereupon one of us sat gently and caressingly upon her lovely head while the other shoveled in snow on one side of her body and out from under on the other until we rolled her over and on to her feet. This took time, for she resented the situation every time she regathered strength and opportunity to struggle. The snow basin had been caused, as is usual in such cases, by the heat of the sun on a large rock, which now lay at its bottom, like a huge ant-lion in its circular trap pit. On the sharp rock the good horse had cut her legs and back shamefully. In fact every horse's feet and legs were bleeding and they left a thin trail of blood on the snow.

After extricating the mare from the snow basin we began to cut a zigzag trail up the shale slide towards the gap of the Pass, some 1,000 feet [*] above us. The slide is so steep that the shale continually slips and slides as the snow and ice melt and rocks frequently roll down.

We would cut fifty or one hundred yards of trail at a time and then lead the horses up to our work. We had as working-tools a hand-pick and a spade. At one turn in the zigzag the shale went out from under a horse's feet and in the consequent plunging the entire pack and sad-

---

[*] Mr. Robert D. Pike, in his most accurate and excellent account of the trip over the Pass from the opposite side of the Divide, has modestly said: "A vertical distance of about 700 feet."

dle slid off and rolled and bumped down to the snow below.

We worked on through the afternoon. Then the sunlight failed and the stars came out. We were not half-way up the slide, although we had worked unceasingly since 1:20 P. M.

About midnight the moon slid into the gap above, and we worked on surrounded by the pinnacles shining with added solemnity and grandeur in the moonlight. It was very cold by this time, and the shale, frozen by the trickling water from the everlasting snows above, held more firmly than it had during the day. It did not slide in small avalanches so frequently, and fewer rocks came down. The animals were so weary—they had had no rest, food, or water since morning—that they were perfectly tractable and quiet both in the shadows and the moonlight of the cañon. I doubt that we could have succeeded in taking them up during the day, but at night they would sleep standing, as we worked at the trail.

About one hundred yards from the top we struck quite solid rock on one side; on the other sheer cliff; in the center solid ice, which we simply could not work with our pick and spade. So we went at the rocks and occasionally turned up pieces the size of small trunks. We had removed all packs and propped them along the trail as we moved up. One pack had been placed under the nose of an old horse who was dozing peacefully in the moonlight, when a descending boulder, loosened in our trail-making, bounded accurately under his chin and carried away a kyack to the snow-field in the glimmering distance below. Hop-skip, down it went, the amphitheater announcing in echoes its downward journey and

SUMMIT OF HARRISON'S PASS, JULY 24, 1902.
From a photograph by Dr. J. H. Johnson.

the scattering of its contents of cans and kettles along the way.

In carrying and recarrying packages and provisions, and in leading horses we crossed Harrison's Pass many times that night.

The last portion of our climb was literally up a flight of stone stairs which we had cut out of the cliff's side. So we stripped the horses of saddles and bridles and of everything except light rope halters around their necks, and up the rocks they climbed each one giving a grunt of relief as the sweeping slope of the Kern Valley broke upon his vision.

It was 4:20 o'clock in the morning as the last horse hooked his fore feet over the last stone step. As we looked back over the vast waves of the snow-capped peaks to the north; the northern lights flashed across the sky their wondrously colored streamers. It seemed a celebration of our success.

But we soon turned to less awesome things and opened a can of tomatoes. We turned the horses loose. The Doctor started out afoot for the water and the wood in the valley below, leading his favorite horse. I watched them until they looked like some stray straddlebug crawling into the timber-line. Then on the top of the Pass, in its very curve, and among the perennial snows, I rolled into a blanket and into a dreamless slumber. The horses hung their heads or nibbled the sparse grass or searched for the snow rivulets.

I do not know how long I slept. I awaked with my eyes staring into an immeasurable abyss of blue without a speck in its infinite expanse, with the sensation that I was falling into it from a vast height; I gave one cry that startled myself into full wakefulness and roused the echoes in the surrounding crags. I was lying on my back in the glowing sunlight looking up into the resplendent azure of the mountain sky and not into a shoreless sea far below me.

LOS ANGELES, CAL., August, 1904.

CALIFORNIA FORESTRY LAW.

[Enacted 1905.]

AN ACT TO PROVIDE FOR THE REGULATION OF FIRES ON, AND THE PROTECTION AND MANAGEMENT OF, PUBLIC AND PRIVATE FOREST LANDS WITHIN THE STATE OF CALIFORNIA, CREATING A STATE BOARD OF FORESTRY AND CERTAIN OFFICERS SUBORDINATE TO SAID BOARD, PRESCRIBING THE DUTIES OF SUCH OFFICERS, CREATING A FORESTRY FUND, AND APPROPRIATING THE MONEYS IN SAID FUND, AND DEFINING AND PROVIDING FOR THE PUNISHMENT OF CERTAIN OFFENSES FOR VIOLATIONS OF THE PROVISIONS OF THIS ACT, AND MAKING AN APPROPRIATION THEREFOR.

The people of the State of California, represented in senate and assembly, do enact as follows:

SECTION 1. STATE BOARD OF FORESTRY.—There shall be a state board of forestry, consisting of the governor, secretary of state, attorney-general and state forester, which shall supervise all matters of state forest policy and management and convene upon the call of the governor or of its secretary.

SEC. 2. STATE FORESTER AND HIS DUTIES.—There shall be a state forester, who shall be a civil executive officer, and who shall be a technically trained forester, appointed by the governor to hold office at the pleasure of the appointing power; and whether any candidate for the position is a technically trained forester shall be determined by certificate from the secretary of the United States Department of Agriculture, or from the Department of Forestry of the State University after such department is established. He shall receive a salary of twenty-four hundred dollars per annum, and shall be authorized and empowered to appoint two assistant foresters, whose salaries shall not exceed twelve hundred dollars each per annum. He shall maintain headquarters at the state capitol in an office provided by the secretary of state, and shall be allowed necessary office and contingent expenses. He and his assistants shall be paid reasonable traveling and field expenses which may be incurred in the necessary performance of their official duties. He shall act as secretary of the state board of forestry. He shall, under the supervision of the state board of forestry, execute all matters pertaining to forestry within the jurisdiction of the state; have charge of all fire wardens in the state, and direct and aid them in their duties; direct the protection and improvement of state parks and forests; collect data relative to forest destruction and conditions; take such action as is authorized by law to prevent and extinguish forest, brush, and grass fires; enforce all laws pertaining to forest and brush-covered land, and prosecute for any violation of such laws; coöperate with landowners, as described in section 4 of this act; and publish from time to time such information of forestry as he may deem wise. He shall prepare annually a report to the governor on the progress and condition of state forest work, and recommend therein plans for improving the state system of forest protection, management and replacement.

SEC. 3. SUPERVISION AND CARE OF STATE PARKS.—The California Redwood Park and the Mt. Hamilton tract, together with all moneys heretofore or hereafter appropriated for the purchase of land for or care of said parks, tracts and stations, shall be in charge of the state board of forestry, said board to take the place of and forthwith shall have all the powers and duties now possessed in accordance with law by persons or commissions with regard to the state parks, tracts of land, and forest stations mentioned in this act, and also any forest or brush land which may hereafter become state property, or be placed definitely in the care of the state; and it is hereby further enacted that, *if the government of the United States or any individual or corporation shall*, at *any time, donate or intrust to* the *state of California*, for state park or state forest reserve purposes, any tract or tracts of wholly or partially wooded land, *such tract or tracts of land shall be administered* at *the expense of the state*, as *provided by law.*

SEC. 4. COÖPERATIVE WORK.—The state forester shall, upon request and whenever he deems it essential to the best interests of the people and the state, coöperate with counties, towns, corporations and individuals in preparing plans for the protection, management and replacement of trees, woodlots and timber tracts, on consideration and under an agreement that the parties obtaining such assistance pay at least the field expenses of the men employed in preparing said plans.

SEC. 5. PUBLICATION OF LAWS AND NOTICES.—The state forester shall prepare and print for public distribution, an abstract of all the forest laws of California, together with such rules and regulations in accord therewith as he may deem necessary, and shall annually print and distribute a list of all fire wardens with their addresses, all such matter to be published with the approval of the state board of forestry. He shall also furnish notices, printed in large letters on cloth, calling attention to the danger from forest fires and to forest fire and trespass laws and their penalties. Such notices shall be posted by the fire wardens in conspicuous places along every highway in brush and forest-covered country, at frequent intervals along streams and lakes frequented by tourists, hunters or fishermen, at established camping sites, and in every post-office in the forested region.

SEC. 6. FIRE DISTRICTS.—The state forester shall divide the state into such number of fire districts as shall be deemed by him most necessary to the efficiency of his work; and, furthermore, any county, or combination of less than four counties, shall be made a separate fire district, upon request of the county board or board of supervisors, in which case such special fire district shall pay the cost of maintaining its district fire warden.

SEC. 7. DUTIES OF ASSISTANT FORESTERS.—The duties of the assistant foresters shall be to devote their entire time to state forest interests according to rules and directions to be determined by the state forester, with the approval of the state board of forestry. They shall take prompt measures to prevent and extinguish forest fires; keep a record of the cause, extent and damage of all forest fires in their respective districts, and perform such other duties as the state forester may direct.

SEC. 8. VOLUNTARY FIRE WARDENS AND THEIR DUTIES.—The state forester shall appoint, in such number and localities as he deems wise, public-spirited citizens to act as voluntary fire wardens, who may receive payment for their services from the counties or from private sources. They shall promptly report all fires and take immediate and active steps toward their extinguishment, report any violation of the forest laws, assist in apprehending and convicting offenders, and perform such other duties as the state forester may direct. The supervisors and rangers on the federal forest reserve within the state, whenever they formally accept the duties and responsibilities of fire wardens, may be appointed as voluntary fire wardens, and shall have all the powers given to fire wardens by this act.

SEC. 9. POWERS AND REQUIREMENTS OF FIRE WARDENS.—The state forester and all fire wardens shall have the powers of peace officers to make arrests without warrant, for violation of any state or federal forest laws, and no fire warden shall be liable to civil action for trespass committed in the discharge of his duties. Any fire warden who has information which would show with reasonable certainty that any person had violated any provision of such forest laws, shall immediately take action against the offender, either by using his own powers as a peace officer or by making complaint before the proper magistrate, or by information to the proper district attorney, and shall obtain all possible evidence pertaining thereto. Failure on the part of any *paid* fire warden to comply with the duties prescribed by this act shall be a misdemeanor, and punishable by a fine of not less than twenty dollars, nor more than two hundred and fifty dollars, or imprisonment for not less than ten days nor more than three months, or both such fine and imprisonment, and the state forester is hereby authorized to investigate and prosecute such violations.

SEC. 10. ASSISTANCE OF CITIZENS IN FIGHTING FIRES.—All fire wardens shall have authority to call upon able-bodied citizens between the ages of sixteen and fifty years, for assistance in putting out fires, and any such person who refuses to obey such summons, unless prevented by good and sufficient reasons, is guilty of a misdemeanor, and must be fined in a sum not less than fifteen dollars, nor more than fifty dollars, or imprisonment in the county jail of the county in which such conviction shall be had, not less than ten days, nor more than thirty days, or both such fine and imprisonment; *provided* that no citizen shall be called upon to fight fire a total of more than five days in any one year.

SEC. 11. FIRE PATROL.—In times and localities of particular fire danger the state forester may maintain a fire patrol through the fire wardens, at such places in brush or forest land as the public interest may require, the expense of such patrol to be paid by the county in which such patrol is maintained; and, furthermore, he may, upon written request by counties, corporations or individuals, maintain a fire patrol on their forest lands, *provided*, that the expense of said patrol be paid by the party or parties requesting same.

SEC. 12. DISTRICT ATTORNEYS TO PROSECUTE VIGOROUSLY.—Whenever an arrest shall have been made for violation of any provision of this act, or whenever any information of such violation shall have been lodged with him, the district attorney of the county in which the criminal act was committed must prosecute the offender or offenders with all diligence and energy. If any district attorney shall fail to comply with the provisions of this section he shall be guilty of a misdemeanor, and upon conviction shall be fined not less than one hundred dollars nor more than one thousand dollars in the discretion of the court. Action against the district attorney shall be brought by the attorney-general in the name of the people of the state on the relation of the state forester. The penalties of this section shall apply to any magistrate, with proper authority, who refuses or neglects to cause the arrest and prosecution of any person or persons when complaint, under oath, of violation of any terms of this act has been lodged with him.

SEC. 13. DESTRUCTION OF WARNING NOTICES.—Any person who shall destroy, deface, remove or disfigure any sign, poster or warning notice posted under the provisions of this act shall be guilty of a misdemeanor and punishable, upon conviction, by a fine of not less than fifteen dollars nor more than one hundred dollars, or imprisonment in the county jail for a period of not less than ten days nor more than three months, or both such fine and imprisonment.

SEC. 14. WILLFULLY, MALICIOUSLY AND NEGLIGENTLY SETTING FOREST FIRES.—Every person, who willfully, maliciously or negligently sets on fire or causes or procures to be set on fire any woods, brush, prairies, grass, grain or stubble on any lands not his own, or allows the fire to escape from his own land, whereby any property of another is injured or destroyed, or accidentally sets any such fire or allows it to escape from his control without extinguishing it or using every effort to extinguish it, shall be guilty of a misdemeanor, and upon conviction is punishable by a fine of not less than fifty dollars, nor more than one thousand dollars, or imprisonment for not less than thirty days nor more than one year, or both such fine and imprisonment. Setting such fires or allowing them to escape shall be prima facie proof of willfulness, malice or neglect under this section, *provided*, that nothing herein contained shall apply to a person who, in good faith, sets a back-fire to check a fire already burning.

SEC. 15. EXTINGUISHMENT OF CAMP FIRES.—Every person who, upon departing from a camp or camping place, leaves fire burning or unextinguished, or who after building such fire allows it to spread, shall be guilty of a misdemeanor and punishable by a fine of not less than fifty dollars nor more than five hundred dollars, with costs of suit and collection, one half of such fine, or such a portion thereof as shall not exceed fifty dollars, to be paid to the person securing the arrest and conviction of such offender, and if the defendant refuses or neglects to pay the fine and costs imposed, he shall be confined in the county jail of the county in which the conviction shall be had, for a period not to exceed one day for every two dollars of the fine imposed, or may be subject to both such fine and imprisonment.

SEC. 16. RESTRICTION OF USE OF FIRE IN DRY SEASON.—It shall be unlawful during what is locally known as the "dry season," this to be considered as the period between May fifteenth and the first soaking rains of autumn or winter, for any person or persons to burn brush, stumps, logs, fallen timber, fallows, grass or forest-covered land, or blast wood with dynamite, powder or other explosives, or set off fireworks of any kind in forest or brush-covered land, either their own or the property of another, without written permission of and under the direction or supervision of a fire warden in that district; these restrictions not to apply to the ordinary use of fire or blasts in logging redwood, nor in cases where back-fires are set in good faith to stop an existing fire. Violation of these provisions shall be a misdemeanor, punishable, upon conviction, by a fine of not less than fifty dollars, nor more than one thousand dollars, or imprisonment not less than thirty days nor more than one year, or both such fine and imprisonment.

SEC. 17. ENGINES IN FOREST LAND.—Logging locomotives, donkey or threshing engines, and other engines and boilers operated in, through or near forests, brush or grass land, which do not burn oil as fuel, shall be provided with appliances to prevent the escape of fire and sparks from the smokestacks thereof, and with devices to prevent the escape of fire from ash pans and fire boxes. Failure to comply with these requirements shall be a misdemeanor, punishable, upon conviction, by a fine of not less than one hundred dollars nor more than five hundred dollars, and any person violating any provision of this section shall be liable to a penalty of not less than fifty dollars nor more than one hundred dollars, for every such violation, or imprisonment for not less than thirty days nor more than three months, or both such fine and imprisonment.

SEC. 18. CIVIL LIABILITY FOR FOREST FIRES.—In addition to the penalties provided in sections 14, 15, 16 and 17 of this act, the United States, state, county, or private owners, whose property is injured or destroyed by such fires, may recover, in a civil action, double the amount of damages suffered if the fires occurred through willfulness, malice or negligence; but if such fires were caused or escaped accidentally or unavoidably, civil action shall lie only for the actual damage sustained as determined by the value of the property injured or destroyed, and the detriment to the land and vegetation thereof. The presumption of willfulness, malice or neglect shall be overcome, *provided* that the precautions set forth in section 17 are observed; *or, provided,* under section 16, fires are set during the "dry season" with written permission of and under the direction of the district fire warden. Persons or corporations causing fires by violations of sections 14, 15, 16 and 17 of this act shall be liable to the state or county in action for debt, to the full amount of all expenses incurred by the state or county in fighting such fires.

SEC. 19. CLEARING ALONG COUNTY ROADS AND LAND AFTER LUMBERING.—Counties, along the county roads, in forest or brush land, shall, when so directed by the state forester, and in a manner and to an extent prescribed by him, cut and remove all brush, grass and inflammable material from their rights of way. If such clearing is not done within a reasonable time after notice, said time to be fixed by the state forester, the state forester shall have it done and the county shall be liable to the state in an action for debt to the amount of the expense thus incurred, and in addition thereto for the expense of any fire patrol rendered necessary by such delay. It is *provided, further,* that all lumber companies, corporations, or individuals shall, when so instructed by the state board of forestry, and at a time and in a manner prescribed by said board, carefully burn their slashings, by which is meant the tops, limbs, and general débris left after lumbering.

SEC. 20. DISPOSALS OF MONEYS RECEIVED AS PENALTIES.—All moneys received as penalties for violations of the provisions of this act, less the cost of collection, and not otherwise provided for, shall be paid into the state treasury to the credit of the forestry fund, which fund is hereby created, and the moneys therein are hereby appropriated for purposes of forest protection, management and replacement under direction of the state board of forestry.

SEC. 21. MONEYS FOR FOREST PURPOSES.—County boards of supervisors may appropriate money for purposes of forest protection, improvement and management.

SEC. 22. PAYMENT OF EXPENSES UNDER THIS ACT.—There is hereby appropriated for the fifty-seventh and fifty-eighth fiscal years, the sum of seventeen thousand six hundred dollars ($17,600.00) for carrying out the provisions of this act, and for the payment of all salaries and expenses herein provided for.

SEC. 23. All acts or parts of acts inconsistent with the provisions of this act are hereby repealed.

SIERRA CLUB BULLETIN.

PUBLISHED IN JANUARY AND JUNE OF EACH YEAR.

Published for Members.   Annual Dues, $3.00.

The purposes of the Club are:—"To explore, enjoy, and render accessible the mountain regions of the Pacific Coast; to publish authentic information concerning them; to enlist the support and co-operation of the people and the Government in preserving the forests and other natural features of the Sierra Nevada Mountains."

ORGANIZATION FOR THE YEAR 1905-1906.

Board of Directors.

Mr. JOHN MUIR (Martinez) . . . . *President*
Prof. A. G. MCADIE (Mills Building, S. F.) . . . . *Vice-President*
Prof. J. N. LECONTE (Berkeley) . . . . *Treasurer*
Mr. WILLIAM E. COLBY (Mills Building, S. F.) . . . . . *Secretary*
    Prof. GEORGE DAVIDSON (Berkeley).
    Prof. W. R. DUDLEY (Stanford University).
    Mr. J. S. HUTCHINSON, JR. (Claus Spreckels Bldg., S. F.).
    Mr. WARREN OLNEY (101 Sansome Street, S. F.).
    Mr. EDWARD T. PARSONS (University Club, S. F.).

Honorary Vice-Presidents.

    Mr. R. U. JOHNSON (*The Century*), New York.
    Pres. DAVID STARR JORDAN (Stanford University).
    Mr. GIFFORD PINCHOT (Washington, D. C.).

Committee on Publications.

Mr. ELLIOTT MCALLISTER (Crocker Building, S. F.) . . . . *Editor*
    Prof. WILLIAM FREDERIC BADÈ (Berkeley) . . *Book Reviews*
    Prof. WM. R. DUDLEY (Stanford University) . . *Forestry Notes*
    Mr. ALEX. G. EELLS (Crocker Building, S. F.).
    Mr. J. S. HUTCHINSON, JR. (Claus Spreckels Building, S. F.).
    Mr. EDWARD T. PARSONS (University Club, S. F.).
    Prof. H. W. ROLFE (Stanford University).
    Mr. WILLOUGHBY RODMAN (Bryson Block, Los Angeles).
    Miss F. B. WHITTIER (Mechanics' Library, S. F.).

Auditing Committee—Directors MCADIE, HUTCHINSON, and DUDLEY.

Outing Committee—Mr. WM. E. COLBY (*Chairman*), Mr. J. N. LECONTE, Mr. EDWARD T. PARSONS.

Committee on Local Walks—Mr. E. G. KNAPP (*Chairman*), Mr. JULIUS CAHN, Mr. GEO. M. CUMMING, Miss MARIAN RANDALL, Mr. R. L. TOPLITZ.

Le Conte Memorial Lodge Committee—Mr. E. T. PARSONS (*Chairman*), Mr. WM. E. COLBY, Prof. J. N. LECONTE.

Librarian—Miss ANITA GOMPERTZ.

REPORTS.

REPORT OF THE SECRETARY,
From May 7, 1904, to May 6, 1905.

The Club has just completed one of the most prosperous and encouraging years of its existence, and has been engaged in some of the most active and effective work since its organization. The act of the last State Legislature receding Yosemite Valley to the National Government was accomplished largely through the efforts of the Club, which also aided in the adoption of the State Forestry Law, in securing the appropriation to be used for continuing the water and forest investigations in conjunction with the Federal Government, and in the transfer of the management of the Federal Forest Reserves to the Bureau of Forestry.

The additions to the membership during the year were one hundred and ninety-two, while ninety-eight names were dropped from the list by reason of death, resignation, or non-payment of dues, making a net increase of ninety-four members for the year. The membership of the Club numbered eight hundred and fifty-eight at the close of the Club fiscal year, and by the end of the next year, if the present members will only exert themselves to interest desirable persons in joining the Club, we ought to have one thousand members.

At the recent Club election, the Board of Directors named on the preceding page were elected, and at their first meeting they in turn named the officers there set forth.

The revised by-laws were adopted without a dissenting vote.

The Club prepared a very attractive exhibit in co-operation with the Pacific Coast Forest, Fish, and Game Association at the Mechanics' Pavilion in San Francisco during April, and was awarded the second prize—a handsome silver cup with horn handles. Great praise is due Mr. M. H. McAllister, without whose able assistance the Club exhibit would not have been possible.

The Le Conte Memorial Lodge Library in Yosemite Valley has been opened for the season, and Mr. H. A. Stout, a recent graduate of the University of California, who is in every way qualified to represent the Club, has been secured to act as caretaker. A friend of the Club has presented twenty-five dollars to be used for the lodge, and a very fine photograph of Professor Joseph Le Conte has been purchased (with a portion of the sum) and appropriately framed for hanging in the lodge.

A large subscription to the lodge fund came from Professor Le Conte's students in South Africa after the lodge had been entirely paid for, and the committee having the matter in charge decided to use this money in securing a bronze tablet, with a bust of Professor Le Conte in bas-relief. Douglas Tilden, the eminent sculptor, is now engaged in modeling this tablet, which, when completed, will be placed in the lodge over the granite fire-place.

Mr. Harrington Putnam, of New York, has presented the following valuable volumes to the club library:—

Conway, Crossing Spitzbergen;
Fillipi, Ascent of Mt. St. Elias by Duke of Abruzzi;
Gribble, Early Mountaineers;
Weston, Japanese Alps;
Edwards, Ramble in the Dolomites;
Saussure, Voyages dans les Alpes.

Mr. Putnam has heretofore presented the Club with some of the finest books in its library.

Mr. Seaver and Mr. DuVal, of New York, have sent Tyndall's "Hours of Exercise in the Alps," and "The Playground of Europe," by Stephens.

Mr. Asahel Curtis, of Seattle, has given the Club a splendid photograph of Mt. Rainier; Mr. E. T. Parsons, several fine ones of Mt. Baker; and Dr. T. J. Patterson, of Visalia, a striking enlargement entitled "A Storm in the Sierras," all of which have been appropriately framed and hung in the clubroom.

The local walks have been resumed this spring and have proven very enjoyable. On May 13th and 14th, thirty-seven persons made a delightful excursion to Mt. St. Helena.

This year's Outing to Mt. Rainier and Paradise Park will be the first club outing to be taken at such a distance, but all indications point to an unqualified success. A large party of Appalachians from Boston and New York will join us, adding to the pleasure of the trip.

Very respectfully,

WM. E. COLBY,
Secretary of Sierra Club.

Report of the Treasurer.

SAN FRANCISCO, May 15, 1905.

To THE DIRECTORS OF THE SIERRA CLUB.

Gentlemen—I hereby submit the following report of the finances of the Sierra Club during the year beginning May 10, 1904, and ending May 9, 1905:—

RECEIPTS.
(From Wm. E. Colby, Secretary.)

From dues 1904-1905	$2,120 00
From advertisements in BULLETINS Nos. 31 and 32	725 00
From rent of desk room in No. 316 Mills Building	72 50
From refund from Appalachian Club for postage	125 38
From sale of publications	6 25
Total receipts from Secretary	$3,049 13
Balance on hand May 10, 1904	580 20
	$3,629 33

EXPENDITURES.

Publications and advertising expenses	$1,190 89
Rent of Room No. 316, Mills Building	300 00
Distributing BULLETINS and letters	289 65
Printing circulars, stamps, and stationery	288 42
Expended on Le Conte Memorial Lodge	243 11
Clerical services	180 00
Typewriting	104 80
On account of Yosemite recession business	55 80
Public meetings	28 75
Furnishing office in Mills Building	13 25
Advertising Sunday walks	9 30
Exchange on checks	4 20
Sundries	14 07
	$2,722 24
Balance on hand May 9, 1905	907 09
	$3,629 33

There is on deposit in the Permanent Fund in the Security Savings Bank of San Francisco $100.00.

Very respectfully,

JOSEPH N. LE CONTE, *Treasurer.*

NOTES AND CORRESPONDENCE.

In addition to longer articles suitable for the body of the magazine, the editor would be glad to receive brief memoranda of all noteworthy trips or explorations, together with brief comment and suggestion on any topics of general interest to the Club. Descriptive or narrative articles, or notes concerning the animals, birds, forests, trails, geology, botany, etc., of the mountains, will be acceptable.

The office of the Sierra Club is at Room 316, Third Floor, Mills Building, San Francisco, where all the maps, photographs, and other records of the Club are kept, and where members are welcome at any time.

The Club would like to purchase additional copies of those numbers of the SIERRA CLUB BULLETIN *which are noted on the back of the cover of this number as being out of print, and we hope any member having extra copies will send them to the Secretary.*

MOUNT WEATHER, VIA BLUEMONT, VA., March 17, 1905.
DEAR MR. COLBY:

I thank you and the Sierra Club most deeply for your kind invitation to the Fifth Annual Outing. I should be most happy if I could be with you. I love the mountain-tops. But my duties are all in the opposite direction this year. Perhaps I may be able to join you next year. I hope to.

"Mount Weather" is but 6,800 feet above sea-level. Still even that is a useful elevation to the meteorologist. Why cannot the Sierra Club raise the funds for a station on the summit of Shasta or Rainier, as the Sonnenblick Club has done for the Sonnenblick in Austria? That would be a "lighthouse in the skies" for American meteorology. With best regards to Professors McAdie, Le Conte, Davidson, and other good friends,

Yours truly, CLEVELAND ABBE.

FROM TUOLUMNE MEADOWS TO YOSEMITE VALLEY BY TUOLUMNE PASS.

The United States Topographical Sheet shows a trail from Tuolumne Meadows up Rafferty's Creek to and across Tuolumne Pass and down the McClure Fork to the Merced River.

The region through which this trail leads is in the High Sierra amongst the head-waters of the Merced River. It is so interesting and so little visited that my companion and I desire to call the attention of the members of the Sierra Club to its accessibility. The two days of last summer in making this trip were two of the most interesting days that I have passed anywhere in the mountains. We thought that the route was known only to the sheep-herders and to Government surveyors, and were quite prepared to send an elaborate article to the BULLETIN. But an examination of our file shows that the ground and much more has been covered in the following articles: "New Routes within Yosemite National Park," by N. F. McClure, Vol. I SIERRA CLUB BULLETIN, page 333; also, "A Route up Merced River," by Robert M. Price, Vol. II SIERRA CLUB BULLETIN, page 197.

The itinerary, therefore, will be briefly outlined in the hope that it will induce others to follow. We left the Club's camp in Tuolumne Meadows and turned up Rafferty's Creek, which comes into the Lyell Fork of the Tuolumne from the south. Rafferty's heads just below Tuolumne Pass. The trail keeps on the right-hand side and near enough the abrupt sides to follow the main stream.

We kept too much to the west, and found ourselves much too high up near Rafferty's Peak, and had to work our way below the crest of the ridge and down to the Pass, which was easily recognized as being the lowest point. Immediately over it were the interesting granite basins draining into Emeric Creek, and thence into the McClure Fork. Here at the Pass we nooned.

From the Pass, instead of following down Emeric Creek, the trail bears off to the east and climbs higher between Vogelsang Peak on the south and Vogelsang Lake on the north, until it comes to the edge of the basin of the McClure Fork. Animals would have had to be taken further to the east, following the monuments on the rock (the friendly "ducks," as my companion dubbed them) to where the descent was possible. As we were without animals, we worked our way down the cliff along a narrow watercourse and came out in the broad meadows below the head-waters of the McClure Fork of the Merced.

Here we should have camped in order to have thoroughly enjoyed the wonderful panoramas about us. Mt. Florence and Mt. McClure were right beyond us to the east, and high peaks and precipitous walls were all about. The afternoon was full of exhilaration, and continuously the panorama changed as we walked rapidly along the well-blazed trail above the McClure Fork. As the afternoon wore on we crossed the waters coming down from the Mt. Florence watershed; and we saw the wonderful dome standing by the side of the beautiful cascade by which Emeric Creek comes in, and understood why the trail did not follow that creek. From high up we saw Lake Merced, and on beyond the unmistakable Le Conte Dome, and on beyond the setting sun.

Our camp was made at dark on the Merced River. Early the next morning we skirted the north shore of Lake Merced to its outlet, and followed the river into Lost Valley and to where the Merced goes into the gorge of Little Yosemite. Further progress by the river seemed impossible, and we worked back and up over to the top of the north wall and had magnificent views of the domes and glaciated walls of Little Yosemite and back over the region whence we had come.

Then followed a climb of a hundred feet or more, and, keeping along the same elevation, through the forest to Sunrise Trail, and thence into Yosemite Valley.

All of this is easily possible for animals, except between the outlet of Lake Merced and Lost Valley. Along this stretch much care must be used. The route gives a glimpse of the wonderful region to the east. Before taking the trip, however, read the articles cited above, and then you will not content yourself with less than two weeks instead of two days.

ELLIOTT McALLISTER.

RENO, NEV., March 18, 1905.

PROFESSOR ALEXANDER McADIE, SAN FRANCISCO.

Dear Sir—Mr. Marsh and I spent eight days on Mt. Whitney, and climbed to the altitude of 13,250 feet, where we could look down on Langley's Lake. At this point the ledge was piled full of drifting snow with a treacherous crust beneath. I now believe that we could have succeeded in crossing this, although the risk would have been great.

The ascent to 13,500 feet could be made at any season of the year, I believe, especially if two or three cabins were constructed along the trail for refuge in case of storm. Access could be had to the summit also during most of the year, Mr. Marsh believes, if a narrow trail for man were cut higher up the pinnacles, where the drift-snow could not lodge in sufficient quantity to prevent the observer from keeping the trail open. The expense would not exceed one hundred and fifty dollars.

The weather was mild, though snow clouds hung over the mountains. The temperature did not fall below 10° F. The wind blew almost constantly from the east, from the subtropical Owen's Valley, and seemed to have an appreciable effect upon the temperature of the mountain, for Lone Pine Lake (9,800 ft.) and Mirror Lake at timber-line (10,450 ft.) were only partially frozen over, while the lakes west of Mt. Whitney at apparently similar altitudes were frozen completely over and covered with snow. The snow also was mealy and unstable, with little hardness anywhere such as I have always found on Mt. Rose above the altitude of 8,500 feet.

As regards the difficulty of the ascent in winter, I should consider Mt. Shasta as not only far easier but also entirely safe, save for the possible fusillade of rocks below the Red Cliffs. There is no horse-trail up Mt. Shasta, however, above the altitude of 9,000 feet.

I wish I were free to do so; I should then venture to volunteer to take observations on Mt. Whitney for you for a year.

If you are willing, I will take the readings of a maximum and a minimum thermometer on Mt. Rose (10,860 ft.), north of Lake Tahoe, nearly every month during the coming twelve months, if you will send me the instruments. The results might have some value. Mt. Rose is the highest point east of the summits of the Sierras and north of Lake Tahoe. The wind is usually very high there; but Lake Tahoe may have an influence on the temperature. If you are favorable, I could place the thermometers on Mt. Rose at once. The temperature early in February at 6,500 feet altitude on this mountain fell considerably below zero, to judge from the frost crystals in my sleeping-bag and frosted feet and from the temperature of $-15°$ and $-25°$ F. at Truckee and Floriston the same night.

Our party had the honor of naming the peak directly south of Lone Pine Pass Mt. McAdie, to commemorate your services in advancing the science of climatology. Its altitude is at least 13,500 feet. If, as Mr. Marsh declares, this peak has not previously been named, we beg that you allow this name to stand.

Very truly yours,

(Signed)   J. E. CHURCH, JR.

Some enterprising and able California and Stanford students, among whom the Sierra Club is represented, have joined in the "University Transportation Company," with headquarters at 653 Market Street, San Francisco, and have undertaken to make the magnificent Hetch-Hetchy Valley accessible from June 1st to the end of August this summer. They are to be commended for their enterprise in opening this beautiful but hitherto little known region, and may be relied on to carry out their agreements. See our advertising columns for details.

SOME FURTHER EXPERIMENTS WITH SLEEPING-BAG AND SLED ON WINTER TRIPS.

After three more ventures under all the evil conditions that the devotee of long winter trips would believe that nature could feasibly prepare for him, I gladly avail myself of the present opportunity to supplement my earlier observations made on the subject of winter trips in previous issues of the BULLETIN.

The first requisite is snow-shoes, and after continued experimenting I have been unable to obtain any shoe superior to the "Algäne Schnee-Reifen," Form *a*, described in volume IV of the BULLETIN, page 64 (January, 1902), for trips requiring both sledging and the traversing of steep incrusted slopes. In newly fallen snow they are too small. But after the gruelling process of treading the feathery snow was over and a treacherous sur-

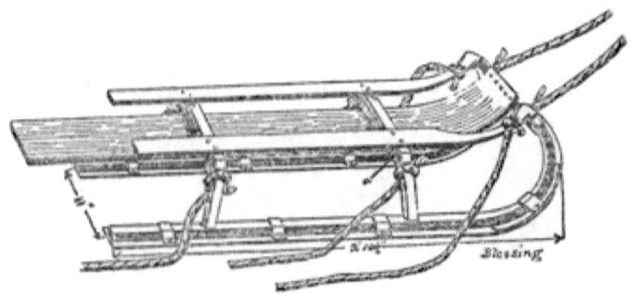

face had to be traversed, they immediately regained their reputation as equal both to the ice-ax and rock moccasin combined.

If possible, the elliptical shoe mentioned in the same article should be taken for use where the snow is not sufficiently packed or incrusted to bear one's weight without sinking more than four inches. When it is considered that one must be a draught-animal on such trips, the uselessness of the ski is at once apparent.

The home-made sled that had been used on our "New-Year Outing in the Sierra" (BULLETIN, Vol. IV, p. 216), had been found altogether too heavy. I purchased a child's sled with bent legs, for one dollar, and by making two simple changes, shown in the above cut, adapted it to the work in hand. Galvanized-iron runners two and one half inches wide were riveted on. At the bend of the runner the iron was doubled to withstand battering. The bed also was removed and a strip of ash board, torn from a dry-goods box, was nailed below the bows to serve as a third runner in case of encountering soft snow.

The legs were wired at the bow *a* to the end of the cross-pieces to strengthen the frame of the sled. This sled was thus fitted to run astride of any low obstruction, which a toboggan would not do, and at the same time to retain the qualities of a toboggan if extra carrying surface should be required. It would be inadvisable, however, to attempt sledging in very soft snow except in an emergency.

Two defects were soon developed. The runners were too short and the sled was too narrow. Such sleds should be rebuilt so as to be four inches longer, if possible, and spring-steel bars should be substituted for the present ones of wood, of such size as to make the sled three inches wider between runners and two inches lower from the ground. The metal shoes should also be increased to the width of three inches.

My sled, even without these improvements, served its purpose well. It held as heavy a load as I could carry in two packs, passed through sagebrush beautifully, and could be hung up in a tree, with pack tied securely in place out of the way of any prowling wolf or cat. It would not and could not naturally stand upright on a slope so steep as to require a zigzag trail to surmount it, as we found on the sides of the cañon of Lone Pine Creek at Mt. Whitney. On the more gradual descents we rode astride on the load; on the steeper descents they rode on their own loads, with runners in the air, or spun side over side or end over end, while we clung to the rope. They also followed readily through the jungle,—that is, as readily as we could crowd a way through the yielding brush.

On the trip to Martis Valley between Truckee and Lake Tahoe, one other weakness was developed, but the snow was then at its worst. It had newly fallen after a heavy rain of long duration, and overlay a stratum of water which froze persistently to the cold metal of the runners, so reducing the sliding power of the sled that I was obliged to drag it down hill as well as up.

The sleeping-bag was successful from the start. It consisted of a large rabbit blanket inside a light duck case. Under the blanket was a light rubber sheet to re-enforce the duck. In the foot of the bag I placed a feather pillow, with a large packet inside to contain my feet. This idea was inspired by frostbite from sleeping out in zero weather with felt boots and rubbers, which probably had grown damp during the day.

A tent is also sometimes advisable. A McCall tent, listed

at $7.50, will serve the purpose admirably. Its weight is twelve pounds; its general size and shape can best be represented by the cut below. Marsh and I slept in one at timber-line (10,450 ft.) on Mt. Whitney for three nights. When it stormed during the day, we turned it upside down with all the parts spread out

as a canopy. A lighter tent should be made, after the same design, of silk for the sides and some light waterproof duck for the floor.

If a rainfall is out of the question, a light cotton sheet apexed over the head of the sleeping-bag as a breathing-hood would be quite sufficient for comfort. The sled, if stood on end, would form a ready support.

But the key to our success on Mt. Whitney was our hip-leggings of light rubber sheeting, made on the sewing-machine. The seams should be placed on the outside of the leg, where the water from the melting snow will not so readily find its way through the needle-holes. These leggings should, of course, be supplemented by felt boots and two-buckle rubbers to hold the bottom of the leggings firmly. Had we not by the merest good luck provided ourselves with these, the water-soaked snow would have wet us so thoroughly the first day that we would have been compelled to beat a retreat on the second at the latest.

Such food only should be taken as can be prepared without much water,—that is, bacon, canned beans, flour, and pemmican made preferably of cornmeal, and meat thoroughly cooked and cased in cloth. Coffee, of course, should be provided if it is craved, and sugar for syrup.

If the trip is to be above timber, an oil-stove of galvanized iron is the cheapest practicable means of cooking. If, however, dry wood can be obtained, it will be far better to take a "Pearl" oil-can in which to build the fire on the snow.

Automobile goggles and knit face-masks are an absolute necessity, and canvas clothing is highly desirable.

With such an equipment we found it possible to be absent ten days from a base of supplies.

Still greater lightness can probably be obtained by improvements in stove, sleeping-bag, and tent. A second pair of felt boots and sufficient food should always be insisted upon, but if either must be slighted, the feet should be given preference to the stomach, for the failure of the former will bring irreparable disaster. In case the weather should become extremely cold, place the sleeping-bag in a hole in the snow and cover it over with the same material, but deep enough so that it cannot be shaken off. With such a blanket of snow, a temperature of $-25°$ F. could readily be met, for according to our tests the thermometer never fell appreciably below $+30°$ F. when buried in the snow.

If the Sierra Club could establish cabins with fireplaces and supplies along King's River, its members could revel in the sports of winter mountaineering from one end of the cañon to the other, and views of winter scenery obtained that would delight the artist's heart. J. E. CHURCH, JR.

RENO, NEV., May 20, 1905.

BOOK REVIEWS.

Edited by William Frederic Badè.

"Check-List of California Birds." An organization that is doing valuable work on the Pacific Coast is the Cooper Ornithological Club. Its leading spirit is Joseph Grinnell. It would be hard to find any one in California who has a more intimate or a more accurate knowledge of its avifauna. This *Check-List of California Birds** makes no claim to be exhaustive, but it is safe to say that important omissions are few. No description of species is attempted, but the range and principal places of occurrence are given. To the Sierran already familiar with the various species of birds this list will prove useful for reference and for the purpose of keeping count. A shorter list of birds of the Sierras, prepared by the late Chester Barlow, is also among the publications of the Cooper Ornithological Club, and may still be obtainable.

The distribution of animals and plants is governed chiefly by the two factors of temperature and humidity. To make clear this principle in its application to the California avifauna the author has added two maps of the State, the one presenting the four principal life-zones on the basis of isothermic areas, the other giving the faunal areas on the basis of isohumic areas.

The check-list is an excellent piece of work, and reflects credit on the author as well as the club whose membership has helped to gather and verify the information. W. F. B.

"Plans for Obtaining Subterranean Temperatures." We are indebted to the author, Professor Grove Karl Gilbert, for a copy of this interesting monograph, reprinted from Year Book No. 3, Carnegie Institute of Washington. It fully covers reasons for the desirability of the information sought, and outlines plans proposed for the investigations, and progress made. E. T. P.

---

* *Pacific Coast Avifauna*, No. 3: Check-List of California Birds. By Joseph Grinnell. Published by the Cooper Ornithological Club. Price, 75c. Address the author at Pasadena, California.

"REPORT OF THE PHILIPPINE CENSUS." The Sierra Club's library has received from the Bureau of Insular Affairs of the War Department the four volumes of the *Report of the Philippine Census.* This is the first census ever taken of the Philippine Islands. The date of its publication, March 27, 1905, is of great importance to those islands and to this country. The Act of Congress of 1902 provided for the taking of this census; and further provided that after its completion, in case general and complete peace with recognition of the authority of the United States shall continue throughout those of the Islands not inhabited by Moros for a period of two years, then a legislative assembly shall be elected by popular vote. From March 27, 1905, commences this period of two years.

The edition of this report is limited, and the library is fortunate in having been presented with this copy. E. Mc.A.

"YOSEMITE LEGENDS." The casual visitor to the foot of Yosemite Falls can read the sign-board "Trail of the Lost Arrow," and possibly may wonder at the touch of romance in the name. The name has in fact a romantic origin, as this is the locality of the legend of Hum-moo, the Lost Arrow. And throughout the valley there are many places about which the Indians have a tale to tell. In this book, *Yosemite Legends,** the author has narrated the principal ones. And in the telling of them, she has clothed them in an atmosphere and a charm that enhance their value, especially to those who can find further enjoyment in Yosemite Valley when they know something of the past tragedies (these present legends) in the lives of the races who for ages have known this place as their only world. E. McA.

"OUT WEST," MAY, 1905. It is pleasant to find that the outings of the Sierra Club are of sufficient importance to the public at large to call for special reference in other publications than our own. The May issue, called the "Mountaineering Number," of *Out West* contains three such articles by members of the Sierra Club. Mr. Willoughby Rodman has written of "An Outing with the Sierra Club," and has described more particularly the outing of 1904; Miss Marion Randall has an article on "Social Phases of Sierra Club Mountaineering," and Mr. Edward T. Parsons contributes "A Sierra Club Fisherman."

---

* *Yosemite Legends.* By BERTHA H. SMITH. With drawings by FLORENCE LUNDBORG. 64 pages. Paul Elder and Company, Tomoyé Press. 1904. San Francisco.

The illustrations alone would attract attention. A careful selection seems to have been made from the best of Mr. Parsons', together with three of Professor Badè's.

Each article appeals to a different temperament, and all will interest and entertain the members of the Sierra Club, and particularly those who desire to revive the memories of last year's Outing.

Miss Randall's article is apparently a rewriting of the one that was contributed to the January BULLETIN; but the latter is somewhat more intimate. Her picture of life in the mountains is most encouraging, although "one is fifty miles from a railroad or post-office and a five days' journey from a bathtub," and those who have experienced the pleasures of an outing realize how they are found in the scene described: "From many a widespread meadow, rimmed about with shadowy pines, have we watched the slow impalpable change from garish day to twilight, from dusk to moon-lit night, until the tranquil stars shone forth again to quiet the restless longing the vanishing day brings." And having experienced such moments, we agree with Mr. Rodman: "To many the greatest benefit derived from these outings is the mental and spiritual elevation which comes from communion with nature."

E. McA.

"A GUIDE TO THE STUDY OF FISHES."   A magnificent work in two volumes, just published, entitled *A Guide to the Study of Fishes*,* by David Starr Jordan, has been presented to the Club's library by Henry Holt & Company. Unfortunately it arrived too late for this issue, but will be reviewed in the next January number.

---

* *A Guide to the Study of Fishes.* By DAVID STARR JORDAN. With colored frontispieces and 427 illustrations. 2 vols., pp. xxvi, 624, and xxii, 598. Published by Henry Holt & Company. New York. 1905.

FORESTRY NOTES.

EDITED BY PROFESSOR WILLIAM R. DUDLEY.

Two things mark the year 1905 as the most important for California, in the whole history of forestry, with the possible exception of 1891, the year of the passage of the Forest Reserve Law. These two events are, first, the vote of Congress transferring the entire forest reserves of the United States from the official control of the General Land Office to that of the Department of Agriculture and its forestry service, and, second, the enactment of a California Forestry Law by the State Legislature.

THE CALIFORNIA FORESTRY LAW. The passage of this law is of far greater importance to the Pacific Coast than has been acknowledged. It is not an ideal law; its resources were cut down somewhat from the original provisions, disappointing its framers thereby; not all interests are satisfied, and claims are made that sections 16 and 17 will work some hardships in lumbering operations. Nevertheless, the acknowledgment by the greatest State west of the great plains that its forestry interests are so great as to need a code of laws, its act in appointing an expert forester and a corps of assistants, whose duties are a scientific treatment of the forest and protection of the State lands against fire, are gains which cannot be overestimated. The law will doubtless be modified and improved by subsequent legislation; but all advocates of forestry will be half-hearted who do not loyally stand by this law until it has been thoroughly tested in the hands of the Forester.

It is printed in full in this number of the BULLETIN, and we ask campers particularly to read sections 14, 15, and 16. This law has been drawn with the greatest care, with the advice of lawyers best informed in regard to forest and park management, and of foresters of the greatest experience. It was submitted to members of several societies interested in forestry in California and to practical lumbermen. Among modifications brought about in this way we particularly call attention to the italicized clauses in section 3. Through lack of a law providing for the reception and care of donations of land, the State has heretofore lost fine tracts of timber.

TRANSFER OF FOREST RESERVES. The "Act providing for the transfer of forest reserves from the Department of the Interior to the Department of Agriculture" became a law February 1, 1905, and contains the following clauses:—

"The Secretary of the Department of Agriculture shall, from and after the passage of this act, execute or cause to be executed all laws affecting public lands heretofore or hereafter reserved under the provisions of section twenty-four of the act entitled 'An act to repeal the timber-culture laws and for other purposes,' approved March third, eighteen hundred and ninety-one, and acts supplemental to and amendatory thereof, after such lands have been so reserved, excepting such laws as affect the surveying, prospecting, locating, appropriating, entering, relinquishing, reconveying, certifying, or patenting of any such lands."

"All money received from the sale of any products or the use of any land or resources of said forest reserves shall be covered into the treasury of the United States, and for a period of five years from the passage of this act shall constitute a special fund, available, until expended, as the Secretary of Agriculture may direct, for the protection, administration, improvement, and extension of Federal forest reserves."

In a letter dated February 1, 1905, from the Secretary of Agriculture to the United States Forester, Gifford Pinchot, he indicates the future policy regarding the administration of the reserves. He says:—

"It must be clearly borne in mind that all land is to be devoted to its most productive use for the permanent good of the whole people, and not for the temporary benefit of individuals or companies. All the resources of the forest are for *use*, under such restrictions only as will insure the permanence of these resources. The permanence of the reserves is indispensable to continued prosperity in the great industries of the Western States, and the policy of this department for their protection and use will invariably be guided by this fact, always bearing in mind that the *conservative use* of these resources in no way conflicts with their permanent value. You will see to it that the water, wood, and forage of the reserves are conserved and wisely used for the benefit of the home-builder first of all, upon whom depends the best permanent use of lands and resources alike. The continued prosperity of the agricultural, lumbering, mining, and livestock interests is directly dependent upon a permanent and accessible supply of water, wood, and forage, as well as upon the present and future use of these resources under business-like regulations, enforced with promptness, effectiveness, and common-sense. In the management of each reserve local questions will be decided upon local grounds; the dominant industry will be considered first, but with as little restriction to minor industries as may be possible, and where conflicting interests must be reconciled the question will always be decided from the standpoint of the greatest good of the greatest number in the long run. These general principles can be successfully applied only when the administration of each reserve is left very largely in the hands of the local officers, under the eye of thoroughly trained and competent inspectors."

These are words of the highest wisdom; use of the reserves without injury to the forests, first to the home-builder, and second to the local industries, always modified by local conditions and local needs. As citizens, men of science, or sentimentalists, we could wish for no better articles of belief. For this transfer of our forests to the trained hands in the Forestry Bureau, we have labored more persistently than for any other end, believing that all the vexed questions which come before the laymen in forestry in the West can only be settled through the dominion of the trained forester over his proper domain, the forests; the above words of promise from the Secretary of Agriculture justify all efforts made to effect this change. It is also ruled that "*Forest Service* is the new official title of the organization having immediate charge of all National forest work under the Secretary of Agriculture. It replaces the Bureau of Forestry in the Department of Agriculture and the Division of Forestry in the General Land Office."

The members of the Sierra Club who can look back to our meeting at the California Academy of Sciences, less than ten years ago, held to arouse public thought upon the condition of our forests at a time when interest in them was at its lowest ebb, can best realize how greatly the public has been educated during this period in a knowledge of forestry problems, and how rapidly a statesman-like policy can advance under the leadership of a few capable men. The time was ripe and the leaders came in the persons of Roosevelt, Pinchot, and Wilson, all of one mind, and of the right mind. The transfer of the reserves has not been heralded with great headlines in the newspapers, but it will so affect business methods in connection with interests so vast in extent and so vital to our well-being as a nation that the historian of a century hence will reckon it as the beginning of one of the most important influences in our national life.

THE LIEU LAND LAW. The last Congress also repealed the law allowing owners of land inside of forest reserves to select equal areas of non-mineral-bearing land elsewhere. This law was the cover to great frauds, because it allowed speculators of the Benson-Hyde type to buy up tracts, often nearly worthless cut-over or brush-lands, inside forest reserves, at a low figure, and locate equal amounts in the most valuable timberlands of the public domain. This law was not wholly baneful, however; considerable tracts of land containing *Sequoia gigantea* in Tulare County, California, passed back to the Government through its operations.

THE YOSEMITE. The boundaries of the Yosemite National Park were modified by the last Congress so as to throw a considerable acreage, most of little forest value, into the Sierra Forest Reserve. This is understood to follow the general lines of the recommendations of the expert commission appointed by President Roosevelt to report on the case, and therefore is unobjectionable.

The so-called "recession" of the Yosemite Valley to its real owner, the United States, was accomplished by a legislative bill passing both houses of the California Legislature, after a vigorous campaign, supported by the best interests and most rational thought in the State. The Sierra Club had much to do in bringing about the desired results under the active and efficient leadership of its secretary. The act simply terminated a trust on behalf of the State, and returns to the wardship of the Nation, where it will be better cared for, the finest piece of natural scenery in the State, and yet it will be freer, after a few years, to the citizens of the State than ever before.

Publications of the Sierra Club

No. 1.—Articles of Association, By-Laws, and List of Members.

Nos. 4 and 5.—Maps of Portions of the Sierra Nevada adjacent to the Yosemite and to King's River, 1893. (Out of print.)

No. 8.—Table of Elevations within the Pacific Coast, 1895, by Mark B. Kerr and R. H. Chapman. *Price, 25 cents.*

No. 12.—Map of the Sierra Region, May, 1896. (Out of print.)

Nos. 2, 3, 6, 7, 9, 10, 11, 13, together forming Volume I., Nos. 1-8, of the SIERRA CLUB BULLETIN.

Contents of Volume I.—Ascent of Mt. Le Conte; Address on Sierra Forest Reservation; California Outing; Crater Lake, Oregon; Diamond Hitch; Explorations North of Tuolumne River; Forest Reservations; From Fresno to Mt. Whitney, via Roaring River; From Gentry's to El Capitan and Yosemite Falls; Grand Cañon of the Tuolumne; Head-waters of King's River; Kern and King's River Divide; King's River and Mt. Whitney Trails; Knapsack Tours in the Sierra; Mt. Bernard; Mt. Tahoma; Mt. Whitney Trail; New Grove of Sequoia Gigantea; Notes on the Pine Ridge Trail; Route up Mt. Williamson; Search for a Route from the Yosemite to the King's River Cañon; Sources of the San Joaquin; Three Days with Mt. King; Through Death Valley; Through the Tuolumne Cañon; Tramp to Mt. Lyell; Upper Sacramento in October; Notes, Correspondence, and Reports.

Nos. 14, 15, 16, 17, 18, and 19, together forming Volume II., Nos. 1-6, of the SIERRA CLUB BULLETIN.

Contents of Volume II.—Ascent of the White Mountains of New Mexico; Basin of the South Fork of the San Joaquin River; Conifers of the Pacific Slope, Parts I and II; Day with Mt. Tacoma; Early Summer Excursion to the Tuolumne Cañon and Mt. Lyell; Expedition of Prince Luigi Amedeo of Savoy to Mt. St. Elias; Explorations of the East Creek Amphitheater, From Mt. Rose to Mt. Shasta and Lower Buttes; Kaweah Group; Lava Region of Northern California; Mountain Trips: What to Take and How to Take It; Neglected Region of the Sierra; Observations on the Denudation of Vegetation—Suggested Remedy for California; On Mt. Lefroy August 3, 1896; On Mt. Lefroy August 3, 1897; Philip Stanley Abbot; Taking of Mt. Balfour; To Tehipite Valley from the King's River Grand Cañon; Up and Down Bubb's Creek; Wanderings in the High Sierra Between Mt. King and Mt. Williamson,—Parts I and II; Woman's Trip Through the Tuolumne Cañon; Yosemite Discovery; Notes, Correspondence, and Reports.

No. 20.—Volume III., No. 1, pp. 1 to 118—price $1.00.—Ramblings Through the High Sierra (Reprinted from "A Journal of Ramblings," privately printed in 1875); Editorial Notice; Ouzel Basin; Forestry Notes.

No. 21.—Ramblings Through the High Sierra. Same as No. 20. (Specially bound; without Editorial Notes, etc.)

No. 22.—Volume III., No. 2, pp. 119 to 188.—Lake Tahoe in Winter; Ascent of "El Yunque"; Another Paradise; King's River Cañon Trail Notes; Ascent of "Matterhorn Peak"; Reports; Notes and Correspondence; Forestry Notes.

No. 23.—Volume III., No. 3, pp. 189 to 270.—Parks and Peaks in Colorado; The Work of the Division of Forestry in the Redwoods; The Mazamas on Mt. Jefferson; Wagon-Trips to the Sierra; The Big Basin; The Re-Afloresting of the Sierra Nevada; The Descent of Tenaya Cañon; An Ascent of Cathedral Peak; A Glimpse of the Winter Sierra; Notes and Correspondence; Forestry Notes.

No. 24.—Volume III., No. 4, pp. 271 to 339.—The Mazamas on Mt. Rainier; Lassen Buttes: From Prattville to Fall River Mills; Zonal Distribution of Trees and Shrubs in the Southern Sierra; Mt. Washington in Winter; Round About Mt. Dana; Notes and Correspondence; Forestry Notes; Reports.

PUBLICATIONS OF THE SIERRA CLUB — *Continued.*

No. 25.—Volume IV., No. 1, pp. 1 to 75.—Joseph Le Conte in the Sierra; El Capitan; Camp Muir in Tuolumne Meadows; The Sierra Club Outing to Tuolumne Meadows; In Tuolumne and Cathedral Cañons; The Great Spruce Forest and the Hermit Thrush; From Redding to the Snow-clad Peaks of Trinity County; Trees and Shrubs in Trinity County; Notes and Correspondence; Forestry Notes; Reports.

No. 26.—Vol. IV., No. 2, pp. 77 to 176.—Into the Heart of Cataract Cañon; My Trip to King's River Cañon (Reprint); Conifers of the Pacific Slope, Part III; Birds of the High Mountains; Notes and Correspondence; Forestry Notes; Reports.

No. 27.—A Flora of the South Fork of King's River from Millwood to the Head-Waters of Bubb's Creek.

No. 28.—Vol. IV., No. 3, pp. 177 to 252.—Among the Sources of the South Fork of King's River, Part I; With the Sierra Club in King's River Cañon; Red-and-White Peak and the Head-waters of Fish Creek; Mt. Whitney, Whitney Creek, and the Poison Meadow Trail; A New-Year Outing in the Sierra; The Ascent of Volcano Mayon; Notes and Correspondence; Forestry Notes; Reports.

No. 29.—Vol. IV., No. 4, pp. 253 to 323.—Among the Sources of the South Fork of King's River, Part II; the Coast Sierra from California to Panama; Ralph Sidney Smith (In Memoriam); Climbing Mt. Brewer; Table of Elevations of Peaks in the Sierra Nevada Mountains over 12,000 feet; King's River Outing, 1902 — Botanical Notes, etc.; Near the Kern's Grand Cañon; Reports; Notes and Correspondence; Forestry Notes.

No. 30.—Vol. V., No. 1, pp. 1 to 85.—The Ascent of the North Palisades; Variations of Sierra Glaciers; How Private Burns Climbed Mt. Pinatúbo; The Hillside Farmer and the Forest; The Notable Mountaineering of the Sierra Club in 1903; On the Trail with the Sierra Club; The Completed Le Conte Memorial Lodge; Reports; Notes and Correspondence; Forestry Notes.

No. 31.—Vol. V., No. 2, pp. 87 to 152.—Mt. Whitney as a Site for a Meteorological Observatory; The Water-Ouzel at Home; The San Francisco Peaks in April; Over Harrison's Pass with Animals; The Ascent of San Antonio; Secretary's Report; Treasurer's Report; Notes and Correspondence; Forestry Notes.

No. 32.—Vol. V., No. 3, pp. 153 to 270.—First Ascent: Mt. Humphreys; Address at Memorial Exercises; Mt. Lyell and Mt. Ritter Ascents by Sierra Club Outing of 1904; A Deer's Bill of Fare; Domes and Dome Structure of the High Sierra; Some Aspects of a Sierra Club Outing; The Evolution Group of Peaks; Reports; Notes and Correspondence; Book Reviews; Forestry Notes.

On receipt, in good condition, of a full set of the numbers comprising Volumes I. or II., together with the sum of $1.50, a bound volume will be forwarded in exchange, postpaid.

Copies of the above publications may be had on application to the Secretary, Room 316, Third Floor, Mills Building, San Francisco, Cal.

Each number 50 cents, except Vol. III., No. 1, price $1.00.

Members may have additional copies of the BULLETINS *at half rates.*

Volume I., Nos. 1, 3, 4, and 5; Volume II., Nos. 1 and 3; Volume III., No. 4; and Volume IV., No. 1, are out of print.

A few copies of Volume I., bound and complete, may be had at $10 each; and Volume II., at $7.50 each.

A few copies of Vol. III, No. 1, separately bound and specially illustrated, may be had for $5.00 each.

www.ingramcontent.com/pod-product-compliance
Lightning Source LLC
Chambersburg PA
CBHW022138300426
44115CB00006B/250